150 YEARS OF THE
CENTRAL SYNAGOGUE

150 Years of the
Central Synagogue

Derek Taylor

VALLENTINE MITCHELL
LONDON • CHICAGO

First published in 2023 by Vallentine Mitchell

Catalyst House,
720 Centennial Court,
Centennial Park, Elstree WD6 3SY, UK

814 N. Franklin Street,
Chicago, Illinois,
IL 60610 USA

www.vmbooks.com

British Library Cataloguing in Publication Data:
An entry can be found on request

ISBN 978 1 80371 039 6 (Paper)
ISBN 978 1 80371 040 2 (Ebook)

Library of Congress Cataloging in Publication Data:
An entry can be found on request

Contents

Central Officers and Members

Ministers

1874-1883	Rev. Aaron Levy Green.
1884-1902	Rev. David Fay.
1903-1934	Rev. Michael Adler, DSO., BA., HCE.
1914-1918	Rabbi Benjamin Michelson (During the war).
1914-1918	Rev. Mendel Zeffert (During the war).
1934-1946	Rev. Philip Cohen BA., HCE.
1939-1945	Rabbi Benjamin Michelson. (During the war.)
1940-1946	Rev. Emil Nemeth (During the war).
1946-1954	Rev. Simeon Isaacs, BA., HCE.
1955-1988	Rabbi Cyril Shine, BA.
1963	Rev. J. Grunwald (Student Minister).
1988-1994	Rabbi Vivian Silverman.
1995-2018	Rabbi Barry Marcus, MBE., PGCE.
2019	Rabbi Barry Lerer (and Rebbetzen Naomi Lerer).
2019	Rabbi Ari Cohen (Assistant Rabbi).

Chazanim

1870-1874	Rev. Aaron Levy Green.
1870 -1884	Rev. Samuel Lyons.
1884-1924	Rev. Emanuel Spero.
1925-1950	Rev. Aron Stoutzker.
1951-1993	Rev. Simon Hass LLCM.
1993-1994	Rev. Moshe Dubiner.
1994-1995	Rev. Shlomo Kreiman.
1994-1996	Chazan Yaacov Reichmann.
1997-2002	Chazan Jonathan Murgraff.
2003-	Chazan Steven Leas.

Male and Female members

1870	260
1880	380
1890	334
1900	355
1910	380
1920	353
1930	374
1940	351
1950	467
1960	685
1970	657
1980	595 & 177 female.
1990	670 comprising 635 households, 28 individual male and 8 female.
2000	465 comprising 431 households 14 male and 20 female.
2010	400-499 by household.

Chairs

2001-2010	Sam Peltz.
2011-2012	Laurie Phillips
2013	Nicola Burns
2014-2021	Barry Townsley CBE.

Vice Chairs

2001-2004	Terry Samek
2008-2012	Nicola Burns
2013-2021	Melvin Lawson.

Women's Officer

2018	Roz Laren

Wardens.

1870	Sir Anthony de Rothschild.
1870	Lionel L. Cohen.

1870	Jacob Waley.
1870	Hyman Beddington.
1870-1871	Baron Ferdinand de Rothschild.
1870-1877	Barnett Meyers.
1872-1874	Louis Lumley.
1874-1875	Edwin Samuel.
1875-1887	Frederick Davis.
1889-1891	Jonah Jonas.
1879-1881	Baron Henry de Worms, MP.
1881-1883	Joseph Benjamin.
1881-1883	Morris Oppenheim.
1883-1885	Henry Isaacs.
1883-1904	Samuel Moss.
1885-1893	Henry Simmons.
1887-1889	Alfred Beddington.
1889-1893	Leonard Cohen.
1893-1901	Joseph Pyke.
1901-1903	Joseph Trenner.
1903-1906	Edward Pinder Davis.
1904-1906	Morris Jonah Jonas.
1906-1910	Sir Robert Waley Cohen.
1907-1920	Edward Pinder Davis.
1910-1926	Sir Adolph Tuck.
1920-1938	Joseph Jacobs.
1921-1923	Alfred Alvarez.
1927-1948	Desmond Tuck.
1933-1947	Gaskell Jacobs.
1940-1947	Josey Freedman.
1940-1947	Hyman Lewis.
1947-1963	Sir Isaac Wolfson.
1948-1963	Jack Harris.
1948-1963	Philip Taylor.
1963-1970	Sir Leonard Wolfs.
1963-1971	Albert L. Levy.
1963-1966	Jack Steinberg.
1966-1971	Lionel Swift.
1970-1974	Sir Eric Miller.
1971-1972	Ralph Djanogly.
1972-1974	Lionel Swift.
1972-1974	Lord Wolfson of Marylebone.

1974-1982	Sidney Diamond.
1977	J. Castle.
1980-1989	Paul Samek, OBE.
1982-1988	Sam Peltz.
1982-1989	Peter Goldbart.
1988-1989	Bernard Jacobs.
1989-1992	Stephen Kay.
1989-2011	Eric Charles.
1990-1993	Peter Goldbart.
1992-1996	Stanley Lewis.
1993-1995	Paul Samek OBE.
1993-1994	David Shilling.
1995-1998	Barry Green.
1996-2000	Dr. Sam Peltz.
1998-2008	Gary Burns.
2001-2007	Leonard Fertleman.
2004-2013	Nigel Gee.
2007-2012	Richard Glyn.
2008-2014	Nicola Burns.
2011	Stanley Salter.
2012	Stuart Lewis.
2013-2019	Harold Schogger.
2019-2021	Mervyn Druian.

Financial Representatives.

1870-1873	S.L. Miers.
1873-1875	Frederick Davies.
1875-1877	Alfred Beddington.
1877-1881	Jonah Jonas.
1881-1883	J. Benjamin.
1883-1885	Henry Isaacs.
1885-1893	Henry Simmons.
1893-1914	Asher Isaacs.
1914-1921	Edward Phillips.
1923-1933	Alfred Alvarez.
1933-1938	Gaskell Jacobs.
1938-1940	Richard Norton.
1945-1947	Hyman Lewis.
1945-1947	Josey Freedman.

1947-1948	Philip Taylor.
1948-1966	Jack Harris.
1965-1966	Alfred Levy.
1967-1971	Lionel Swift.
1972	Harry Djanogly.
1973	Lionel Swift.
1974-1979	Daniel Questel.
1980-1981	Paul Samek.
1982-1989	Peter Goldbart.
1990-2011	Eric Charles.
2011-2021	Stanley Salter.
2021	Ronnie Harris.

Beadle.

1855-1905	Philip Vallentine.
1906-1927	Max Schulman.
1927-1958	Morris Roth.
	M. Wozner.
	Jeremy Tarlow.

Secretary.

1868	Rev. Aaron Levy Green.
1874-1888	Rev. Samuel Lyons.
1888-1902	Rev. David Fay.
1902-1913	L.J.Solomons. (Ass.Secretary 1902, Acting Secretary 1903-1906)
1906-1913	L.J.Solomons.
1914-1918	J.H.Taylor.
1918-1919	H. Kintzler.
1920-1926	H. Winston.
1926-1936	S.Cohen.
1937-1940	Rev. Philip Cohen.
1945-1947	Rev. Philip Cohen.
1948-1955	Philip Jacobs.
1956-1968	Michael Stoller.
	S. Ehrlich.
	Mrs. Unsdorfer.

1988-2002	Coral Jewel.
2002-	Craig Levison.

Hebrew Classes

1900	20
1901	70
19/05	80
1907	70
1910	64
1911	70
1914	104
1916	123
1917	138
1919	110
1920	80

2021 officers.

Rabbi: Barry Lerer.
Rebbetzin: Naomi Lerer.
Assistant Rabbi: Ari Cohen.
Cantor: Steven Leas.
Chairman: Barry Townsley.
Vice Chairman: Melvin Lawson.
Wardens: Mervyn Druian, Stuart Lewis.
Women's Officer: Roz Laren.
Financial Representative: Ronnie Harris.
Synagogue Council: Kenny Arfin, Roger Cohen, Valerie Cohen, Andrea Druian, Diana Goldsmith, Susan Grant, Jennifer Green, James Hyman, Jonathan Metliss, Daphne Schogger, Harold Schogger, Maurice Shamash, Rosalie Stevens.
US Council Representatives: Nicola Burns, Adrienne Phillips, Laurie Phillips Representatives at the Board of Deputies: Jonathan Metliss, Maurice Shamash Central Community Cares Chairperson: Susan Grant.
Children's Service: Raquel Amit, Yoav Amit.
Administrator: Craig Levison.
Community Development Officer/Personal Assistant: Raquel Amit.

Building Management Team Douglas O'Halloran, Jayson Pillay, Sylvia Drimba.

Security Team Nina Tetra (Head of Security and Compliance Officer) Kenny Arfin, James Leof.

Sons of the congregations who fell in the First World War.

Major Montague Abrahams	16th Rifle Brigade
Gunner M. Bernstein	Royal Field Artillery
Rifleman Noah Boss	Queens Westminster Rifles
Second Lieutenant David Cohen	7th Royal Sussex Regiment
Second Lieutenant Brian Davis	7th London Regiment
Second Lieutenant Oscar Frankenstein	5th Welsh Regiment
Second Lieutenant Braham Franks	8th West Riding Regiment
Second Lieutenant Cecil Freeman-Cowen	Royal Field Artillery
Second Lieutenant Victor Grossman	24th Northumberland Fusiliers
Lieutenant Harry Harris	10th West Riding Regiment
Lieutenant Cyril Henry	2nd Worcester Regiment
Lieutenant Rudolph Leveson	10th Durham Light Infantry
Second Lieutenant Norman Raphael	2nd Royal Warwick Regiment
Private Alfred Rosenbaum	7th Royal Sussex Regiment
Major Evelyn de Rothschild	Bucks Yeomanry
Second Lieutenant Arthur Samuel	Royal Army Service Corps
Lieutenant Gerald Samuel	10th Royal West Kent Regiment
Second Lieutenant Leonard Solomon	1st Kings Own Scottish Borderers

Central Synagogue Jewish fatalities in the Boer War 1899-1900

F. Aaron, Private *Imperial Yeomanry* died Marandellas 10.10.1900

S. Abraham, Corporal *East Kent Regiment* killed Driefontein

W. Abrahams, Private *New South Wales Mounted Infantry* killed at Abraham's Kraal 10.3.1900

C. Abrams, Sergeant *King's Royal Rifles* killed Glencoe 20.10.1899 [S. Abrams?]

J. Bamberger, Private *West Riding Regiment* died Bloemfontein 14.5.1900

B. Bettelheim, Private *East Kent Regiment* killed Paaredeberg

G. Blumfield *12th Lancers* killed Modder River

Benjamin Blumson, Able Seaman *H.M.S. "Powerful"* died Ladysmith
    22.12.1899
S. Cappleman, Private *King's Royal Rifles* died Vryheid 31.5.1900
I. E. Cohen, Trooper *Border Mounted Rifles* died Ladysmith
John Barrow Cohen, Trooper *Natal Carabineers* killed Ladysmith 6.3.1900
Samuel Cohen, Private *Cape Vol. Medical Staff Corps* died Bloemfontein
    3.5.1900
Barnett Davis, Private *Natal Vol. Medical Staff Corps* died Standerton
    [23.11.1900?]
M. B. Davis, Private *Rhodesian Regiment* killed Mafeking
S. E. Davis, Private *Imperial Yeomanry* died Marandellas 25.7.1900
A. Diamond, Private *14th Hussars* died Ladysmith
H. Dreher, Private *Royal Lancaster Regiment* killed Spion Kop 24.1.1900
G. Eddlestone, Private *King's Royal Rifles* died Chieveley
Manuel Enoch, Private *Connaught Rangers* killed Tugela River 15.12.1899
A. Franks, Private *King's Royal Rifles* died Maritzburg 24.12.1899
J. Freedman, Private *Rifle Brigade* killed Bergendal
Leonard Golden, Trooper *British South African Police* killed Mafeking
    18.5.1900
A. E. Goldschmidt, Private *Prince Alfred's Volunteer Guard* killed Kroonstad
    14.5.1900
Mark Goldstein, Trooper *Natal Carabineers* killed Monte Christo 16.2.1900
H. J. Goodman, Sergeant *Australian Horse* killed Koeks River 21.7.1900
George Edward Halford, Private *City Imperial Volunteers* died Karee
    15.5.1900
H. Hergold, Private *West Riding Regiment* killed Paaredeberg
G. Hirsch, Private Cape *Pioneer Railway Regiment* died Pretoria 18.5.1900
H. Hoffman, Private *Norfolk Regiment* died Karee 16.5.1900
Lancelot Isaacs, Private *Welsh Regiment* died Germiston 7.12.1900 [Isaac?]
Reuben Isaacs, Driver *Army Service Corps* died Maritzburg 24.3.1900
C. Isaacson, Private *Royal Army Medical Corps* died Bloemfontein 31.5.1900
Joseph Jacobs, Private *Cape Vol. Medical Staff Corps* accidentally killed
    Machadodorp 13.11.1900
Benjamin Lawson, Trooper *Border Mounted Rifles* killed Ladysmith
    6.1.1900
A. Levitt, Private *Middlesex Regiment* killed Spion Kop 27.1.1900
Edward Levy, Private *Prince Alfred's Volunteer Guard* died Cradock
    16.2.1900
Henry Julius Levy, Trooper *British South African Police* killed Mafeking
    21.10.1899

Adolph Lewis, Trooper *Kitchener's Horse* killed Houtnek 30.4.1900
C. Lewis, Trooper *South African Light Horse* Tugela River 15.12.1899
S. Mack, Private *Royal Scots Fusiliers* died Maritzburg 19.12.1899
Harry Aaron Marks, Private *City Imperial Volunteers* died Bloemfontein 17.4.1900
Ben Mayer, Private *Manchester Regiment* killed Elandslaagte 21.10.1899
D. Moses, Private *South Wales Borderers* died Bloemfontein 24.5.1900
J. H. Moses, Labourer *Army Ordnance Corps* died Bloemfontein 25.5.1900
A. Oppenheim, Private *New Zealand Mounted Infantry* killed Reitfontein 29.11.1900
Frederick Melchior Raphael, Lieutenant *South Lancashire Regiment* killed Spion Kop 24.1.1900
James Soloman, Private *Bethune's Mounted Infantry* died Newcastle 9.6.1900
O. Strauss, Trooper *Border Mounted Rifles* died Ladysmith 16.12.1899
F. Wolfson, Corporal *King's Royal Rifles* killed Ladysmith 6.1.1900

Second Year of The War 1900-01

Henry Abrahams, Private *7th Dragoon Guards* died of disease, Warringhams 30.8.1901
J. Adler, Private *Royal Dublin Fusiliers* died of disease, Charlestown 18.12.1900
A. Baker, Private *Manchester Regiment* died of disease, Bethlehem 3.2.1901
S. J. Barnard, Private *Victorian Mounted Infantry* killed in action, Wilmansrust 12.6.1901
Lewis Barnett, Private *Western Province Mounted Rifles* killed on patrol, Calvinia 10.6.1901
Benjamin Collins, Private *Cheshire Regiment* died of disease, Ventersdorp 27.5.1901
Louis Daniels, Private *Imperial Yeomanry* died of disease, Germiston 21.8.1901
Albert W. Davis, Private *Queensland Bushmen* died of disease, Standerton 2.6.1901
Isaac Drukker (J. Duper), Corporal *Royal Warwickshire Regiment* died of disease, Newcastle 25.12.1900
E. Dytch, Private *South Staffordshire Regiment* died of disease, Reitz 18.12.1900
Joseph Freedman, Private *14th Hussars* died of disease, Germiston 15.4.1901
J. Freedman, Private *King's Royal Rifle Corps* killed in action, Roodepoort

Joseph Freeman, Private *Shropshire Light Infantry* died of wounds, Steynsburg

Abraham Charles Josua Garish, Private *Piquetberg Town Guard* killed on duty, Piquetberg 7.11.1901

I. Harlbuth, Private *Imperial Yeomanry* killed in action, Vlakfontein

Ellis Horwitz, Private *Western Province Mounted Rifles* died of disease, Glanwilliam 23.3.1901

C. Isaac, Gunner *Royal Field Artillery* died of disease, Standerton

Robert Henry Isaacs (Morris), Trooper *Kitchener's Fighting Scouts* killed in action, Cloosfiesdoorn

John Jacobs, Constable *South African Constabulary* died of disease, Bloemfontein 30.3.1901

John Jacobs, Sergeant *7th Dragoon Guards* killed in action, Klipplaat 6.2.1901

F. Jacobson, Sergeant *Army Ordnance Corps* died of disease, Engocobe

Theodore Isaac Levin, Trooper *Brabant's Horse* died of wounds, Hanover

A. Levine, Private *East Lancashire Regiment* killed in action, Rensburg Drift 22.4.1901

R. Levinson, Private *Duke of Edinburgh's V. Regiment* died of disease, Porterville 26.1.1901

Abraham Levy, Constable *South African Constabulary* killed on duty, Mafeking District

S. Lewin, Private *Leicester Regiment* killed in action, Honing's Kloof 30.7.1901

E. Mendes, Corporal *Cheshire Regiment* died of disease, Burghersdorp 3.2.1901

Alfred Henry Marks (Marsh), Trooper *Scottish Horse* killed in action, Brakenlaagte 30.10.1901

A. L. Meyer, Private *Oudtshoorn Volunteer Rifles* killed in action, Kruis River 1.9.1901

J. R. Meyers Private *Royal Army Medical Corps* killed in action, Wynberg 14.12.1900

Nathan Moss, Trooper *Steinacker's Horse* died of disease, Lorenzo Marques 12.3.1901

Aaron Myers (Robert Harvey), Able Seaman *H.M.S. "Terrible"* died of disease, Haslar Hospital

J. Myers, Private *West Yorkshire Regiment* accidentally drowned, Warrenton 21.12.1900

J. Myers, Private *West Yorkshire Regiment* killed on patrol with Smith-Dorrien 6.2.1901

Frank Nathan, Private *Imperial Yeomanry* killed in action, Lichtenberg 12.3.1901

Jack Rabie, Private *Western Province Mounted Rifles* killed on patrol, Calvinia 10.6.1901

Harry Robinson, Private *Colonial Defence Force* killed in action, Cheviot Fells 3.1901[?]

G. Ramus, Private *Rifle Brigade* died of disease, Standerton 4.9.1901

H. Sagar, Private *Army Ordnance Corps* died of disease, Maritzburg 21.12.1900

F. Sampson, Gunner *Royal Garrison Artillery* died of disease, Lydenberg 1.2.1901

B. Simmons, Private *Royal Lancaster Regiment* died of disease, Dundee 26.10.1901

Harold Solomon, Constable *South African Constabulary* died of disease, Bloemfontein 25.3.1901

Herbert Solomon, Private *West Australian Mounted Infantry* killed in action 15.4.1901

Walter Solomon, Private *Colonial Defence Force* killed in action, Zuurberg 16.10.1901

Harry Weiler, Trooper *Marshall's Horse* killed in action, Ladysmith

Arthur Wolf, Private *Colonial Defence Force* killed in action, Cheviot Fells 15.3.1901

TOTAL (including first Memorial list, Chanuach, 5661): Killed in action, or died of wounds, 46; died of disease or accident, 49.

1901-2

Louis Alexander *Imperial Military Railways* accidentally shot, Viljoen's Drift 28.2.1902

E. H. Braun, Trooper *Cape Police* died of wounds, Windhoek 25.2.1902

Walter Chapman, Private *Kitchener's Fighting Scouts* killed in action, Zoutpansdrift 30.12.1901

Arthur Charet, Private *Kitchener's Fighting Scouts* killed in action, Zoutpansdrift 30.12.1901

Joseph Coleman, Private *5th Rifle Brigade (Militia)* died of disease, Zoutpansdrift 23.5.1902

H. D. Elkin, Lance Corporal *Royal Irish Fusiliers* died of disease, Standerton

Woolf Gabriel, Trooper *Imperial Light Horse* died of wounds, Newmarket Farm 5.2.1902

Samuel Goldman, Private *Canadian Scouts* died of disease, Elandsfontein 27.2.1902

David Goldstone, Private *Western Province Mounted Rifles* accidentally drowned, Wittedrift 10.2.1902

Eugene Gros, Q.M. Sergeant *Colonial Light Horse* died of disease, Ceres 26.3.1902

Benjamin Harris, Private *Army Service Corps* died of disease, Rietfontein West 1.1.1902

Edward Hart, Private *18th Hussars* died of disease, Standerton 23.2.1902

Coleman Joel Hayes, Orderly *Imperial Hospital Corps* died of disease, Harrismith 15.3.1902

J. Hesse, Private *Imperial Yeomanry* killed in action, Tweefontein 25.12.1901

B. Hyams, Sapper *Royal Engineers* died of disease, Pretoria 3.2.1902

Ingram (Isaacs) father and son, Troopers, *Colonial Horse* killed in action

S. E. Levy, Corporal *Army Service Corps* missing, found dead 8.6.1901[?]

Israel Lewin, Orderly *Imperial Hospital Corps* died of disease, Newcastle 5.2.1902

Samuel Lyons, Private *16th Lancers* killed in action, Calvinia Road 22.12.1901

E. Mayers, Private *Royal Lancaster Regiment* died of disease, Pretoria 29.1.1902

B. T. Meyer, Private *Imperial Yeomanry* killed in action, Tweefontein 25.12.1900

E. Meyers, Private *7th Hussars* died of disease, Heidelberg, T.V.L. 23.7.1902

J. Moeller, Private *New Zealand Rough Riders* killed in action 3.7.1900

A. Morris, Private *Johannesburg Mounted Rifles* died of disease 7.3.1902

C. Moses, Private *3rd Wiltshire (Militia) Mounted Infantry* died of disease, Kroonstad 7.12.1901

A. Salmon, Conductor *attached Army Service Corps* killed in action, Klipdrift

A. Strauss, Driver *Royal Field Artillery* killed in action

Isaac Tanvitch *attached Army Service Corps* died of disease, Kroonstad 7.5.1902

Joseph Tobias, Corporal *Essex Regiment* killed in action, Tweekopjes 9.3.1902

Victor Woolf *Imperial Military Railways* died of disease 19.12.1901

Lewis Yates, Trooper *South African Constabulary* died of disease, Pretoria 2.2.1902.

Foreword

Veasu Li Mikdash Veshachanti Betocham

They shall make for me a Sanctuary and I will Dwell Among them.
(Exodus 25:8)

The Central Synagogue is one of the most well-known and beautiful Synagogues in the world. With an illustrious history dating back more than 150 years, it is the only one of the five original constituent Synagogues of the United Synagogue still in existence.

Throughout the years, some of the most important names and figures in Anglo Jewry have belonged to this great community and have prayed in its majestic and hallowed sanctuary. Their stories, and the story of the Synagogue are interwoven to create a wonderful and colourful tapestry.

Derek Taylor is truly a scholar of Anglo Jewry. And as he has proved in his previous books, his research, level of detail, and historical accuracy are unparalleled. In these pages he has written a book for the historian and the casual reader alike who might be interested in gaining a glimpse of the history of a community and Synagogue that is steeped in the annals of Anglo Jewry and the jewel in the crown of the United Synagogue.

For me it is a true honour to lead this wonderful community, continue the work of my eminent forebears, and to build on the over 150 years of legacy and tradition and carry Central Synagogue into the next chapter of its amazing story.

Rabbi Barry Lerer, London, January 2023.

1

The story so far

Central Synagogue is now the oldest in London, dating from a decision in 1848 to start a branch of the City's Great Synagogue in the West End. It is the last of the original group of United Synagogues. Central has now been a fixture near Regents Park for 150 years though much has changed over that time. For one thing, the West End of London has moved from the Strand to Mayfair which makes the Synagogue even more at the heart of London's most fashionable area. The name of the Synagogue has changed too. It was always known as The Central until 1995 and became Central from that time onwards.

The original restructuring of the vista along Regent Street, from Piccadilly to Regents Park in the time of George IV, was designed to offer an uninterrupted view from one end to the other. This grand concept was obscured in later years, however, by the building of the Langham Hotel and the BBC building. Regents Park, with its magnificent Nash terraces has also transformed the whole area up to St. Johns Wood and beyond, from being countryside with rural fields to becoming an upmarket suburb.

The whole of North London has been built up as well. Slowly over this period, by contrast, the City of London has ceased to be where people live and has become a great financial, shopping and tourist centre, with many skyscrapers. This too is an innovation as a building's height in London was restricted to eight floors for many years.

There are still residents in the West End, but most of the Jewish families who used to live there and had moved from the East End to the West End, found their children moving still further North. They chose Hampstead Garden Suburb, Edgware, Stanmore, and went on to Borehamwood and Rickmansworth. The Central Synagogue is now part of London's West End heritage. Besides its local resident members though, it serves West End workers who want to attend a morning or evening service, families visiting patients in nearby hospitals, students from local London University colleges and tourists from all over the world. Over the years its raison d'étre has markedly diversified.

The present building is the third in which the congregation has worshipped. The first synagogue was opened in 1855 and the second magnificent structure was consecrated in 1870. The third, after the second was destroyed in the Blitz, was opened in 1956. The present synagogue is a totally modern building, but then unlike the 18th century Sephardi Bevis Marks shul, the architect could start from scratch after the Second World War. Bevis Marks, for example, is still only lit by traditional candles.

There have been a number of brief histories of Central. The first by Rev. Michael Adler in 1905, was to mark the Synagogue's silver jubilee; the second by Rev. Simeon Isaacs in 1948, was when the Synagogue was a blitzed ruin; the third was by Rabbi Cyril Shine in 1970 and the fourth in 2020 by Leonard Fertleman and Mervyn Druian. They all described the history of the synagogue with diligence and skill, but the workload in writing history is considerable and a certain amount of abbreviation was inevitable.

The history of a Synagogue is, of course, also the history of its members. Many of Central's over the years had distinguished careers in the professions, business and politics. A large number were originally from poor immigrant families, but they didn't abandon their heritage when they became wealthy and successful. Many also devoted time and money to charitable causes outside the Synagogue and merited the memorial services which marked their passing. What the vast majority supported was Orthodox Judaism. There were those who went over to the Progressive congregations when they were created, but there were always replacements to fill their seats.

Whatever changes have occurred in society, in demography or in the views of the British people as a whole, the congregation of Central today would be quite at home in the services conducted in the Victorian age.

The history of the Jews in Britain, of course, goes back a great deal further than the time of Central. It was as long ago as 1070 that William the Conqueror invited a number of Jewish merchants from his hometown of Rouen in Normandy to settle in England after he had won the Battle of Hastings. There was a second wave of Jewish immigrants from Angevin and Capetian territories in the fifty years after Henry II came to the throne in 1154.

William recognised that the Jews could fill two gaps in the mediaeval system of feudal government. First, in feudalism, there were three kinds of people; the aristocracy, the soldiers and the peasants. There were no shopkeepers. No specific traders. Second, Christians, by the rules of the Church, couldn't charge interest on money loaned to those who needed it.

It wasn't, however, contrary to the Din (Jewish law) and trade and farming, as always, involved a need for capital which some Jews could and did offer. Aaron of Lincoln (c1125-1186) was just one of them and he became the richest man in the country.

William recognised that he needed to build up England's trade and he was confident that the Jews could help. A structure, however, needed to be developed. For example, from the Jewish point of view, there was one distinct problem. If there were trade disputes in Anglo-Saxon England, the contemporary custom was for them to be resolved by the plaintiff and the defendant fighting each other on horseback. The winner of the joust was considered to have won the case.

Now jousting was not a skill at which many Jews excelled and they, therefore, suggested another solution to such disputes to William. The recommendation was that there should be six men nominated for the plaintiff and six for the defendant, who would sit down and thrash out the problem. If this idea was rejected, William knew that the Jews would seriously consider going home to the Continent. From that dilemma came the jury system.

The Jews were not independent citizens. Unlike an ordinary Englishman they belonged to the King, who protected them and used them as useful sources of taxation, as well as appointing them tax collectors, which didn't make them popular. Over the years that followed, the aristocracy borrowed more money from the Jews than they could repay.

Magna Carta might be the foundation of British democracy, but it had many antisemitic conditions concerning debts to Jews. Jews were useful but not liked. As a consequence of the difficulties created by the indebtedness, the community was expelled by Edward II in 1290. The interest rates charged could indeed be exorbitant, but the excuse was, of course, the refusal of the Jews to acknowledge Jesus as the Messiah.

Only the occasional Jew came to England in the next 350 years. For instance, Henry VIII called in rabbis to try to make the case that a divorce from his wife, Catherine of Aragon, was legitimate according to the Bible; it wasn't in Catholicism and when the Pope refused to grant a divorce Henry turned the country Protestant.

In time Queen Elizabeth I would have two Jewish doctors and the King of Aragon would send a Jewish doctor to accompany his daughter, Catherine, when she married Charles II. The Jews remained banned from living in Britain until, in 1656, Oliver Cromwell, the Protector, made it quite clear that they were not to be harassed if they came back to the country.

A conference on the subject at the time identified that, by law, there was in fact nothing to stop the Jews living in Britain. The expulsion order had to be made by the monarch himself and nobody had suggested to Edward's successor, Edward III, that he do so in his turn. The expulsion order was therefore automatically annulled but nobody noticed.

In Cromwell's time there wasn't sufficient support for a new law to be passed to officially allow the Jews back into the country. This was in part fortunate for the Jews as almost all of Cromwell's legislation was abolished when Charles II regained the throne. The new King insisted on the abolition of the legislation of the regicides.

The original Jews came from Amsterdam and were largely traders, which could mean anything from a jeweller to an insurance broker. During Cromwell's rule, a number of Jews were able to become effective constituents of the City of London. For example, only 24 non-English brokers were licensed in the capital from all over the world. Twelve of these appointments were restricted to Jews.

Their reputation was that good, but then they had been traders for centuries; North African Jews were trading with China in the 8th century. The Jewish rules for trading were laid out in detail in the 6th century Talmud in a large section called Nezikin. The rules were applicable all over the world and if there were disputes, any Beth Din, the Jewish court, could hand down decisions which would be according to the Talmud and therefore accepted.

Jewish merchants were also innovative. One Jewish broker in London even created cargo insurance. Non-Jewish traders in Europe didn't have common rules with, say, Asian businessmen and they found trading much more difficult as a result.

Charles II made the Jews' residence legal in 1661. It was not a popular decision. In that year a delegation of Christian London merchants had appealed to the restored King to expel the Jews again, as they were becoming considerable competition in the City. Charles, however, had received financial support from the Jews in Amsterdam when he was exiled there in recent years. There is still a document in the Scottish Records Office from Charles' emissary, General Middleton, writing to the Jews in Amsterdam. It reads:

> To assure them that if they shall in the coniuncture be ready by any
> contributions money, ARMS or ammunition to advance that service
> which wee have entrusted you, they shall find that when God shall
> restore us to the possession of our right and to that power which of

right doth belong to us, wee shall extend that protection to them which they can reasonably expecte, and abate that rigour of the Lawes which is against them in our several dominions.

Which was an offer the Jewish community, still barred from living in certain Dutch towns, were unlikely to reject. In the event, considerable funds had been forthcoming. Charles was pragmatic throughout his reign. He probably felt he needed to be cautious in case his restoration was short-lived, in which case he might require further financial support from the Jews, who needed him in return.

There was also a promise to be kept; Charles refused the delegation's request. His brother, when he became James II, did likewise. The Jews settled down and are now the oldest ethnic minority in the country.

The original Stuart immigrants were Sephardim from Spain and Portugal via Holland, after their expulsion in 1492 from the Peninsula. They originally worshipped about 1670 in London in a small synagogue in a house in the City, before they built Bevis Marks in 1700. Queen Anne donated a large rafter to its structure. A gift from the monarch offered the ultimate support for the community. The Jewish immigrants also bought land for a cemetery, which is Judaically more important for a community than a Synagogue.

The Ashkenazi followed the Sephardim but were far less affluent. They were refugees from the Thirty Years War, which had wiped out two thirds of the entire German population through massacres, sickness and military operations. It had done immense harm to the Jewish communities as well.

The Sephardim and the Ashkenazim were equally Orthodox but when they were expelled from the Holy Land by the Romans, the Sephardim had moved across North Africa and into Spain, while the Ashkenazim had travelled North to Eastern Europe. Their rituals and traditions had developed minor differences over 1,000 years but they both remained true to Orthodoxy.

The Ashkenazi immigrants initially scraped a living in London, often taking menial jobs serving the Sephardim, though there were exceptions who managed to flourish. One such was Moses Hart, who became a prominent Ashkenazi merchant, and built the Ashkenazi Great Synagogue near Bevis Marks in the City of London in 1722. It cost him £2,000, which is over £300,000 today. Moses Hart had been born in Breslau in Germany, the son of a rabbi. The earliest relic of Jews in that town is a tombstone from the 13th century. From there you can finish up back in Biblical times. The author's wife's ancestry can be traced back to 80AD.

The stories in the Pentateuch are well known, but what is long forgotten is the religions which existed in the days of the Bible, but which have now vanished. The gods of the Canaanites included El and Baal, the Philistines had Dagon and the Moabites Chemosh. Faithful to the Pentateuch were the Samaritans, but they were often at daggers drawn with the Jews in the Holy Land and equally numerous. They are almost forgotten today but in Biblical times the Samaritans were as important as the Jews.

It has never been easy to maintain a religion, particularly when you are conquered by other, much more powerful, nations. The Greeks and the Romans had their own household gods, and it is only necessary to look at the Pyramids to see the power of the Egyptians in their prime. The Romans had so much trouble conquering the Jews, however, that the eventual peace treaty allowed the Israelites to continue to follow their own religion. They were the only people in the Roman Empire to be granted that privilege.

The new Christian church grew over the years from the teaching of Jesus and was officially made the religion of Constantine's empire in the 4th century. The Church then spent well over a millennium trying to convert the Jews. To achieve this they tried persuasion, massacres, discriminatory taxation, expulsion, blood libels, accusations of poisoning wells which led to pogroms, and accusations of murdering Christian children to use their blood to make matzas.

Jews survived all of that and it was only half of their problems. The other opposition to Orthodox Judaism came from segments of the Jews themselves over the centuries; the Karaites, Sabbateans, Conservatives, Reform, Liberal and Masorti, and many others.

The Sephardim had the support of the established Amsterdam Jewish community, though they had their fair share of the impoverished as well. Over the next 200 years the Sephardim remained the more senior element of the Jewish community in Britain. The Ashkenazim, however, became more numerous and settled in many ports around the country. They spoke foreign languages and could trade with the ships which visited the ports. The emigrants often came from the same areas in Europe and they created Synagogues like the 18th century building in Plymouth. Their relationship with each other was, however, tenuous and many are still sturdily independent to this day.

Naturally, those who prospered were the likely leaders of the community, because creating a Jewish community infrastructure is expensive; ideally, a Sefer Torah, a Synagogue, a cemetery, a mikvah (a ritual bath), and a school are needed, besides the spiritual leaders, a shochet (animal slaughterer), mohel (circumciser), and other Synagogue officers.

Providing the necessary finance led to those who did so becoming the leaders of the community and that meant that the congregation's ministers had a lower status. While they could be relied upon to maintain the Orthodox ritual, they were treated as servants of the community.

Nationally, Jewish brokers played a major role in supporting the government in several crises. Francisco Lopez Suasso gave William III an interest-free loan of two million crowns to finance the 1689 invasion. Solomon de Medina had the bread contract to feed the army in the War of the Spanish Succession from 1707-1711, and incidentally paid Marlborough, the British General, £63,000 in bribes to keep the contract. (At least £9 million today).

The crucial decision for the community came in 1715 when Queen Anne had died and James Francis Edward Stuart, the Old Pretender, claimed the throne. He had the best case by far, but the government was Protestant and he was a Catholic. The government's choice was George of Hanover who was the 45th in line but was the first Protestant. It was known that the Old Pretender intended to invade the country to win the throne and might well win in battle with the government's forces. The question for the Jews before the invasion was who to support.

They were fortunate to have as their spiritual leader the Italian David Nieto, who was a very talented Talmudist and a strong minister. When consulted, David Nieto referred the lay leaders, the Mahamad, to a third century Jewish law, Dina de Malchuta Dina. In English it meant that the law of the country in which the Jews were living, was to be the law of the community as well.

The Mahamad accordingly voted to support the government by 18 votes to 5, and when the Old Pretender was defeated, the loyalty of the Jewish community was proven – particularly as one of their members, Menassah Lopez, steadied the pound when the invasion came. This avoided a financial crisis and Samson Gideon did the same when the Young Pretender invaded in 1745.

Later in the century the Rothschilds supported the pound during the Napoleonic Wars, and generations later raised the money to enable Benjamin Disraeli to buy the shares in the Suez Canal, which proved such a profitable investment for the country. When antisemites question the influence of Jewish financiers, the support they have given successive governments in difficult economic times is very seldom mentioned in their favour.

Henry Pelham, the prime minister in 1745, was grateful to Samson Gideon and a bill was passed in the House of Lords in 1753 to allow Jews to apply for naturalisation. It was called the Jewish Naturalisation Bill or more commonly the Jew Bill. It was, however, the cause of a considerable outbreak of antisemitism by those who held that such a law should only apply to Christians and it was repealed in 1754.

The Sephardim were recognised as the senior body by the government. When, for example, a delegation of the Sephardim called on King George III to tender their respects on his coronation, the Ashkenazim were not included in the group. They protested, however, at their absence and a new body called the Board of Deputies of British Jews emerged where both were represented. In the early part of the 19th century the leader of the Sephardim, Sir Moses Montefiore, became the accepted lay leader for the community as a whole and was also the chair of the Board.

The Sephardim were paternalistic towards the Ashkenazim. For example, it was reported to them on one occasion that a Jew was lying dead in the street. The Sephardim established that he was Ashkenazi and promptly rooted the Great Synagogue wardens out of their beds in the middle of the night to deal with the body appropriately. The Great wardens were suitably embarrassed.

Besides London, the immigrant Jews who created communities in many parts of Britain did not form a national body. They often did come, however, to consult the rabbi of the Great Synagogue in London when they wanted rulings on spiritual matters, but they remained independent. They would also seek the Chief Rabbi's help in finding suitable candidates for Synagogue positions. The minister's office became an unofficial labour exchange. He was eventually acknowledged as the Chief Rabbi, which was an unusual distinction for Jews internationally. This relationship would influence the way the Central came to develop in the future.

Reminiscing at the turn of the 19th century, it was remembered as a time when the wealthy Jews occupied only four streets in the West End and their spiritual needs were satisfied by one small Synagogue in the Strand. There were said to be less than ten worth £10,000 and the only benevolent association was the Bread, Milk and Coal charity. It was not unusual for a warden to serve twenty years, as occupying the office was considered becoming a member of the Jewish peerage. Only at this time were moves afoot to found the Jewish Hospital and Jews' Free School. It was solemnly recorded in the obituary of one of the wardens that he had always been a gentleman.

The Reform movement started in Hamburg in 1818 and spread over the years to be predominant in America and Germany. Originally it had a higher social status in its home country and was favoured by those more anxious to fit in with the general population. Just over a century later the Holocaust reduced the number of every kind of Jew by millions, but over the preceding period few British Jews had joined the Reform and Liberal movements. The great majority of British Jews remained Orthodox. One of the reasons for this was the Central Synagogue.

Over the centuries most of the new immigrant Jews were poverty-stricken refugees and in Britain, their new country, many became old clothes men and pedlars, or worked in sweat shops making clothes. There were again some major exceptions, one of whom was the Rothschild family. When the Napoleonic Wars were raging, the family patriarch, the German Jewish banker, Mayer Amschel Rothschild, was handed the fortune of the Elector of Hesse Kassel to invest abroad when the country was invaded.

The sum involved was very large as the Elector had, over the years, made a fortune by hiring out his men as mercenaries to rulers who needed more soldiers. There were 350 German states at the time within the whole country. Mayer Amschel gave the funds to his son, Nathan Mayer, who came to Britain and started a business in the thriving town of Manchester.

Rothschild was like so many Jewish entrepreneurs over the centuries. Jews were usually forbidden to join the Guilds which ran the traditional industries in a European country. They were only permitted to operate in undertakings which were potentially viable but risky in developing, such as the importation of Indian diamonds in the 18th century. The Jews became expert at spotting the hole in the market and Nathan Mayer Rothschild saw the opportunity provided by the British government's need for capital to pay for the war. He used the Elector's money to invest in gilt edged stock to support the pound and to buy and sell in the money market, both in Britain and overseas.

The pay for Wellington's army in Spain, for example, was clandestinely sent from London, through the Rothschild's office in Paris, even though Wellington was fighting the French in the Peninsula. Moreover, when London bankers were charging the government high interest rates, the Rothschilds were far more patriotic in their terms.

Nevertheless, over the period of the Napoleonic wars the national debt rose from under £300 million to over £1,000 million. The finances of many European countries also came under great strain and equally looked to the Rothschilds for help.

By such activities the Rothschilds became extremely wealthy, though they paid the Elector back every pfennig to which he was entitled when the war finally ended. In future years the family opened branches of business in Vienna, Rome and Paris, as well as Frankfurt and London. Religiously, the sons didn't stray. They continued to follow in their father's footsteps and remained very Orthodox.

Nathan became a warden of the Great Synagogue in 1818, together with his brother-in-law, Solomon Cohen, and was influential in creating a treaty in 1835 which saw the three main London synagogues, the Great, the Hambro and the New, agreeing to centralise their distribution of aid to the poor; the Great gave half the annual charity and the two other synagogue a quarter each. Nathan had recognised the increased efficiency which would result from the centralisation of the efforts of the Synagogues as early as 1823, but it took twelve years to achieve agreement.

Charity is a fundamental in Judaism. On the day of the great Fast, Yom Kippur, the Almighty is believed to decide the fate of every individual in the coming year. The only ways of avoiding a poor outcome are penitence, prayer and charity. It is considered wise not to neglect the poor and the elderly.

What was particularly noticeable about the Rothschilds was the strength of their family feeling. They did everything together and looked after each other whenever there was any need. Nathan died in 1836 and Lionel Nathan de Rothschild succeeded him as a warden of the Great. He would also be the first Orthodox Jewish MP. In addition, he was also behind the appointment of Chief Rabbi Nathan Marcus Adler in 1845 and the Rothschild family continued to serve as wardens of the Great for many years thereafter.

By the middle of the 19th century, however, a considerable proportion of the London Jewish community had moved from the East End City area to the more upmarket West End and walking to the Synagogues in the City proved onerous, particularly for the children. What was long forgotten in modern times was that the City walls in the 18th century were accepted as an Eruv. (An enclosed space which could be treated as your house and therefore not subject to all the sabbath rules upon movement.)

Chief Rabbi Hart Lyon is on record in the 18th century as criticising the Great Synagogue congregation for carrying packages "outside the City walls" on the Sabbath. Which must logically mean that inside the City walls were acceptable as an Eruv and, for instance, you could push a pram there. There was another Eruv in the East End which Chief Rabbi Solomon Herschell approved.

This came about after a cholera epidemic had subsided in the 1830s, when a Jewish entrepreneur decided to build some houses for the poor as a thanksgiving. He obtained the Chief Rabbi's permission for the area to constitute an eruv. In attempting to get one approved in the North of

London against some pretty stiff opposition in the 20th century the precedent was never recalled, which strengthens the case for recording history thoroughly.

Solomon Herschell set the standard for observance within the main Synagogues. For example, on Rosh Hashonah it is the Din that one should wash away one's sins by throwing bread into a river. So, Solomon Herschell threw bread into the Thames. The only problem for Londoners was that when he set out from his house in the City to walk to the river, the community followed in his footsteps and caused a dense traffic jam.

Within the Sephardi community there was a rule from Stuart times that none of their members could form a synagogue within six miles of Bevis Marks. The ruling lay leaders, the Mahamad, refused the suggestion that one be allowed to be built in the West End. The rationale was that additional congregations would result in splitting the synagogue's funds, to the detriment of its many charitable enterprises. As a consequence of this, however, a number of Bevis Marks Sephardim and Great Synagogue Ashkenazim broke away, to found a new synagogue in the West End in 1840.

They were called Secessionists but there was concern that they might follow the example of several Jewish families in Hamburg and try, as they saw it, to modernise the religion itself. It wouldn't be correct to call the Secessionist Synagogue Reform at the time, though, for their practices differed very little from the Orthodox until almost 100 years later.

By contrast, the German breakaway movement was called Reform and the British Chief Rabbi from 1845, Nathan Marcus Adler, was determined to prevent it making progress in Britain. It wasn't the first breakaway from Orthodox Judaism in history by any means.

The laws in the Talmud had only been settled in the 6th century and movements like the Karaites and the Sabbateans had briefly been popular until they had declined and many vanished. The changes they tried to institute often suited the founders; for example, Sabbatei Zevi, the 18th century Sabbateian leader, made Tisha b'Av a festival instead of a fast because he had been born on Tisha b'Av. He eventually became a Moslem and there is still a small sect in Turkey, called the Donme, who observe a combination of Jewish and Moslem practices.

The Secessionist minister, David Woolf Marks, also tried to make changes but he was controlled by his Honorary officers, who wanted to remain within the Orthodox Jewish fold.

The old Chief Rabbi, Solomon Herschell, had pronounced a Herem on the Secessionists in 1840 just before he died, which was a form of excommunication. Although this was relaxed after some years, the Secessionist lay leaders were always conscious of the contumely of the community, which would fall on their heads if they made substantial changes in their Synagogue ritual. By far the majority of the British Jewish community rejected becoming Secessionist. It had no influence outside London for many years.

The Orthodox communities were, however, anxious to maintain their independence. For instance, Herschell's proclamation did not gain the approval of the small 18th century Orthodox Western Synagogue in London who refused to have anything to do with it, and that became another cause of dissension between the London Ashkenazi Synagogues.

While Chief Rabbi Adler was always concerned at the progress of Reform on the Continent, agreement to form a Branch synagogue in the West End was not solely a defence measure against the Secessionists. It was mostly a recognition that a number of the community was moving from the City to the West End, creating a need to make their journey to synagogue easier. As a snobbish side effect, it also enabled them to divorce themselves from their less wealthy neighbours. The lay leader of the community, Sir Moses Montefiore, might walk from his home in Park Lane to Bevis Marks, even when he was an old man, but it was considered too far for most of his community.

As a member of a Jewish Orthodox congregation in Britain today, it would be difficult to recognize the community as it existed in 1845. There had been a Chief Rabbi attached to the Great Synagogue since 1705, but the recently deceased Solomon Herschell had concentrated his attention on the Synagogues in London and did not have a great deal to do with the provinces.

There were no common prayer books and there were many minor differences between the various congregations throughout the country. Sermons were given on very few occasions, and then in Yiddish, a polyglot language, part Hebrew, part German with words from other tongues as well. It was also only a small community; while there are 280,000 Jews in Britain today, there were only 35,000 in 1845.

The expectation of life at birth in those days was about 40 and there were many fatal diseases. For example, in the 1860s, 50,000 Londoners died of cholera. Child mortality was considerable and heart-breaking, there was no old age pension, no unemployment benefit and if a poor person lost their job, the family could often suffer from malnutrition. Britain was effectively run by its landowners. The Corn Law tax, which penalised foreign corn imports, maintaining a higher price for bread than necessary for many years and hurting the poor, was only abolished in 1846.

Since George I came to the throne in 1715 there had been legislation to restrict the civil rights of people who were not members of the Church of England. Non-conformists and Catholics were not allowed to sit in Parliament, any more than Jews could. This legislation had been abandoned in favour of the Catholics in 1829, but remained applicable to Jews, who also weren't allowed to hold public office, own commercial property in the City or become military officers. They were also excluded from the Freedom of the City, were only selectively admitted to the Stock Exchange and had limited access to the legal profession.

The leaders of the community set out to achieve similar emancipation to the Catholics and slowly they achieved their objective. In 1830 they were finally allowed to own shops in the City and in 1835 David Salomons, who would become a member at the Central, was elected an Alderman. In 1855 he became the first Jewish Lord Mayor of London and the Oath Act which enabled Jews to sit as members of parliament, was passed in 1858, allowing the elected Lionel de Rothschild to finally take his seat in Parliament by swearing allegiance on the Old Testament.

Before, when taking the Oath of Allegiance on entering parliament, it was necessary to promise it "on the true word of a Christian." A number of Jews, like the economist, David Ricardo, had been prepared to swallow their principles, and swear the Christian oath but Rothschild, a pillar of the proposed new Branch synagogue in the West End, had no intention of doing so. There still remained restrictions in society though; for instance, Jews were only finally able to obtain degrees at Oxford and Cambridge by the terms of the passing of the Universities Test Act in 1871.

For the community there were consequently two distinct objectives; emancipation and Orthodoxy. They were usually promoted harmoniously but not always. For instance, where the government was prepared to sanction Jewish marriages without their municipal involvement, those Jewish lay leaders who wanted equality with their fellow citizens, did not want to be made exceptions. The religious and secular leaders disagreed, normally the Chief Rabbi and Sir David Salomons, and a civil certificate is still needed to legalise a Jewish wedding, besides a religious ketubah. Only now has a law been passed to make the giving of a *Get*, a divorce, mandatory for husbands, and it is a very contentious ruling.

The Din is that a divorce means that a husband voluntarily gives his wife a legal divorce document called a Get. The wife, however, does not have to accept it. She did up to 1,000 years before Victorian times, but in the early Middle Ages the German Rabbi Gershom ben Judah decided that this was unfair to the wife. Rashi said that every rabbi was Rabbi Gershom's student, and his ruling was accepted. It was a rare instance of a Din being changed.

Above all, the Victorians were a class ridden society. The ultimate social achievement was to be accepted as a gentleman. To be rejected was to suffer humiliation. There were still all kinds of rejection even after emancipatory legislation. You could be blackballed when you tried to become a member of a London club. Your children could be refused admission to public schools. There were any number of societies which could turn Jews down as members and these included golf and tennis clubs, Freemasons' lodges, universities and local political clubs.

The government might emancipate Jews by the passing of the Oath Act which allowed them to be MPs, by the University Test Act which let them take degrees at Oxford and Cambridge, and acts which enabled them to take public office, but British society could still refuse to accept them. The Jews who left the East End knew that they were more likely to be considered gentlemen and treated as such if they had a West End address.

Within the London community there was also both cooperation and discord. There were five major Ashkenazi London synagogues in 1845; the Great, (1722) Hambro, (1725) New, (1760), Western (1761) and Maiden Lane (1810). The Hambro and the New were founded by members who fell out with the Great, and Maiden Lane by members who fell out with the Western. Jews can be as argumentative as anybody else.

This was the community Nathan Marcus Adler inherited when he was appointed Chief Rabbi in 1845. His election had been surreptitiously fixed, even though it was claimed to be democratic. Admittedly, to decide the successful candidate, for the first time, all the British Jewish communities could have a vote, but only if they agreed to give £5 a year to support the Chief Rabbi's office. Most communities were poor and could only afford one or two votes. The wealthy Great, Hambro and New synagogues in London finally had 95 votes out of 141 and cast them for Adler after a great deal of lobbying.

Adler had been Chief Rabbi in Hanover in Germany for over a decade and his father was a great friend of the Rothschilds. It therefore mattered that Lionel de Rothschild was the warden of the Great, as this ensured their votes. The seat holders at the Synagogues each had a vote to see which candidate they would nominate and when Rothschild made his personal preference known, there was sufficient support for his wishes to be approved.

Adler also had the support of the former governor general of Hanover, the Duke of Cumberland. When his Duchess was very ill in pregnancy in

1835, she was not expected to live. As a consequence, Adler had held services in the Hanover synagogue to pray for her recovery. When she did survive, the Duke felt indebted to Adler ever after. Cumberland recommended Adler to Rothschild, and Adler was also supported by Sir Moses Montefiore, whose company had lit the streets of Hanover and who approved of Adler's sermons. There were very few sermons given in Britain at the time. The Chief Rabbi, himself, was only committed to speaking from the pulpit before the festivals of Passover and Rosh Hashonah.

The relations between the Adler and Rothschild families could hardly have been closer. In Germany when Amschel Rothschild, the founder, went to Hanover he always called on Adler's father, Rabbi Mordecai, for his blessing. The bond, once formed, was maintained as part of the family ethos.

The Rothschild family was immensely important in the City of London, raising money for many nations. They were rich beyond the dreams of avarice and they considered that their success was entirely due to the beneficence of the Almighty. Although they were also extremely family minded, what seems to have never come out was that Nathan Marcus Adler had married a Rothschild.

His first wife, Henrietta, was the granddaughter of Jeanette von Rothschild who was the sister of Nathan Rothschild, the head of the clan. If there was dissension on religious matters in the community, the Adlers could always rely on the support of the Rothschilds if it came to the crunch. The first Lord Rothschild, the future head of the United Synagogue, was his younger cousin. The impression has been given that Rothschild dominated Adler but all the evidence is that he backed up the Chief Rabbi whenever it was necessary.

One of the first things Adler had done on entering office was to send a questionnaire to all his congregations, asking them about the practice in their shul. Then he issued a list of forty-seven instructions in 1847, which set down a single approach for all the Synagogues which acknowledged his authority. This would apply to the Central in the future as much as any other shul. As Adler said:

> The following regulations which are in strict conformity with the Law, are laid down for general guidance, and it is confidently hoped that all congregations, as well as all the individuals who attend the Synagogues, will adhere to these laws, remove all differences, and conduct themselves so that everyone shall feel impelled to exclaim "How awful is the place; this is truly a house of God.

The Secessionists did not acknowledge the authority of the Chief Rabbi. They were few in number, but they came from powerful families. Their secession often split relations, parents and children and caused much sorrow. There was, however, as is so often the case, a hidden agenda. It went back all the way to when the Spanish started to shell Gibraltar in 1779. Over the years they fired 250,000 shells on the Rock and the whole Sephardi community had to be evacuated to London, along with the other citizens, where they joined Bevis Marks.

One year, on the death of one of their number, mourning services were held in the home of the deceased. This was within the rules of the London Sephardim, but not when prayers were also said at the same time to mark the festival of Shavuot.

These, according to the Ascamot (rules) of the congregation, should have been held in the Synagogue. The Gibraltar Jews involved were severely criticised and fined, much to their resentment.

By 1835, however, they had gained control of the Bevis Marks lay leadership and it was the older, longer-established non-Gibraltarian families who wanted a Synagogue in the West End. The rebuff the Gibraltarians had suffered 50 years before had not been forgotten. With the agreement of Chief Rabbi Herschell, they punished the Secessionists by having the Herem issued. The Secessionists had not intended to depart from the ranks of the Orthodox. As was pointed out:

> West London was not a German Reform congregation. Its innovations were sermons in the vernacular, an organ and a shorter service....the slow emergence of the Reform Synagogue of Great Britain evidenced the majestic gradualism and spirit of compromise of the British scene.

For 100 years this majestic gradualism proceeded at less than a snail's pace, and the compromise was to not stray from the Orthodox ritual in any serious way. The official history of the Reform movement in Britain states:

> The West London Synagogue of British Jews was run by its Council of Founders and their committees, not by the Clergy. The Minister had to refer to the governing laity on nearly all Synagogue matters, taking instructions as to when and where to preach.

Ministers in those days were effectively treated as second class citizens and the rationale of the approach of the West London Honorary officers was summed up by their warden, Moses Mocatta, nine of whose family had been among the original Secessionists:

> For any least deviation, unqualified censure will be heaped upon us and the self-styled Orthodox of our co-religionists will gladly seize on the minutest point to vilify our minister and cast obloquy on our congregation.

Many years later the popular journalist, Chaim Bermant, coined the phrase 'The Cousinhood', to describe the old Jewish families; they did marry among themselves and tried to keep out those who came from families not considered gentlemen. To lose the exclusive, if informal, membership of the group was a fear that greatly concerned the likes of the Mocattas.

Even so, there was competition among the Orthodox and the Secessionists for members. The Great Synagogue Orthodox wanted to retain the loyalty of their congregation and the Burton Street Secessionists wanted to win them over to their point of view. When the Central Synagogue was finally built, in 1874 the *Jewish Chronicle* summed up the situation as it had developed:

> We may say that the members of the new congregation deny altogether the impeachment of having renounced the Oral Law. Professor Marks and Mr. Elkin, in the earlier days of the Reform, strenuously maintained the general fidelity of their congregation to the Jewish tradition....there is probably less discrepancy between the Jews forming what are called Orthodox congregations and Jews who are members of the Reformed Congregation of London than is apparent within the bosom of a single denomination of Christians, we will say the Church of England. [The Reform synagogue] cannot be characterised other than as a secession.

That situation wasn't guaranteed to last forever though. It wasn't just a matter of religious practice either. There were commercial considerations. Sir Anthony de Rothschild (1810-1876) was now the senior warden at the Great and both Rothschilds and Mocatta & Goldsmid were powerful firms in the City. When a committee was set up to daily fix the price of gold in 1919, Rothschilds would chair the meeting and Mocatta & Goldsmid would be one of the five companies setting the price. It would have been in neither family's interest to fall out.

The other major player was Nathan Marcus Adler, the Chief Rabbi. He had seen the growth of Reform Judaism in Germany and was determined that the British community would not go down the same path. He had maintained the Orthodoxy of the Jews in Hanover when he was the Chief Rabbi from 1831-1845. When he came to London, he followed exactly the same principles with the congregations in Britain and the Empire who acknowledged his authority. Behind the scenes Nathan Marcus Adler was the creator of the United Synagogue when it was formed.

The growth of the Reform congregations in Germany aroused a great deal of criticism within the British community. The new *Jewish Chronicle* reflected the views of their readers:

> These men in fact did not desire a reformed but a more convenient Judaism; not a spark of religious fervour animated their deliberations; not an item of religious zeal stimulated their doings. A desire of assimilating with their Christian neighbours under the mask of reformed Jews, all their proceedings betray and they have forfeited the sympathy of religious Israel.

It was in that atmosphere that the recommendations for changes in the ritual and the creation of a Branch Synagogue needed to be seen. There was, however, another factor which influenced the country as a whole; this was the Chartist movement which campaigned for political reform. Its programme was considered so dangerous that when they proposed to petition parliament, the government arranged for the Queen and Prince Albert to leave London for the safety of the Isle of Wight. They were so concerned that they also armed the staff at the Foreign Office and recruited tens of thousands of special constables. The Chartist petition was alleged to have six million signatures.

Although the movement petered out, rather than face thousands of troops at their main gathering in April 1848, the possibility of radical change was in the public's mind and could be seen to lead to successful uprisings in Europe in that year. Where the Great, the Hambro and the New Synagogue had been the undisputed Jewish main centres of worship for the past 100 years, the alteration of established norms was now far more feasible for the Great's Honorary Officers. Having avoided the revolution that affected most of Europe, successive governments were very reluctant to change anything radical for many years, but this did not affect the efforts of the Honorary Officers of the Great. The Rothschilds continued to press for a more acceptable oath.

It did, however, make it very difficult to get sufficient support to pass an Oath Act to allow Jewish MPs to swear allegiance on the Old Testament. Bills were raised for some years after the Chartists but were not passed. It would take a very hot summer to drive most of the MPs away from parliament and enable the Oath Act to be passed by a small number of votes in 1858. The building of a new synagogue in the West End may have been considered desirable, but many in the community were content to keep a low profile.

1. Shul interior

2

A tender Branch

The Jews had emigrated to Britain over the centuries since Charles II approved their return, for a number of reasons. First, and most important, was because it was safe. The majority came through the London docks and settled in the East End near the fashionable City area. As London was the financial and commercial centre of the country, the Jewish merchants and brokers made their homes in the City. As it was a major port, poor emigrants settled down in the vicinity when they arrived at the docks, because they didn't have to travel any further and it was the least expensive place to lay their heads.

There were also communities in the major ports, like Plymouth, Liverpool and Portsmouth, and in a number of provincial towns like Manchester and Birmingham. The members often acted as agents for companies in the countries from which they had come. They created their own Synagogues and ran their own affairs.

All of them spoke foreign languages, so they were able to communicate with the sailors on the ships calling at the ports, and enable them to replenish their stocks. Among themselves, they used Yiddish socially but obviously spoke the language of the countries from which they originally came. From time to time duty had to be paid on the imports the ships carried as cargo, and there were arguments with the Customs.

When he became Chief Rabbi, what Nathan Marcus Adler immediately recognised as a major problem was that the community didn't have anything like enough home-grown ministers, who could guide their congregations. Chief Rabbi Herschell had formed a Beth Din in 1808, but the dayanim who were rabbis, were usually Poles. There were a few Synagogues with Talmudically able ministers, but those few were normally foreigners as well. There was no national approach and where there was more than one congregation in a town, the different bodies often fell out.

So, when Nathan Marcus Adler was appointed Chief Rabbi in 1845, he set out to strengthen the organisation and infrastructure of the community. One of his objectives was to create a college to train British ministers. The fact was, however, that in this endeavour he was starting his efforts almost from scratch; the college didn't exist, he had to raise the finance, and there wasn't a structure or a curriculum; he had to solve all these problems and it took him 10 years.

There was also another major problem for the community; education was always considered to be fundamental to the maintenance of the religion, and there was concern when, in the early part of the 19th century, evangelists set up a number of conversionist schools to try to attract and convert Jewish children to Christianity; the substantial bribe many of them offered Jewish parents was a suit of clothes and lunch every day for their children. A few succumbed to the bribe and to combat this problem, the Jews' Free School was built up, until it became the largest school in the country by the turn of the 20th century, with over 4,000 pupils.

It had been created originally in 1732 as the Talmud Torah (Hebrew school) of the Great Synagogue, to educate orphan children. The wealthy members from the early days of the Synagogue tried to help their poorer brethren and were to be commended for it, but they wanted their own children to attend more prestigious academies. The Jews' Free School moved to Bell Lane in the East End in 1822 but still attracted primarily poor children. The main objective of the governors, though, was to teach the pupils how to earn a living, rather than to join the ranks of Synagogue ministers or become Talmudic scholars.

From its earliest days the school attracted the support of the Rothschilds, notably Hannah, Nathan Meyer's wife. It was said that the Rothschilds provided "suits and boots, spectacles and scholarships" and in addition their financial support was munificent. Educationally, for most of the 19th century, the day-to-day running of the school was in the very capable hands of Moses Angel, an exceptional headmaster, even though it was public knowledge that his father was a con man and had died in Tasmania after being sentenced to be transported.

The Chief Rabbi was fully supportive of the Jews' Free School but he also wanted a college specifically to train ministers because, as he said at his inauguration:

> [It is] extremely difficult to guard it [the law] at a time in which one party seeks its glory in pulling down existing structures of religious theory and practice; the other in preserving everything hallowed by age, though opposed to the foundations of the law; in which one minister worships progress and the other adores conservatism.

Adler did a great deal to solve the problem during his ministry, but it is still the cause of much contention to this day. On the one hand are the Progressives who consider change is permissible, and on the other the Charedim who stick rigidly to conservatism. The Central, over the years has usually tried to take a middle path.

The low status of synagogue ministers also militated against the comparatively few wealthy Jewish families wanting their sons to join their ranks. Professionals, like lawyers or doctors, were better rewarded and attracted a higher regard in the very class-conscious Victorian society. As a consequence, pupils at what would become Jews' College were also primarily from poor families, who were seldom considered as belonging in the ranks of so-called gentlemen.

They were initially also just boys 'and had to be trained in the fundamentals before they were ready for a curriculum which was designed to make them able to serve congregations. Many wouldn't stay the course.

In 1848 the authorities of the Great Synagogue had decided that the removal of the homes of many of its most influential supporters to the West End, would become a source of danger to its viability. The only solution was to establish a Synagogue in the new neighbourhood. The City was becoming only the financial centre it is today, rather than equally residential. Alternatively, there were fields in the West End on which fine houses could be built. The problem for the Honorary Officers of the Great had become more urgent because the Secessionists had built their first Synagogue in Burton Street in the West End in 1842 and they were attracting as members many of those who now lived in the district.

In 1848 the foundation stone was laid of a new Secessionist synagogue in Margaret Street. For the most part, though, it wouldn't be religious differences that drew Great Synagogue members to Margaret Street, because the secessionist Honorary Officers deliberately ensured there was little difference in the rituals. It was the convenience of the Margaret Street location to their new homes which was the attraction. The media were certain this was the reasoning of the Margaret Street members:

> Their motives are obviously not to pull down but to uphold the walls of Judaism....

> They do not aim at touching the pillars, but to repair them and prevent their decay.

The Written Law and the Oral Law were seen to remain sacrosanct.

The senior members of the Great became increasingly concerned over time but they were busy men and months passed before a committee meeting in November 1848 agreed:

> That it being considered of the utmost importance that a place of worship in connection with this synagogue be established at the West End of the metropolis, this Committee do take the subject into consideration at the next meeting.

"Utmost importance" did not translate into immediate action, but who were these families who were moving to the West End? For the most part they were only two or three generations away from living in poverty in European ghettoes themselves.

As Shakespeare had suggested, they had "taken arms against a sea of troubles and, by opposing, ended them". It is not sufficiently appreciated how courageous a decision was needed to leave friends and family in their native lands, to give up rewarding occupations and to go to live in a country where they probably didn't speak the language. In many cases, however, their very lives were at stake and then there was little option. The descendants of so many of those who didn't emigrate died a century later in the Holocaust.

Large numbers of the emigrants who had come to Britain after the 1848 revolutionary uprisings in Europe had petered out and the old regimes had returned to power. The common language of the immigrants remained Yiddish and certainly not English. When Nathan Marcus Adler was appointed Chief Rabbi, it was one of the conditions that he learned English within two years; he managed it in one.

Nathan Marcus Adler always had a German accent, as did his son and successor, Hermann Adler. This was quite acceptable in society. The many German states had been the allies of the British for more than a century; the British monarchs had also been Kings of Hanover from 1715 to 1837; it was the last-minute arrival of the Prussian army under Marshall Blucher which enabled Wellington to win the battle of Waterloo, even though in June 1815, addressing his troops and in his seventies, the general announced that he was pregnant by an elephant! At home, in royal circles too, Prince Albert of Saxe Coburg was a popular consort of Queen Victoria. The French were the traditional enemies, and it would be many years before Germany even became a single state, a possible competitor and threat. Queen Victoria's oldest daughter married the King of Prussia and became the Empress. By the end of the century, most of the royal families in Europe were related to Queen Victoria.

Although there were a few wealthy exceptions like the Rothschilds, who remained very independent, most of the families leaving the City were anxious to fit in with their Victorian neighbours, by becoming more English than the English. For example, including the Rothschilds, gentlemen wore top hats which was one way of fitting in with the upper and middle classes. Top hats were not restricted to the Synagogue Honorary Officers but were worn by many members in the streets and shul as well.

On the religious side, the tallish (prayer shawl) was a typical example of conformity. It was, of course, always worn in Synagogue on the Sabbath. For centuries it had been made of white wool with black stripes. When, however, a manufacturer produced a silk tallish with a light blue stripe, it became recognised as a mark of class superiority. There was also a version which was not so all-enveloping. The time would come in the middle of the twentieth century when wearing black and white woollen tallish would be considered common.

Fashions change though, and after many years of declining observance, those who remained particularly traditional started to wear the black and white tallish again. More years elapsed and the black and white tallish became an outward sign of greater Orthodoxy, as against the blue and white. Today blue and white is not fashionable in Orthodox circles.

There was nothing in the Talmud about the correct dress for rabbis. The policy on mandatory canonicals came in future from the United Synagogue authorities. Before that time a lot of Ashkenazi ministers wore a hexagonal black cap, a black gown and neck bands. There was a High Holyday version in white. Clerical dress was the tradition of the church and associated with it, but it had originally been academic dress and not clerical anyway.

There was also no definite ruling about the dress of the ladies, except that it should not distract the men from their prayers. As the emigrants who arrived in the East End in the 1880s were often more observant than the existing community, their ladies would cover their hair with a sheitel, a wig.

This was designed to reduce the attractiveness of their public appearance and it was not popular with many of the wives of those who had moved to the West End. It still isn't, but it is a very ancient tradition. The potential attraction of the ladies was taken seriously by the newcomers. The possibility of men's apparel distracting the ladies was not an issue, any more than there was a serious campaign for equal rights for women at the time.

There was a clear distinction, however, in one aspect of the ladies' dress. Unmarried women had never had to wear a hat in Synagogue and it was now decided that married women did not have to do so either in the proposed new Branch Synagogue. This is still the policy at Central today. There is another aspect of the Din which applies here. When the practice in a community has been in effect for a long time, it becomes a law; that now covers the hat of the married ladies at Central.

It wasn't easy for the emigrants to communicate with the general public when they didn't speak their language well. There are about half a million words in English, four times as many as any other language. There are innumerable nuances and pronunciations, and dialects like Oxford English and the Scottish brogue are far apart. Provincial accents were considered down-market too, but these differences are not always recognised by people who come from poor homes and who may not be well educated.

There are, for example, the expressions "gentlemen" and "ladies". The abbreviation "gents" has been used for years to recognise the superiority of gentlemen who have made the grade. "Gents" is also, of course, used as a name for a toilet.

When the minutes of the Central Board of Management in the 1950s were written, there were references to Ladies' seats in the new synagogue and "Gents" seats. It wasn't Oxford English, but the wealth of members did not always equate with an in-depth knowledge of the English language. Today the future of the tie is in doubt, but efforts to keep up with the Jones will, no doubt, continue. It was in the Victorian days that the term "posh" emerged.

The best cabins to enjoy the sun by liner to South Africa were on the port side of the ship. Coming back, the best cabins were on the starboard side. Hence "Port Out, Starboard Home", equals posh. The unspoken aim of the Central's members was to be posh, as was the ambition of every West End Synagogue congregation. The members did not want the accusation of being common or foreign; they too wanted the status of gentlemen.

Their polyglot language, Yiddish, was not upmarket. It was severely attacked by Lord Rothschild when he became head of the United Synagogue. Yiddish didn't help the ambitions of the community to fit in with the general population and Lord Rothschild wanted it abolished. Over the years it declined, but it is still widely used in the very Orthodox communities. Their teachers often give the lessons in their schools in the ancient language. Yiddish does, in fact, have a commendable literary history and great 20th century authors, like Isaac Bashevis Singer, still wrote in Yiddish. A lot of Yiddish words are now part of the English language as well and are to be found in the authoritative Oxford English Dictionary; words like shtick, shtook, chutzpah and shtum, for example.

Another formality came when a member was offered a part in the service; they would shake the hands of the wardens sitting in their box, before resuming their seats. They still do, though the Sephardim bow instead of shaking hands. Top hats for the wardens were only generally discontinued as the 21st century dawned. Barmitzvah boys wore top hats in the Central before the Second World War. As a concession, they were allowed to wear trilby hats during the conflict.

There were other signs of affluence which distinguished gentlemen and ladies. One was what would be called today being overweight. If people were stout, it meant that they could afford plenty to eat; meals could easily run to six or seven courses. The dangers of obesity and cholesterol were only to be discovered well into the future.

In addition, a typical Branch male congregant would have either a substantial beard or at least a moustache. There were fashions in hair styles as well; sideburns and handlebar moustaches were popular. The wealthy used moustache cups to avoid the luxurious growth getting wet in their tea. A casual appearance was a sign of poverty. Jeans had yet to be invented, though a Jew, Adolf von Baeyer, would win the Nobel prize for inventing artificial indigo which is always used to colour the trousers.

From the outset, the Great committee were determined that any new synagogue in the West End should be erected under their own auspices. At the time there was an 1808 treaty between the three City Synagogues on the one hand and the Western Synagogue independently. It was agreed that no additional synagogue would be encouraged within six miles of the Strand, where the Western Synagogue was located. The Western broke the agreement, however, so the City Synagogues didn't feel bound by it. The Western's refusal to display the Herem against the Secessionists was another cause of dissension.

Some progress was made when a subcommittee was appointed in 1849 to report the views of the Great on a new Synagogue in the West End. It took them a further two months to register their approval of the idea and a meeting of 29 members of the Great vestry then resolved unanimously:

> That it is highly necessary that a branch Synagogue in connection with this congregation should, without delay, be established in the West End of the Metropolis in order to afford the numerous members of the Synagogue and their families, residing in that locality, the means to attend a place of divine worship.

This is what they had minuted the previous November. The committee was very representative of the members. It consisted of Lewis Jacobs, the president, who was a shirtmaker in the Strand, the merchant, Samuel Moses, who was the Treasurer, Sir Anthony de Rothschild, the banker, Dennis Samuel who was with Samuel Montagu in the City and Joshua Alexander, the father of David Alexander, the future president of the Board of Deputies.

There was also Samuel de Symons who had emigrated from Russia, now a member of the Stock Exchange. He had played a large part in the creation of the Branch. He was highly regarded in the community and took a keen interest in the Jewish schools. When he died in 1860 a group of JFS schoolboys, out of respect, came to his burial, which the Chief Rabbi conducted. Morris Emanuel died some months after his appointment and there was also Simon Samuel, Mark Woolf and Baron S.B. Worms, a cousin of the Chief Rabbi's wife.

In February 1850, more than a year after the first resolution, it was decided that the new synagogue should be a quarter of a mile west of Regent Circus and £6,000 was allocated for its construction. It was agreed to invite the Sephardim, the Hambro and the New to join in the new enterprise as well. At a meeting to discuss this, it was decided that the delegates would consult with their congregants about the idea, but the Sephardim soon came to the conclusion that they couldn't see their way clear to cooperate, because of their different traditions.

> They were animated by an equal desire with that of the Wardens and the Committee of the Great Synagogue to promote so important an object as affording to the numerous residents of the West End of the Metropolis in connection with the City Synagogues the opportunity of attending a place of worship in their locality, but that there were insuperable difficulties in regard to the difference of ritual and the usage, customs and practices of the Synagogues, which the members of both communities must be equally anxious respectively to preserve...a friendly and cordial union with them and the other City Synagogues, and with a view to contribute their aid in supplying the spiritual wants of the Jewish community in the two existing Minhagim.

The Sephardim were in a minority in the London community and did not want to become in any way subservient. They had been the senior community since 1660 and they valued their status. Indeed, if a Sephardi girl married an Ashkenazi boy, there were Sephardi families who would sit shiva, as if the girl had died.

The Great now said that they were perfectly agreeable to the suggestion that the new Synagogue should be a branch of the united Ashkenazi congregations in the City. It was suggested that a quarter each of the cost should come from the New and the Hambro, and the Great would provide half. However, neither the Hambro nor the New were keen on finding that kind of money and it soon became clear that the new Synagogue would only be forthcoming if it was solely financed by the Great.

The discussions presaged the difficulties that would hamper the formation of the United Synagogue in the years to come. The trouble which often occurs with bodies getting together to cooperate is that it creates a new power structure and those who, as a result, become of lesser importance than in their previous role, can well resist the union.

On the question of altering the ritual, the Chief Rabbi wrote back to the Great Board of Management and warned them of his experience in Germany:

> Where the greatest variety of innovations had been introduced in the mode of worship, proved that the organic changing of the ritual throws a firebrand into the Congregation, which not only weakens the bond of union, but rends asunder the most sacred ties of relationship, and plunges the rabbis or ministers from the moment they leave the rabbinical precept into the greatest inconsistencies and forces them to proceed from reform to reform until it leads them to the undermining of those pillars on which the whole edifice rests, and moreover it is far from advantageous to Judaism at large, as the places of worship, after the first charm of novelty had subsided, were deserted.

Nathan Marcus Adler had seen this happen in Germany when he was the Chief Rabbi of Hanover. The ritual did remain under discussion for a time. Warden Dennis Samuel proposed that the new synagogue ritual should be:

> Based upon the true principles of our faith, congenial to the rising generation. [and that the services were] to be conducted upon a revised Orthodox foundation.

Dennis Samuel's views were not adopted. What the rising generation found congenial was hardly likely to be a unanimous view. For the time being the subject was dropped. The Chief Rabbi did allow the proposed new Branch synagogue to have a Choir and agreed that the first part of the Sabbath service could start at 8 o'clock and the second at 11. Otherwise, by their absence, he realised that members were likely to show that they didn't want to get up early in the morning and, to avoid this, would often neglect the first part of the service. They might find that congenial but the ritual wouldn't change fundamentally. For example, there are certain prayers which should be said within a few hours of dawn and the Chief Rabbi was going to keep to the rules. He did compromise in one area though, by agreeing to omit the majority of the piyutim [penitential prayers] which Aaron Levy Green, the future Central minister writing as Nemo in the *Jewish Chronicle*, attacked on many occasions in later years. The Chief Rabbi modified his views on other aspects of the ritual to a slight degree as well, but hardly at all. He said, however, that he hoped:

> that the various views on this important matter will be reconciled by my propositions, and that whatever contradictory feeling may be existing, all will give way to the paramount necessity of maintaining concord and union amongst our community.

A revised Orthodox foundation was not likely to appeal to Nathan Marcus Adler, even if members of the rising generation approved of the alterations. There were still those who were anxious to introduce changes in the ritual as far as the timing and the length of the services were concerned. The Chief Rabbi had, however, dealt with similar approaches when he was chief rabbi in Hanover and constantly opposed any real alternatives. He had approved a choir for the musaph service at the Branch Synagogue and agreed that there should be fewer misheberachs, (blessings), but nothing much else changed.

Who could oppose "concord and union" though? Attending Synagogue is an individual decision and many Orthodox Synagogues find it difficult to attract a congregation of ten men for morning and evening services, without which the mourning prayer for dead relatives cannot be said. Many churches have abandoned daily services now as well. Having fought a losing battle, a number of Synagogues gave up the attempt. Central though has always had a minyan, and the present congregation are still determined to do so. The ten come from a large core group. The Synagogue's existence as a place of divine worship remains its primary function.

Adler continued to urge the Great committee to get on with creating the Branch Synagogue, but the arguments for and against a Synagogue in the West End were not immediately resolved. It was only in July 1853, five years after the original decision, that fifteen members of the Vestry of the

Great visited a warehouse in Great Portland Street and agreed that it might make a suitable Synagogue.

They decided to take the building on a lengthy lease, so long as they could get agreement to raise the roof. Sir Anthony de Rothschild was one of the representatives, which gave it additional authority. The Rothschilds donated a third of the money needed. and it was agreed that the official address of the Branch would be 120, Great Portland Street. The eventual site included a block of leasehold houses.

It was now necessary to appoint a Chazan, a Second Reader and a Beadle. In choosing a minister Rev. Aaron Levy Green (1821-1883) had become very popular at the Great since he joined them as Second Reader at the age of 14 in 1851. He had come into contact with the leaders of the community, as Secretary of the new Jews' College a number of years later. He was also related to Rabbi Nathan Green, one of the ministers in Amsterdam.

At the early age of 32 he was appointed First Reader of the new Branch Synagogue without any other candidates being considered, at a salary of £300 a year plus a rent-free house, and in November 1853 the committee of the synagogue agreed that he could be "excused from the performance of certain of his duties for the purpose of study." He was not appointed the Minister, though. The First Reader at the time was designated the chazan and did not have the Minister's rank.

The new Chazan's father was a trader in Petticoat Lane in the East End and Aaron Levy Green was educated in the Talmud Torah section of the Jews' Free School. He came from a poor family, but he was a very bright child and had been allowed to conduct a service at the Great when he was only nine years old. At the age of 17 he was appointed minister of the Bristol congregation and held the post from 1838-1851.

Admittedly, he had no religious qualification, but in the provinces at the time those with a good voice and capable of taking a service were hard to find. Aaron Levy Green had no academic training either, but when he came to Bristol he adopted the title Reverend, by which he was known, and he was very studious all his life. Solomon Schechter, another power in the Jewish clerical land, said of him:

> Attending all sorts of meetings and performing all kinds of parish work during the day, he devoted his nights mostly to the study of Jewish literature. Once every month he would sit up the whole night for mental stock-taking, to review the studies that had occupied him for the previous four weeks.

There was nowhere in the country at the time – and for many years in the future – where Aaron Levy Green could get semichah, the rabbinic diploma. The Chief Rabbi kept the title of Rabbi to himself, partly to diminish the authority of the other ministers in other Synagogues by comparison, and partly because he genuinely had semichah and the others were usually insufficiently qualified Talmudically.

All the candidates for Chief Rabbi when Nathan Marcus Adler was appointed in 1845, were from Germany. Aaron Levy Green only became the official Central Synagogue minister in 1874. It wasn't until long after Nathan Marcus Adler's son, Hermann Adler, succeeded him, that a Jews' College student was awarded semicha.

As the *Jewish Chronicle* recalled in Aaron Levy Green's obituary about his time in Bristol:

> At that time a Reader was no more than a Chazan whose sole qualification used to consist in his voice. It was only natural that his social position was no higher than that of a Sheleach Tsibur (Messenger of the Congregation) as Mr. Green used often to point out. Against this degraded state of things Mr. Green protested with all the energy of his nature. He made it an established institution that an English sermon should form an integral part of public worship.

Well, in fact, the Chief Rabbi had encouraged English sermons and gave one at the Great every month, but Aaron Levy Green was an enthusiastic devotee and Nathan Marcus Adler was an excellent guru to his ministers.

There was little point, however, in the JC railing against "this degraded state of things" if nothing substantial was going to change. When the Central Synagogue was blitzed in 1941, there was a Board of Management meeting a couple. of weeks later. The minutes of the meeting recorded "Rev E. Nemeth, A Stoutsker and E. Roth attended by invitation." It was nearly 100 years later but normally the ministers would not be considered important enough to attend the Board of Management meetings except in unusual circumstances. If they weren't invited, they weren't welcome.

That was how synagogue ministers were regarded and treated. Praise might rightly be heaped on the head of Rabbi Cyril Shine when he died, but certainly in the 1960s he was not invited to attend the Board. The idea of inviting his colleague, the notable chazan, Simon Hass, was never suggested. In 2020 the president of the United Synagogue referred to the dynamic leadership of the Synagogue's rabbis:

Great rabbis lie at the heart of the United Synagogue. The respect
and affection for Rabbi Marcus, both within the Jewish community
and far beyond, are a real testimony to his status.

If they were considered great rabbis, they hadn't been treated as such in the
early days. In most Synagogues this respect and affection usually depended
on the personality of the incumbent and the Central had some very senior
lay leaders for many years, who had no intention of giving up their pre-
eminent authority. The Central would normally be run effectively and
efficiently by lay members, like all but the Synagogues of the ultra-religious
congregations.

There the rabbi was a very senior figure and ruled on many aspects of
a member's life, which in a United Synagogue would not be considered part
of the rabbi's responsibilities. Advice would always be available, but
instructions would not.

There was no tradition, though, of rabbinical families in Britain and
there were often complaints in the Jewish media that the ministers were
not treated as well as they should have been. The salary was always poor
unless it was the Chief Rabbi. There was no pension in the early days and
the minister's standard of living depended a good deal on charity. When he
became too old to work, his last years were often spent in penury. There
are too many examples, particularly in provincial communities, which were
not members of the London-based United Synagogue, for this to be an
exaggeration.

There had also been a tradition for centuries that Rabbis should not be
paid for the work they did. The position of high priest had started with
Aaron in the Bible and the tradition evolved that rabbis are appointed to
serve the Almighty and this they should consider sufficient reward in itself.
It was, therefore, necessary that the Rabbis find another occupation to pay
the bills.

Great rabbis might earn a living as wood choppers, like Hillel, or, as
with Rashi, as a vintner. Rabbis were not given a salary by their
congregations until the 14th century. One tradition which did emerge from
this was that rabbis often became doctors, like Moses Maimonides in the
Middle Ages, and this explains the attention given to health in the Talmud
and the Jewish approach to health in general.

Where most ancient civilisations in Biblical times believed that illness
was the diktat of the gods and nothing could be done to cure it, the Jewish
position was that every effort should be made to understand and cure the
maladies. Over 200 of the laws in the Talmud have to do with health.

The Coronavirus pandemic has seriously affected all Synagogues, but the Talmud, in dealing with the plague, specifies that hands must be washed and those with the disease isolated; recommendations which were reinvented only recently by governments around the world. An astonishingly large number of Jews have won the Nobel prize for Medicine; 60 in all, even though for many years Jews were not accepted as students by medical colleges as late as the 20th century. Antisemitism was not condemned in those circles.

Jews' College was known as the Cinderella of Jewish charities and although most of the United Synagogue ministers were recognised as coming from poor backgrounds, the organisation took the benefits of their studies but gave them inadequate financial aid. The Central's Sir Adolph Tuck was a United Synagogue councillor and complained regularly at meetings of the lack of sufficient support, but in vain. As there were far better rewarded professions, the wealthier families also tried to send their children to fee-paying public schools, even though their religious education would probably be totally neglected by the school governors. It did enable many of the former Jewish pupils to go on to better paying occupations than the ministry.

As a consequence, the British community were fortunate over the years to attract men who had a vocation for the pulpit and a strong desire to serve their fellows. You cannot, however, judge the past by present-day standards. It is only possible to try to improve the situation. The daughter of Rev. Stoutsker remembers:

> The family were often hosted to tea by Isaac Wolfson, which was a highlight for them as the cakes were so memorable.

Sometimes, it is only possible to blush for one's ancestors.

In Bristol Aaron Levy Green had attacked the views of an academic, Dr. George Croly, who was against Jews being elected to parliament without having to take the oath of allegiance on the true word of a Christian. Aaron Levy Green entitled his attack "Dr. Croly Lld, versus Civil and Religious Liberty." It brought him to the attention of Sir Moses Montefiore, who took an interest in his career thereafter.

Aaron Levy Green had strong views on many subjects, but the reality was that the Synagogue had been the brainchild of Sir Anthony de Rothschild, who was one of the richest and most powerful men in the world. He was the third son of Nathan Mayer Rothschild and would become the first president of the United Synagogue when it was formed. Socially, the two were in no way on a par.

Where Aaron Levy Green, over the years, tried to establish charitable and educational bodies to strengthen the community, he could count on Anthony de Rothschild's help. Where he wanted to change the format of the services, he had to change the Chief Rabbi's mind and that was going to be firmly resisted. In a crunch situation the Rothschilds would support the Chief Rabbi, who was a member of the family.

For example, successive portions of the Pentateuch are read on each sabbath of the year. This is a key and lengthy part of the service. Aaron Levy Green and several other ministers wanted the process to take three years, instead of one which would make the weekly portion, and therefore the service, shorter, but both Chief Rabbi Nathan Marcus Adler and his son, Hermann Adler, who succeeded him, were very much against this.

The reading of the Pentateuch had always been the most important part of the service; the part that started at 11 o'clock. No one suggested that there was any Biblical justification for a three year cycle. As the Rothschilds were both Orthodox and cousins of the Adlers, this was just one idea that was never going to be adopted, but Aaron Levy Green still advocated change. The three-year cycle would never be agreed by the Central.

Judaism is a strict religion. There are over 600 laws. It is very difficult to keep them all, and conscientious Jews are always aware of their shortcomings, often with a resultant guilt complex. One of the side effects of the development of the Reform synagogue was that their rules were eventually made less strict. As one Reform rabbi put it later in the 20th century:

> In a modern post-enlightenment world where individual autonomy has taken the place of divine sanction.

Who had the authority to decide that the Almighty's divine sanction should be abandoned was not explained. This was a long way from the original manifesto of the Secessionists in 1840:

> We, the undersigned, regarding Public Worship as highly conducive to the interests of religion, consider it a matter of deep regret that it is not more frequently attended by members of our Religious Persuasion. We are perfectly sure that this circumstance is not owing to any want of a general conviction of the fundamental Truths of our Religion, but we ascribe it to the distance of the existing Synagogues from the places of our Residence; to the length and imperfections of the order of service, to the inconvenient hours at which it is

appointed; to the unimpressive manner in which it is performed and to the absence of religious instruction in our Synagogues.

By implication, the "fundamental Truths of our religion" include the Written and Oral Law. Divine sanction was expected to remain firmly intact in the time of the Secessionists and the intellectual Enlightenment didn't abolish them, because divine sanction is a matter of faith and not science. The Secessionists accepted that. As late as the 1920s any proposal to change the original Secessionist ritual was firmly resisted, including the suggestion that men and women should sit together.

Aaron Levy Green was a dedicated minister and, of course, this involves many stressful challenges. The minister may be seen by the congregation in the pulpit as emotionally uninvolved, but on many occasions he is called upon to comfort bereaved members in private and to try to lessen the pain that the stricken family is suffering.

If the loved one was taken when young, the task is even more difficult and yet there will be many occasions every year when a minister is called upon to try to lessen the grief. Only the family of the bereaved know how hard he tries and their thanks cannot eliminate the emotional upheaval he must inevitably go through. Visiting seriously ill members in hospital is equally upsetting and after the day's work, the evening prayers for the mourners may take him to homes far away from his own, occupying much of what would otherwise be his spare time, besides circumcisions, brissim, weddings and barmitzvahs. It is a very difficult and demanding profession.

Aaron Levy Green attracted large congregations because he gave excellent sermons when these were still something of a novelty.:

> The order and decorum there are admirable. The weekly discourses delivered by the Rev. Mr. Green have not contributed a little towards this pleasing change. These pious effusions are always animated, often truly elegant, and not rarely stirring and thrilling to the soul. The Rev. preacher has evidently known how to strike the right chord to the minds of his flock, as evinced by the sympathetic response reverberating from their hearts.

The world would change in the future, but film evenings and bowling contests would not inspire a congregation to the same degree as a powerful sermon. Of course, the shortness of life expectancy was a powerful incentive to attend services in Victorian times, particularly when illness struck, but

Aaron Levy Green's sermons were worth hearing for their own sake and were often reported at some length in the Jewish media.

They ranged from an appeal for Moroccan Jews who had fled to Gibraltar because of the war with Spain, to the case for true religion rather than superstition. Of course, sermons are likely to be more effective when the minister has been in office for some years, and Aaron Levy Green had spent a lifetime mastering his profession. Then again, the minister was part of a team. At the Central a teacher at the Jews' Free School, Rev. Samuel Lyons, in 1855 was appointed Second Reader and Secretary after a keen contest, and Philip Valentine was made the Beadle.

Samuel Lyons came from a poor family and was born two months after the death of his father. He was educated at the Jews' Hospital in Mile End and taught at the Jews' Free School as a young man. One of the advantages Samuel Lyons offered was that he had been born in England and "trained and destined for an engagement of the present character." Talmudic studies were not neglected at the Jews' Hospital school. As a teacher at the JFS Samuel Lyons was well known to the Honorary Officers at the Branch who also took a keen interest in the school.

The main argument about the appointment of Samuel Lyons was whether preference should be given to English candidates or to treat the English and foreign nominees simply on their merits. The fact was that foreign candidates could be obtained who were Talmudically more qualified than the home-grown variety, but they would have a different outlook and have trouble with the English language. Samuel Lyons was chosen where other applicants were more Talmudically competent. Philip Valentine stayed in post for the next fifty years and died in 1908. Mrs. Valentine was his helper for thirty-five years.

Outside the Synagogue, 1855 was a notable year for the Jewish community, in that David Salomons was elected the first Jewish Lord Mayor of London. He would be a member of the Central and when he was introduced to the Barons of the Exchequer by the Recorder of London, nobody had any doubt, as the Recorder said, that his election was a major step forward in the British history of religious freedom. The Recorder waxed lyrical about David Salomons' career, commercial, political and charitable, and he had undoubtedly brought great credit to his community. The Recorder only regretted that other countries were not as tolerant towards their Jewish citizens as was Britain.

The form of the new Synagogue continued to be thrashed out. To help the chazan there was to be a choir with a leader and six youngsters at a cost of not more than £100 a year. They needed to be recruited from families living in the district because, of course, they weren't supposed to ride to the Synagogue on the sabbath. It was unlikely, though, that the Honorary Officers would look too deeply into how they reached the shul, as the choristers might well have to be replaced when their voices broke.

In the future they included a poor boy whose father was a local tailor. This was Philip Taylor, born Harry Schneider, who was in the choir in 1905 and would be a warden of the Synagogue for fifteen years in the 1950s and 1960s at the same time as Sir Isaac Wolfson. Coming from a tailoring family, Philip Taylor was always immaculate and wore formal dress on every possible occasion. He married into the Central's prominent Freedman family who never dropped their Victorian standards of dress.

In a class ridden society, however, the London Jewish community always remained divided into poor and rich. Those who married into more affluent families often spent their lives as strictly cadet branches of the predominant clan. Behind the facade there were often clashes. A lot of hard work went into making the Synagogue a centre of harmony.

When the First World War began Philip Taylor was typical of the Jewish community. There were the majority who were prepared to join up and fight for the country, although conscription was not introduced in the early years of the conflict. There were also, however, a substantial number of Jews who were immigrants from Russia and didn't want to fight on the side of the Czar.

Philip Taylor knew nothing of the Czar and falsified his age to be enlisted in the army. He changed his name as well, as did the Royal Family from Saxe Coburg to Windsor. His emigrant father was furious at him for joining up and didn't speak to him for three years. The solution for the government was to deport those who wouldn't enlist, back to the countries from which they had come originally.

The Western Synagogue opposed the idea of the new Synagogue. They said it would affect their membership adversely and suggested that there were quite sufficient seats already available in the West End. The Maiden Lane Synagogue members were also concerned at the influence of a new Synagogue on their membership. The Great had its own agenda, however, and it was decided to go ahead anyway. In 1868 a public meeting chaired by Sir Anthony de Rothschild approved the building of a new Synagogue and in March 1869 he laid the foundation stone.

There would be many occasions when the largest Ashkenazi Synagogues would work together but, fundamentally, they remained individual congregations until they were brought together as the United Synagogue many years later. Even then the new organisation would be confined to the London Synagogues and would not include any from the provinces.

In the meantime, the question was how to actually build a permanent Synagogue in the West End.

Past and Present Officers of the Central Synagogue.

2. Collage

3

Aaron Levy Green

Six and a half years after the idea was first put forward, the new Synagogue in the West End was finally consecrated on March 25,1855. Simon Ascher, the chazan at the Great officiated, and there was a choir trained by Julius Mombach, the choirmaster at the Great. He enhanced the service by playing a serefina, which was a kind of harmonium, to accompany the choir. To add additional status to the occasion, children strewed flowers in front of the parade of the Sifrei Torah and the Chief Rabbi preached. The icing on the cake was when Sir David Salomons, the new Lord Mayor, attended a special service to mark the occasion.

The Chief Rabbi said that he had decided the services would continue to be split in two, although he had approved this timing with reluctance because he thought the early part of the services would continue to be neglected. The Din, however, remained undisturbed, which was always his intention and his unswerving aim.

When Nathan Marcus Adler was elected Chief Rabbi in 1845, he was wholeheartedly determined to set appropriate Orthodox standards in a country with many minor variations to Synagogue rituals. All that was agreed, however, was that the ritual would be that of the Polish and German Jews, but they still needed to be made uniform. Each Synagogue had its own version of the prayers. It wasn't easy to get everybody to sing from the same prayer book as there was no uniform prayer book.

Indeed, it was not until the last year of Adler's ministry, more than 40 years later, that he supervised the production of a standard version of the ritual, which we now call the Singer Prayer book. It wasn't; it was the 'Adler Prayer' book and acknowledged as such by Simeon Singer in the first edition. The Chief Rabbi edited everything before he died, up to the prayer for mourners at the end of the book.

Referring to it as the Singer Prayer Book was a typical Adler ploy. He knew his days were coming to an end, but the problem of the difference between the emigrant East End communities and the richer West End congregations had still not gone away. Simeon Singer was a special case among the ministers of the London congregations; he had served communities in both parts of the metropolis and was popular in each.

The prayer book therefore had a better chance of being accepted as authoritative if his name was attached to it; the Chief Rabbi was more associated with the West End leaders. Therefore, the Chief Rabbi was happy for the. book to be known by Singer's name, but he had been careful to check every prayer.

Nathan Marcus Adler achieved his objectives, throughout his life, by such strategies; his policy of giving credit to others for initiatives he favoured was a brilliant strategic approach. His favourite expression when arguments broke out, was to say, "Let there be peace for my sake". It invariably worked and the opposition had the necessary excuse for agreeing to his wishes that they were ensuring peace in the community. As a consequence they didn't lose face.

The design of the Synagogue building was much admired and that in itself was an achievement:

> It is a pure chaste Moresque, free from the meretricious decorations which bedizen some buildings alleged to be built in this dignified style of architecture.

Within six months of its consecration the new Branch Synagogue had sold 80 men's seats and 60 women's. Another 50 men and 60 women had transferred their seats from the Great. The Synagogue had a total of 212 seats downstairs and 144 in the gallery. It was agreed that £200 a year would be allocated to paying back the debt to the Great and, financially, the Branch Synagogue finances soon exceeded the surplus of the founding shul. There were some substantial additional costs when the Synagogue had to be closed from June to August 1858 for building improvements but these were financed easily enough.

Despite the divided times of the Sabbath services being approved by the Chief Rabbi, Aaron Levy Green was always against the second service now starting at 10.30. It continued though until a completely new Synagogue was opened in 1870 when Aaron Levy Green was successful in abolishing the practice. It was, however, unique, as the Chief Rabbi wouldn't allow a divided service at the New when they asked for his permission.

One of the most important desired effects of the building of the Branch Synagogue was to keep many members of the Great from leaving the community and joining the Secessionists. Aaron Levy Green played a part in this as well. His singing and sermons ensured a large congregation coming to the Branch every week. It was so unusual for ministers to give regular sermons at the time that Aaron Levy Green's contributions were always publicised with the wording "has kindly consented to give a sermon."

He was also very persuasive in an emergency. One Friday in 1874 the barge Tilbury was going through the Regents Park Canal near London Zoo with a load of petrol and gunpowder. Unfortunately, it blew up, killing those on board in an explosion heard twenty miles away.

Aaron Levy Green's appeal in shul on Shabbat the next day for contributions to help the victims, brought £2,000 from the congregation. (£190,000 today). The Explosives Act in 1875 avoided a similar disaster, but there was a great deal of local damage, and the Branch played a substantial part in financing the repairs, thus gaining a reputation in the local community as a welcome newcomer. It wouldn't be the last time the Synagogue helped its neighbours.

It was accepted that the British Jewish community had now effectively split into three. The ultra-Orthodox would reject any changes and were to be found in small congregations in the East End, adhering to the practices they had brought with them from Europe. The main body would develop into what would become known as Anglo-Jewry, though the expression only appeared in the *Jewish Chronicle* in the 1920s.

While they kept to the Din, there wasn't the same local condemnation and ostracism if members strayed from the strict Orthodox line. Finally, there were the Secessionists who wanted to set their own rules, but at the same time not differ that much from those of Anglo-Jewry.

Judgment on the superiority of the London Synagogues was based on many criteria. One was the result of the charitable offerings over the High Holydays which were publicised in the media. In 1853 the members of the Great gave £830, The New £620 and Bevis Marks, £520, out of a total for the six London Synagogues of £2,470. In today's money that is at least a quarter of a million pounds.

The Sephardim had decided to create their own Branch Synagogue in the West End and Nathan Marcus Adler consecrated it in October 1853, years before the Ashkenazi Branch of the Great Synagogue. It could seat 250 worshippers and to mark its opening, there were donations of £1,000. There was no Sephardi Haham at the time as the relations between the Mahamad and the last Haham, Raphael Meldola, were so contentious that the Sephardim were concerned not to repeat the experience for many years.

The desirability of cooperation in such bodies as the Board of Deputies, however, was widely recognised and delegates from provincial Synagogues became more numerous. Where they had connections with the

Secessionists, however, there were disputes about whether they were eligible to be members. Aaron Levy Green also took a great interest in the new Board of Guardians, which was founded by Ephraim Alex in 1859. It was formed to look after the raising and distribution of charity for the poor and it did a great deal of good work.

The growing reputation of the Branch community owed a great deal to Aaron Levy Green's personality. He involved himself in many good causes; he was an assiduous visitor to hospitals, asylums and prisons and he lobbied for Visitation Committees to be created for both the United Synagogue and the Board of Guardians to carry on his work. He set a good example in a whole range of charitable endeavours.

When he'd finished recruiting support, there was scarcely an institution, charitable or educational, where some of its Honorary Officers didn't belong to the Branch synagogue. For his own part, Aaron Levy Green would visit provincial communities to help resolve differences, inspect schools and bring his own wide Talmudic knowledge to bear in providing the congregations with memorable sermons. He became popular in many parts of the country.

It was a Jewish tradition for congregations around the world to answer appeals for help from Jewish communities suffering from persecution. Of course, there were admirable charities doing equally good work who were not Jewish, but the history of the Central over the next 150 years would be studded with efforts to ameliorate disasters. They helped the emigrants after the 1848 revolution in Europe collapsed, and the refugees from the pogroms in Russia after the assassination of the Czar in 1881. Then there were the refugees fleeing the Nazis in the 1930s, the survivors of the Holocaust and the destruction of the Jewish communities in the Arab countries in the Middle East. These were just some of the notable examples.

Today we are concerned with the possibility of catching Covid. It doesn't compare in virulence with relatives dying in concentration camps, the confiscation of one's capital, discriminatory legislation, and state sponsored antisemitism. Helping the oppressed is by no means automatic. The world did little to stop genocide in Manchuria, Rwanda, Nigeria and Cambodia.

With the help of congregations like the Central, a lot of the emigrants struggled out of poverty over the years but there wasn't just a need for financial help. The emotional stress the communities suffered needed to be reduced by friendship and societal support and that was the task of Synagogue congregations as well.

As the arguments about building a new synagogue dragged on, Aaron Levy Green gave a particularly powerful sermon in 1860. It was on the day when Jerusalem was destroyed by the Romans and Aaron Levy Green pointed out that the city fell because of internal dissension among the leaders, rather than by the might of the centurions.

"Today", he said "the chiefs of the community are not agreed on the subjects most vital to us and all wish to be leaders". He pointed to "meaningless objections" and the large administrative costs which reduced the money originally raised to help the poor. It was not surprising that a full congregation listened to his criticism. He was still under 40 but he had now served the community for nine years and was a powerful voice against irresponsible lay leadership.

He met the community far more than halfway. There were particularly popular invitations to his Sukkah at his home during the festival of Sukkot. In addition, his writings in the *Jewish Chronicle*, under the name of Nemo, were often very influential, though these were anonymous, if widely suspected to come from his pen. They had started in 1853 and were one of the ways in which the views of the clergy could be heard outside the pulpit. Using the pseudonym, Aaron Levy Green could address all the problems of the community, from the desirability of a Jewish hospital to the contradictory results of the Marriage Act and the non-attendance of members in Synagogue on the sabbath. As was said after his passing:

> The good-natured acuteness, the sarcasm which wounded only to chasten, the learning which gave weight and force to an ephemera of criticism, the drollery which enlivened the learning, have gone, but will not be forgotten.

One of his constant concerns, for example, was the status of the people hired by the United Synagogue Burial Society to prepare the bodies. They were paid very little and often did not treat the cadavers with the respect they merited. Nemo was very critical but, in this instance, not a lot changed.

When the pogroms started in Eastern Europe, Aaron Levy Green became a member of the Romanian Mansion House Committee, set up by the Lord Mayor to try to help the victims. He also served on the Romanian and Turkish Relief Committee and was a founder of the Jewish Association for the Diffusion of Religious Knowledge.

It was convenient that when the new Synagogue was constructed, a considerable number of the community's charitable organisations took to meeting in its council room.

Michael Adler, who would become the minister at the Central in the future, said of Aaron Levy Green:

Amiable personality, powerful and witty preaching, decorous
rendering of the service ....excellent hazan, delivered a sermon every
week, and as a rule preached extempore [without notes]. Especially
successful with his appeals for charitable funds....the Central
Synagogue owed its prominence in the community as much to the
remarkable personality of its minister as to the social status of its
worshippers....no man of his generation was more intimately
connected with all the interests of English Judaism....education,
religious culture, state of the poor, revival of Hebrew literature, closer
union of Jews....uplifting of the religious tone of the community.

Even if Michael Adler naturally eulogised after Aaron Levy Green's death, it
was a handsome portrait, reflecting the popularity of the minister. Although
treated in many ways as just servants of the community, a forceful personality
could energise the congregation and Aaron Levy Green had achieved that.

A Building and Finance Committee was appointed at the Synagogue
with Edward Beddington as Treasurer. He had the help of Alderman
Phillips, Samuel Montagu, who would create the Federation of Synagogues,
Alfred Beddington, and Baron Henry de Worms.

The Baron (1840-1903) had been given the title by Emperor Franz Josef
of Austria and was given a British peerage as Lord Pirbright in 1895. His
paternal grandmother was Jeanette de Rothschild, so he was a member of
the family as well. He was also related to Nathan Marcus Adler's first wife.
Politically, he was a Conservative MP from 1880-1895 and served in the
government. He also had large plantations in Ceylon and even managed to
find the time to write a number of history books. He fitted well into the
Building and Finance committee.

The reconstruction of the warehouse involved many delays, including
one because the walls hadn't dried out, and it was not until March 1855 that
the building could be consecrated. The design of the new synagogue had
been a matter of lengthy discussion. The architect, a Mr. J. Clarke, described
its final appearance:

The interior of the synagogue is about 40 foot square, with a lofty
dome in the centre 20 feet in diameter, richly ornamented with
emblematic designs in bold relief, supported by four Corinthian
columns. The remaining portion of the ceiling is groined. [Two
Barrel Vaults intersecting]. The light is introduced by means of a
lantern of stained glass in the dome, and also by windows over the
ends of the gallery, which latter runs round three sides of the

building. Under the dome is the reading platform. The principal feature of the building is the Ark, the effect of which is very striking and novel. It is elevated on a platform of veined marble, and approached by three steps of the same material. On each side of the Ark are three Corinthian columns which support a canopy. The recess in which the Ark stands has a dominical [dome like] ceiling, elaborately painted and gilt, with the light radiating from above through painted glass. On each side of the Ark are marble pedestals sustaining costly and gigantic candlesticks. The doors of the Ark are of rich damson wood, with gold mountings. The Synagogue contains 212 seats in the body, and 144 in the gallery.

The inscription over the front door was part of King Solomon's prayer at the consecration of the Temple in Biblical times and the words formed a gematria (numbers replacing letters) for the date 5630, corresponding to the year 1869. Dr. Asher, the Secretary of the Great Synagogue, had carefully worked this out, copying another old tradition.

It was noted that:

the porch entrance is fitted with a pair of iron gates of such remarkable pattern that one cannot forebear wondering how anything so light, delicate and complex could be worked in so inflexible a material as cast iron. The design of these gates can only be compared with a number of giant cobwebs, interlacing and intersecting one another in all possible positions.

The curtain in front of the Ark was the gift of Mrs. Barnett Joseph and there was a silver cup from Charles Moseley, a mantle from Mrs. S.I. Joseph and two silk mantles from Baroness Lionel de Rothschild. In 1910 David Isaacs would present the Synagogue with an organ and this time the members accepted it gratefully. In 1928 the second Lord Bearsted gave a splendid almemar in memory of his parents.

It was significant that there was a prayer at the consecration service appealing to the Secessionist Jews to return to Orthodoxy:

O lead in thy lovingkindness also those who have forsaken the old paths, for their desire is not to anger Thee, but they err in their heart.

The West End congregation had been founded as a branch of the Great and it remained in that form, run by the Great, until 1870. The Great took care of the management and the services. The fact that the new synagogue was a branch of the Great was emphasised by weddings not being permitted in the shul and visiting wardens from the Great being given the "posts of honour".

The wardens of the Great were automatically wardens of the Branch synagogue and from 1855 till 1870 these were Sir Anthony de Rothschild, Professor Jacob Waley, Samuel de Symons, Louis Nathan, David Davidson, Ephraim Alex, S.A.Jones, Lionel Louis Cohen and Henry Beddington.

The Beadle appointed in 1855 was Phillip Vallentine, whose father, Isaac, had been instrumental in founding the Jewish Orphan Asylum. Isaac Vallentine was an East End printer and when a horrific outbreak of cholera affected the area in 1830, he worked to start the orphanage which looked after many children who had lost their parents.

To further emphasise the close relationship between the Synagogues, elections of the Branch Committee and the Great Vestry were held on the same day, emphasising again the Branch's subservience to the founder Synagogue. Philip Vallentine then had to take the Branch voting boxes to the Great for counting.

In addition, the Great appointed a subcommittee to look after the affairs of the Branch, consisting of Baron Lionel de Rothschild, Samuel de Symans, Lewis Jacobs, Benjamin Cohen and Aron Joseph. Joseph was a distinguished architect and in later life was particularly associated with the new Bayswater synagogue and in the founding of the Jewish Religious Union, which became the Liberal Synagogue after his death.

The new Branch Synagogue was so popular that many members of the Great transferred to it. The Honorary Officers of the Great were eventually largely drawn from Branch members. Of course, the problems of the New and the Hambro didn't disappear with their withdrawal from the creation of the Branch. In 1859 the Board of Management of the New passed a resolution:

> with a view of prevention of the necessity of this congregation having a Branch Synagogue of their own....some endeavours be made with the Great and Hambro Synagogues to effect an amalgamation and these two agreed to appoint delegates to a meeting of the three. On April 27 the delegate committee resolved: Considering the present social conditions of the Jewish community in London – and with a view of their future well-doing - and to afford to the respective members and their families residing in the West End of the Metropolis increased accommodation by the establishment of

another Synagogue, it is the opinion of this committee that before entering into the details for building the said Branch Synagogue there should first be an amalgamation of the three City and such other Metropolitan Synagogues as may desire to unite with them.

The United Synagogue organisation was the eventual solution, but it took another eleven years to bring it about. It was a form of amalgamation which still left the individual Synagogues with a good deal of independence. It also took years to get a new West End synagogue constructed in the warehouse used by the Branch.

At last it was achieved and the opportunity existed to build a community on a sound foundation. It would take those additional fifteen years in all, however, for the congregation to be completely independent in a newly constructed building, and it would result in giving up a degree of its individuality when it joined the United Synagogue. Still, there would be plenty of volunteers to help establish it.

The American Civil War and the overproduction of cotton led to widespread unemployment in Lancashire and the Lord Mayor of London formed a fund in 1862 to relieve the distress. The Chief Rabbi asked all his Synagogues to support the fund and appeals were made from the pulpits on the eve of Chanukah. Aaron Levy Green made a spirited appeal and the members of the Branch were happy to support the cause, even though they were hardly affected by what went on in Lancashire.

With so many people moving to the West End there was now further talk of the City Synagogues getting together in some way. There were discussions on the amalgamation of the Great and the Hambro, but these broke down because the Hambro wanted to maintain its traditions and insisted that the Synagogue continue to be open for daily services. The Great wouldn't agree to the cost that this would involve.

By 1861 the Hambro had withdrawn, and it was left to the Great and the New to create the Bayswater Synagogue. As Jews moved to the Hyde Park area there had emerged the need for another West End Synagogue and consequently the Bayswater Synagogue was built and opened in 1863. Its minister for many years was the Chief Rabbi's son, Hermann, and it too became part of the United Synagogue when it was founded.

Unlike the Central, however, the Bayswater had to be allowed to be more independent because there were two sponsor Synagogues rather than one. It had influential members and the congregation insisted, for instance, on having its own marriage secretary. The Board of Deputies did not want to grant them a secretary and the arguments over this reached the Attorney

General, Roundel Palmer, who sided with the congregation. In the end, the members got their way and the first wedding in the shul was on October 23, 1865.

It also took years for a constitution to be agreed between the communities which eventually made up the United Synagogue. This was partly because the Charities Commission naturally insisted on every aspect of the new United Synagogue constitution having unanimous approval before it went to parliament.

At the end of the day the new Branch Synagogue was still a converted warehouse and would not compare in design with the new Bayswater Synagogue. Indeed, when the Bayswater opened, a considerable number of Branch members left the congregation, but the vacant seats were filled in a couple of weeks. Although it was a relatively new institution, many members did not make an allowance for the time it takes to build permanently high standards.

Typical was a seat holder's letter which criticised the singing of the choir over Passover in 1860. It was said to be:

> anything but harmonious and at times was so defective and jarring as to exact more than the usual condemnation.

In the West End, generally speaking, the larger the Synagogue, the greater its financial resources and, to that extent, the Central and the Bayswater became competitors for members to swell their coffers. To get all the Synagogues to join together was an even more tortuous process.

Where, in 1845 the only major Synagogues in the West End were those of the Western and the Secessionists, by 1870 there were four, as the Central and the Bayswater were built to look after the newcomers to the district. The community in London was now splitting into West End and East End congregations and this was exaggerated in the 1880s when the refugees from the Eastern European pogroms started to flood into London's port area. They naturally came with their own traditions from their former homes and these carried much sentimental appeal for them. After all, they could be centuries old. They did not welcome what they saw as interference.

The ministers worked hard. Aaron Levy Green was a great attraction at the Central and Hermann Adler did sterling work at the Bayswater. It was important that they both started Hebrew classes for the children and the first Batmitvah ceremony was held at the Bayswater in 1864. Twenty years later when the idea of the Batmitzvah was more popular, the Chief

Rabbi's office granted permission for the ceremony but stipulated that "the model of the service [should be the one] adopted by the Central Synagogue".

In 1862 the problem of renewing the Branch Synagogue lease had to be addressed. After considerable negotiations over four years, an 80-year lease of the present site of the building was bought in 1866. The annual balance sheet in the Branch Synagogue was still by then showing a surplus even larger than the Great Synagogue; its positive balance was £1,176, exceeding the Great's £1,024.

The Branch Synagogue was not universally welcome. One Christian conversionist tried to distribute religious tracts during the Shabbot service in 1865 and was charged in court with disturbing the community, He complained that he had been hit in the face when expelled from the shul, but the magistrate told him he was very fortunate that nothing worse had befallen him. This judgment would have been very different from Eastern Europe.

One member who escaped serious injury on another occasion was Lionel de Rothschild when he was aboard a train which crashed in France. According to custom, he said the prayer of thanks for his escape, before the ark was opened in the Branch Synagogue on the next Shabbat.

In 1866 over fifty requests for seats had to be turned down and early in 1868 a public meeting, chaired by Sir Anthony de Rothschild, finally passed a resolution to build a new Synagogue. The Great gave £6,000, the Rothchilds gave £4,000 and the fixtures of the old synagogue were given to the Brighton and Stepney Synagogues; the building would become a concert room.

With the Rothschilds and the Great involved, the plans for the new Synagogue were well publicised. It was different with a new Synagogue in the East End in Sandys Row. The building had formally been a church, created in 1766 to serve Huguenot refugees. When they moved out of the district it became a Baptist chapel and in 1867 was bought to be a synagogue by the local Dutch Jewish community.

The community had come from Amsterdam and retained Nathan Solomon Joseph to redesign the building. It was consecrated by the new Haham, Benjamin Artom. It was Ashkenazi, but Nathan Marcus Adler refused to do the honours, as he didn't want more competition for the City Synagogues, and he made his views very clear. The Synagogue eventually became one of those whose annual deficit the United Synagogue helped to underwrite. It is today the oldest surviving independent Ashkenazi Synagogue in London.

When it was decided to build the Synagogue on the site in Hallam Street, it was Nathan Solomon Joseph who was appointed as the architect, and he built a number of other Synagogues during his lifetime, such as Garnethill in Glasgow and the Great, in Belfast. He also designed the new cemetery in Willesden. There was no competition for the appointment and Nathan Solomon Joseph had the additional advantage for his nomination that he was the chief rabbi's son-in-law.

The style chosen for the new Synagogue was Moresque, which is Moorish. There were many questions to decide. How was the Synagogue to compare with the great number of new churches which were springing up all over the country and were primarily Gothic in architecture. How was it to compare with the Bayswater and whose architecture should be adopted? How much should it cost?

One decision was that the new Synagogue would not have an organ, a proposed innovation which at the time the members soundly rejected. Some of the Jewish congregations in Europe did have organs, but playing them on Shabbat was considered working by many communities and, therefore, by rejecting an organ, the temptation to potentially break the sabbath rules was avoided.

As the building committee again included Samuel Montagu – later Lord Swaythling – Baron Henry Worms, and other financial worthies, the necessary donations were soon forthcoming. The congregation produced £12,000. The whole bill was over £37,000, (about £3 million today) including the houses of the ministers. The £6,000 from the Great was augmented by £8,000 selling debentures and another £10,000 from the public.

To a considerable extent the necessary elements of a Synagogue dictated the design of the new building. In a Synagogue the magnificence of lofty Gothic arches in Churches would not be possible because the vista would be broken up by the ladies' gallery. The Ark would dominate one end of the Synagogue and the Bima either the centre of the shul, or at the ark. There could be no busts or statues as these were held to be forbidden graven images, and a belfry wasn't needed either.

Nevertheless, a number of the new Synagogues around the country were very fine. The size and decoration of them led to them being referred to as Cathedral Synagogues. Typically, the magnificent Princes Road Synagogue in Liverpool was opened in 1874 and the equally ornate New West End near Hyde Park in 1879. There were still points of discussion about the new Synagogue; some congregants still wanted an organ, but that suggestion was again turned down. As was a recommendation that there be ladies in the choir.

The Branch Synagogue was first called the Central when Baron Lionel de Rothschild MP laid the foundation stone on 18 March 1869. The Baron sounded exactly the right note:

> I am proud to see that so many members of the community are in the enjoyment of a great position on account of their talents and intellectual attainments, and I am gratified at the high municipal and Parliamentary offices to which others have been elected. But these advantages would, indeed, be dearly bought if they were not accompanied by increased attention to their Institutions and an increased observance of their holy religion.

The modern idea that a synagogue interior is also part of a community centre was never likely to have credence, or even be considered in the Victorian era. As an institution, the Synagogue had replaced the Temple in Biblical times, as the Jewish communities spread far and wide. Agreed, it was understood that a school to teach the faith was even more important, but apart from that, the Synagogue itself was the rationale for the building.

If members did not come to Synagogue there was no likelihood that their alternative tastes would be catered for, and there was no demand for the Synagogue to be a subsidiary location to committee rooms. The Greek word Synagogue means a place of gathering, but for prayer rather than social amusements.

The architecture of Synagogues cannot compare with the great cathedrals, but these magnificent buildings could take hundreds of years to build and while Jewish communities were often made to help finance their construction, they were frequently, by the 19th century, expelled long before they had lived that long in a country.

Even so, the ability of the Victorians to build large new structures in a short space of time was remarkable; constructing the new Central Synagogue only took a year. It was opened in April 1870 and consecrated by the Chief Rabbi. It was 20 metres tall and 22 metres wide. The report in the *Jewish Chronicle* waxed lyrical on every aspect of the building:

> The ground floor of the tower is occupied by the principal porch - a grand archway supported on richly carved shafts of Rutland stone and red Mansfield stone. The voussoirs [tapered stone] of the arch consists of the same varieties of stone, placed alternately, and

beautifully carved with Moresque devices, the keystone alone being left without adornment....the almemar is highly decorated, being panelled and moulded. The corner posts are carved and surmounted with solid brass candelabra....even the carpets, the gas fittings and the new curtains are distinguished by their Moresque details.

The architects were not always as sanguine. One member of the Joseph family of architects was Delissa who was responsible for the Hampstead, Hammersmith, Cardiff and the Manchester Higher Broughton Synagogues. He was asked by a critic when he was 50 years old why Synagogues were so ugly, by comparison with Churches on the Continent.

> The English national taste does not demand the standard of fine architecture that the Continental taste demands. You see the same in regard to courts of justice and municipal buildings. The English are not prepared to pay for fine architecture. If the demand existed... we could find many architects who would be able to produce buildings as fine as any to be found on the Continent.

It was an excuse, because there were great British buildings and great British architects, like Christopher Wren, Inigo Jones, Giles Gilbert Scott and Augustus Pugin, to name just a few.

For the consecration the Chief Rabbi and the new Sephardi spiritual leader, Haham Benjamin Artom, conducted the afternoon service at the old Synagogue and the Chief Rabbi then carried the Sefer Torah to the new building. He was accompanied by the Dayanim, and during the consecration service, Sir Moses Montefiore, now aged 85, opened the ark:

> Beneath the tender gold light which streamed from the crown of the sanctuary.

The historic programme for the consecration commemorates those who had worked so hard to create the Synagogue. The wardens were Sir Anthony de Rothschild, Lionel Cohen, Jacob Waley and Hyman Beddington. The treasurers were Joseph Lazarus and Edward Beddington. There were also fourteen overseers, Moses Symons, Ephraim Alex, Joshua Alexander, Alfred Beddington, David Benjamin, Saul Isaac, Lewis Jacobs, Lewis Lazarus, Frederick Marcus, Samuel Montagu, Henry Moses, Louis Nathan, Sir Benjamin Phillips, the Lord Mayor in 1865, and Henry Worms. The secretary was Asher She.

The community, all over the country, was much impressed. When the first service on Shabbat was held the following week, it was reported with due solemnity in the press. The first part, as decided by the Chief Rabbi, lasted from 8.45 till 10.15 and the only criticism was that the choir under Mr. Oppenheimer was said to need some more trebles if suitable schoolboys could be found.

The novelty of the new building even attracted a group of non-Jews, who wandered around the shul making notes and upsetting the congregants, who didn't know how to stop the disruption. The visitors were, however, often very impressed. One non-Jewish reader of the *Jewish Chronicle* took the opportunity to congratulate the singing of the choir when he attended a service.

The report of the first shabbat was far more emotional than we expect today.

> May the new Central Synagogue, thus dedicated to the Holy Service of the Divine Religion of our Fathers, be to ourselves, our children, and our children's children, a joy and a blessing. Though in these days the cloud no more fills the Houses of Worship which we raise, and the Mystic Presence no longer dwells in ineffable glory in the Sanctuary, still may that Presence – that testimony of a Father's care, which we call, and best know by the name of Love – rest on the Building raised for His worship and consecrated to His name. May no prayer be uplifted there save such prayers as it is well and wise for men to offer and may those prayers be heard within this roof. May the happiness of this United Congregation rest, in their obedience to the behest, and their hopes in the promise, of their Divine Faith.

One of the first weddings in the new Synagogue was that of Solomon Weinstein who was born in Cracow and was married by the Chief Rabbi, Nathan Marcus Adler, to Elizabeth Trenner, in 1872. Happily, they would celebrate their 65th wedding anniversary in 1937 in America.

The competition for members between the Secessionist and the Central Synagogue was well known to the community. It was brushed over in the press, however, where:

> we need not here revert in detail to the causes which have led to its erection, nor to the circumstances connected with its establishment.

Things settled down though and the Central soon became very prosperous. In 1873, however, they lost their Financial Representative when S.L. Meier died. Barnett Meyers remained a warden until 1877. He was devoted to Jewish charities and was also the President of the Jews' Deaf & Dumb Home and Treasurer of the Stepney Jewish Schools. He had been the treasurer of the Jewish Schools for many years and was very well known in the community. As many as 200 mourners came to his funeral in East Ham in 1889, including the Chief Rabbi. Barnett Meyers was succeeded by Sir Philip Magnus, who was a Secessionist but keenly interested and involved in the schools and Jews' College.

One of their prominent wardens was Louis Lumley (1828-1906) who served from 1872-1874. He started his business life as secretary to his uncle, the Director of the Royal Opera House, and introduced the renowned Swedish singer, Jenny Lind to the London stage. As a solicitor he ran a very successful practice and was one of those recruited by Aaron Levy Green to support Jewish charities. With his encouragement, Louis Lumley spent much of his spare time on the Building Committee of the United Synagogue, and at Jews' College where he sat on the Council and was chair of the classes committee.

In 1873 Aaron Levy Green went on the warpath in the pulpit discussing Theism. This was a creed created by Rev. Charles Voysey, (1828-1912), a Church of England cleric, who had been dismissed for his views. These were that only the belief in G-d was relevant. Otherwise, an individual had to rely on his conscience. All the dogmas and rites of all the other religions in the world were mistaken.

The problem for Aaron Levy Green was that Rev. Voysey was holding services at St. George's Hall, up the road from the Central, and Judaism was as much criticised as the Church of England. Rev. Voysey had also been condemned by the Privy Council and his views did not survive his death for long. Nevertheless, it was one of the fashionable theories in its time and was given more attention than it really deserved.

By 1875 every seat in the Synagogue had been sold and forty new seats had been added. The fact that the Central was a brand-new Synagogue enabled it to avoid the annual squabble between the communities comprising the United Synagogue, when it came to the budget for repairs. Any expenditure over £25 had to be approved by the United Synagogue Council and the conflicting claims for precedence made for many arguments.

When the new Synagogue opened, and it seems unlikely that it was a coincidence, the Central Board of Management met in June 1870 and recorded in the minutes:

The Board of Management are of opinion that the following alterations (a-p) on Sabbaths and Festivals are desirable, and unanimously recommend that the necessary steps be taken for carrying them into effect.

There followed fifteen requests for changes and it was further unanimously resolved:

That an extract from the Minutes of this Meeting, referring to the proposed alterations a to p, be sent to the Boards of Management of the Bayswater, West End, St. Johns Wood, Borough and North London Synagogues, informing them of the suggestions which have met with the approval of this Board for the purpose of improving the Services of this Synagogue, and inviting them to consider the same with the view to a combined representation on behalf of the Six Congregations to the Rev. the Chief Rabbi, in accordance with the Deed of Foundation and Trust (Clause 2) That this Board will be glad to appoint three delegates to meet delegates from the other Synagogues, for the purpose of considering any representations or modifications they may suggest, with a view to concerted action; and will feel obliged by the earliest possible reply. That the Board is of opinion that any changes which may be ultimately adopted after they have been approved by the Chief Rabbi should be submitted to the seat holders for ratification.

The idea that lay members should ratify changes approved by the Chief Rabbi implied that they considered themselves equally competent to make decisions on the ritual. Their qualifications for this role were not specified. Among the changes they required were the abolition of the repetition of the Amidah, the singing of the 84th psalm and, when a second Sefer was taken from the Ark, Vzous Hatorah should only be sung once.

This list of alterations was a direct challenge to the authority of the Chief Rabbi who did not approve of the majority of the suggested changes anyway, but the dividing of the Sabbath services was now stopped. He hadn't wanted it in the first place. The Board's proposals would reemerge later in the decade.

On any Board of Management there are members who wield more authority than newer, less knowledgeable, and younger colleagues. It is, therefore, difficult to identify the members who obviously resented their inability to set down the rules by which the Synagogue ritual was decided.

Their decision to question the principle of the Chief Rabbi's overall authority in spiritual matters is therefore concealed in a joint decision to put forward their recommendations.

Aaron Levy Green had his own agenda. Writing as Nemo in the *Jewish Chronicle,* he advocated changes in the Synagogue ritual which were revolutionary. One of his bête noire were the piyyutim, which were poems dating back in some cases to the Temple, but written for contemporary circumstances. They included such much-loved prayers as Adon Alom and Yigdal, Nemo wrote in 1872:

> The piyut was most likely a necessity of the age. It is now a menace. Despite the melodies, men will and do ask themselves the meaning of the words they utter, and who can justify, however he may admire, the literary ingenuities, the attributes, the verbal quibbles, the erroneous history, the false morality, the liturgical verbosity, of much that goes by the name of prayer.

Nemo's problem on gathering support for changes, in this and other aspects of the ritual, was that he was talking way over the heads of the average congregant.

The offer of a gift to the Synagogue of a pulpit was now turned down and a lectern, running on wheels, was pulled out from the side of the ark whenever there was a sermon. There were additional gifts to further enhance the Synagogue; a chupah would be presented to the shul in 1872 and the choirboys were given white dress neckties to wear on Yom Kippur in 1874. Alfred Beddington gave the synagogue a Nar Tamid (perpetual light) in 1876, a carved wooden pulpit was installed in 1880 and a handsome marble one in 1901. The members were setting down very firm roots.

There were always appeals to the community at large for new charitable donations. The Willesden Cemetery, for instance, was necessary, according to the United Synagogue committee which had been set up to develop it, because when poor German immigrant Jews passed away, the responsibility for burying them fell on the organisation. Its more favourable location for the West End members was skipped over. At the same time, by 1875 the income of the Central, at £4,500, exceeded the other United Synagogues, while their own expenditure was only £2,500. Most of the remainder went to the US to balance the books of the poorer Synagogues, like Sandys Row.

The United Synagogue Visitation Committee met at the Synagogue in 1875 with Nathan Joseph in the chair and was able to report on the results of their work over the previous three years. There were problems, of course,

Typically, the religious service they intended to hold at the Colney Hatch Lunatic Asylum had to be abandoned as the inmates were not able to appreciate the event. They had, however, visited 9 lunatic asylums, 340 hospitals, 46 workhouses and 382 prisons in that time.

The Synagogue was closed for redecoration and reopened in September 1876. The members had raised the money to pay for the work. Architectural improvements were important news and detailed descriptions of the improvements were forthcoming. Typically:

> Colour and gold are mainly used for the Sanctuary and Ark. The oak columns supporting the ark are replaced with pairs of slender marble columns. The gallery fronts are treated as cabinet work, with moldings gilt and panels inlaid in ivory colour.

Nathan Joseph was supervising the work as he had done before. The general comment was that:

> It has been executed in a bold but highly successful manner, the richness of the colours harmonising well with the general plan of the building.

A number of the members now wanted to learn more of Hebrew literature and in November 1876 a series of lectures were arranged under the auspices of Aaron Levy Green to address this shortcoming. The Synagogue was a hive of activity.

3. Lord Rothschild – One of the families who have always supported the Synagogue

4

The First Synagogue

In 1870 the Synagogue had 260 members. By that time the main London Synagogues had joined together as the United Synagogue and the Central was one of the original five congregations. The wardens at the Great were inducted in December 1870, but there was no similar ceremony at the Central. In July 1870 the 'United Synagogues Act' had received the Royal Assent and as a consequence the Central had become a Synagogue independent of the Great. The United Synagogue is still the only Jewish religious body in British history established by an act of a basically secular legislature. It says a lot for the paternal attitude of successive British governments towards the community that this is the case.

Three of the most regular attenders at the Branch Synagogue, Sir Anthony de Rothschild, (1810-1876), Lionel Louis Cohen (1832-1887) and Professor Jacob Waley, (1818-1873), were prime movers in the creation of the United Synagogue, though they were nudged into action by the Chief Rabbi during a visit to his sukkah in 1866.

Once again it was typical of Nathan Marcus Adler that other people would get the credit for initiatives he had promulgated; it remained his method of getting his own way and it was still invariably effective. The Chief Rabbi had obviously benefited from his experience of dealing with a far less helpful regime in Hanover. The town council there had often perpetuated anti-Jewish legislation during his time in office as chief rabbi.

Sir Jacob Waley was the fourth Jew to be called to the Bar and was a noted conveyancing counsel. He was a member of the 1867 Royal Commission on the transfer of real property and Joint Secretary of the Political Economy Club. In addition, he was the first president of the Anglo-Jewish society and president of the Jewish Orphan Society. A nephew of Sir Moses Montefiore, like his uncle he would try to help Jews abroad, notably the Romanian community.

Sir Anthony was elected the first president of the United Synagogue and Lionel Louis Cohen a vice president. For the sake of impartiality and to lessen his already heavy workload, Anthony Rothschild resigned from his office at the Central. The Rothschild family would act as presidents of the United Synagogue for over 70 years; Lord Nathaniel Rothschild succeeded Anthony and was in office until his death in 1915. After Lord Nathaniel Rothschild came Leopold till 1917 and Lionel until 1942. The first treasurer of the United Synagogue was also a member of the Central: Assur Moses.

Aaron Levy Green was still anxious to improve the Synagogue ritual. The seventh day of Sukkot is Hashonah Rabbah which the rabbis at the time of the Talmud considered a mini-Yom Kippur, as the Almighty was believed to decide on the future level of the winter rainfall on that day. Rain is so important in the Holy Land that Jewish communities all over the world still pray for rain during the winter months, although they are guaranteed ample supplies in many of their own countries at that time.

The festival had, however, become less observed over the years, as the following eighth day is a festival, Shemini Atzeret and so is the next day, Simchat Torah, which sees the end of Deuteronomy and the start again of reading the book of Genesis. Now the choir were brought in once more on Hashonah Rabbah and a full service was recited by a substantial congregation.

In December 1870 the Central members elected their own officers. Those originally appointed by the Great insisted on resigning. Baron Ferdinand de Rothschild and Barnett Meyers were elected in their stead. At the election in the Vestry Room there was a considerable effort by the members to get the wardens to remain in office and Nathan Joseph made a powerful appeal to them to do so, but to no avail. The Rothschilds could always find replacements within the family.

Ferdinand de Rothschild needed to be resilient as he had been widowed only four years before, which was a grievous blow. He turned his attention to building Waddesdon Manor in Buckinghamshire, now one of our finest stately homes, though he didn't neglect the poorest in the community; he served as Treasurer of the Board of Guardians from 1868-1875.

Enthusiasm for running the new shul ran high. There were thirty candidates for the five seats on the Board of Management of the Central and thirty-eight for the seven members of its Council. The Synagogue soon became fashionable and in the first year 365 men's seats and 269 women's were let.

In 1871 the new Synagogue became a fitting location for prayers to be said for the Prince of Wales. Albert Edward had an attack of typhoid that year, an ailment which had killed his father less than a decade before. The congregation were strong royalists and were moved by Aaron Levy Green's appeal from the pulpit for the safe recovery of the prince, which eventually did occur.

While both the Central and the Bayswater fulfilled the needs of people in their localities, it was recognised that they should not be in competition. So, the favourable relationship between the two Synagogues was strengthened at Passover in 1871 when Aaron Levy Green and Hermann Adler exchanged pulpits.

The image of the Central was further enhanced that year when the Emperor of Brazil, Dom Pedro II, decided to come to the Synagogue one Friday night in July after the service had ended. His visit was quite unexpected and the shul was actually closed. It was quickly reset again and:

> The Ark was opened and a Sefer Torah was brought out and shewn to the Emperor, who addressed the clergymen in excellent English. He read and translated Hebrew fluently from a Pentateuch handed to him.

On Saturday morning:

> As His Majesty entered, the congregation rose to receive him, and the Rev. A.L.Green pronounced the blessing ordained by the Rabbis to be said in the presence of a sovereign.

The Emperor was taken to the wardens' pew and was said to pay great attention to the service. It was reported that he was given an illuminated address, though how this was written on Shabbat is not explained. Perhaps sent on afterwards. *The Times* was impressed:

> We understand that the visit of the Emperor to the Central Synagogue is the first that has been paid in this country by a reigning sovereign to a Synagogue during Divine Service. We may add that his majesty is versed in the Hebrew language and was consequently able to read and understand the service.

Brazil had, of course, been part of the Portuguese empire for some years and the language of the country is Portuguese rather than the Spanish of the rest of the continent. There had been a fair amount of antisemitism in Portugal in the 18th century and an earlier King, José I, had considered making Jews wear yellow hats. His prime minister, the Marquis of Pombal, brought two to a discussion on the proposal. The Marquis was in a minority in disliking discrimination, and he had the presumption to tell the king that one hat was for him and one for the King, as the royal family in Portugal had Jewish blood. It was not surprising that the Emperor could understand Hebrew. Jose I gave up the idea.

There was a marriage at the new Synagogue of art dealer Asher Wertheimer and Flora Joseph. It took place on a Wednesday in July and the chuppah featured four ornamental 'pineapple' shaped finials on top of the chuppah poles. These are still in safe keeping at the present Synagogue, having survived the destruction of the former building in the Blitz.

By 1872 the community included five MPs, six Barons, two Aldermen, the Solicitor General (Sir George Jessel), and one member of the Royal Academy. (Professor Solomon Hart). The status of these members was well known and gave the congregation added *naches* (gratification), but there were other members who were very prominent behind the public scenes.

George Lewis, for example, was a fashionable solicitor and a confidante of the Prince of Wales, who needed his services when he ran into difficulties. This happened on more than one occasion, thanks to the Prince's Bohemian lifestyle. George Lewis was very discreet and although the prime minister and Arthur Balfour opposed him being granted a knighthood in 1893, the Prince of Wales overruled them. There were many Jews in the Prince's circle, known as the Marlborough House Set, which aroused envy in the upper classes. When he eventually came to the throne there was a lot of gossip about whether the new King's Jewish friends would be dropped, but they remained strong supporters in his circle.

If there were now a number of Synagogues in the West End, they emphasised the problem that the only Ashkenazi cemetery was in East Ham in the East End. It still had space, but its location was unattractive for the West End members. One of the members of the Board of Management, Joseph Freedman, had given the lamps for the chapel at East Ham to commemorate his father who was buried on the Mount of Olives in Jerusalem. The record in Jerusalem describes him as a rich Jew from London. Another family who had prospered. Joseph Freedman became the forefather of the Freedman family's support of the Synagogue over many years.

East Ham being in a poor district, it was, therefore, decided in 1872 to buy land for a new cemetery and Willesden in North West London was chosen. A Jewish cemetery has to be in the country to make infection less likely and security easier. Another Din that was way ahead of its time. Graves in churchyards are very common.

Willesden offered both attributes and the Synagogue officers decided to try to raise the necessary funds by appealing to the community. The estimated cost was £7,630, which would be close on £700,000 today, and it was a year before the cemetery saw its first burial. This was Samuel Moses, a long-time member of the Central who had specifically asked to be buried in Willesden.

The Chief Rabbi had been consulted and approved the arrangements. Approval was then given by the president and vice president of the United Synagogue, but the Council were not consulted and the Central Honorary Officers asked for a retrospective bill of indemnity for their action. An aggravated member tried to get a bill of censure passed instead, but this was rejected.

The Chief Rabbi then pointed out that anything to do with the cemetery came under his jurisdiction and not that of any lay body. He received an apology for the member's interference. The cemetery is so highly regarded today that it has been designated a Heritage Site and provided with a substantial sum to pay for the necessary upgrading.

There were, of course, the ongoing expenses in running the Synagogue itself which had to be carefully apportioned. For example, from an early stage the choir at the Central was highly praised, but this was because of the hard work they put in rehearsing, and the question arose of whether they should be compensated to a greater extent for their efforts. Each chorister received £5 a year and as it was widely felt that treble voices were the most sonorous, many were youngsters whose voices hadn't broken and whose parents needed the money to help support the family.

The choristers could be exploited though. At the Great, for example, at the end of the High Holydays in 1872, the Board of Management sent £2 to be distributed among the fourteen members of the choir. The High Holydays take place over four weeks and the services are much longer than usual. Two pounds divided by fourteen is 14 contemporary pence. The choir were offended and sent it on to the 'Penny Dinners Fund for Poor Children'. They were not complimentary about the Board either. It was not surprising that advertisements for Bass, Treble and Tenor voices for the Synagogues appeared regularly in the papers.

The annual cost of the choir ten years later was only £265, and this had to cover not only the choirmaster, all thirty or so men and boys, who comprised the singers, as well as their lodgings when they came from far afield and meals on most festivals. Their contribution to the services was particularly important during Yom Kippur when considerable numbers of the congregation tended to go home rather than stay for the concluding

Neilah service. Aaron Levy Green, on occasions, would be asked by the wardens to give a second sermon before the conclusion, to keep the members involved.

There were greater problems to consider though. In November the United Synagogue lost its chair of the Building Committee when Edward Beddington (1819-1872), died of heart disease. The family name had, in fact, been Moses; Beddington is a suburb in Sutton in South London, but it seemed a more dignified name to his sons. Edward Beddington's father, Henry Moses, left £500,000 (£47 million today), when he died in 1875. He had been a major supporter of the Jews' Hospital.

Edward Beddington, like his father, was a successful woollen merchant. The family would also manufacture what they called Abdullah cigarettes, but he still found time to work very hard on the creation of the Synagogue. He was also the treasurer of Jews' College, as well as being instrumental in promoting the new proposed cemetery and with three other members guaranteeing its cost. So the Central were responsible for the creation of the cemetery but Edward Beddington was only 53 when he passed away. The Synagogue and the community could ill afford to lose him.

His brother, Alfred, had been the Financial Representative from 1875-1877 but the interests of the family moved to military careers. His son, Lieutenant Colonel Claude Beddington, would be a good friend of the Synagogue's future minister, Michael Adler, on the Western Front in the Great War. Claude Beddington was the commander of the Westmoreland and Cumberland regiment and the Mounted Troops of the 20th Division. He also had a long and distinguished military career thereafter.

At the age of 72 and promoted to Deputy Director of Military Intelligence, he would be tragically machine gunned and killed off the Welsh Coast in 1940 while sailing his yacht on Admiralty business. His brother, William, was a notable soldier as well. He was commander of the 2nd Dragoon Guards in the Second World War and finished up as a Major General. In all, 37 members of the family served in the forces, which was exceptional, as until the 19th century Jews were not allowed to be army officers, though Wellington had a Jewish General at the Battle of Waterloo.

The wardens continued to serve Jewish charities. Louis Lumley in 1873 went with the Chief Rabbi to the Jewish Deaf and Dumb Home and encouraged greater support for the institution. As he said:

> It is impossible to express in words the impact made upon me this day by the successful efforts produced by Mr. Schonthell's teaching. If our Jewish community were more sensible of the great good the

institution does, it would be more liberally supported and its benefit more fully expanded.

The home had been founded in 1865 by Baroness Meyer de Rothschild and eventually became the Norwood Home in Wandsworth. Mr. Schonthell worked there for many years and was given a chased silver dish at a presentation in 1902 when he had been there for 30 years.

It was by now considered a privilege to be appointed to the Central Board of Management. Asher Isaacs actually bought space in the *Jewish Chronicle* to thank the members for electing him. The congregation still wanted to improve the building and in 1876 the Synagogue was completely redecorated. It had to be closed for all of January and the cost was £1,300, (a million and a quarter today), which the congregation provided. When it was reopened the first service coincided with Aaron Levy Green sitting shiva (mourning) for his brother, Michael, and so there was no sermon. In his early days Michael Levy Green had been the minister in Exeter. He died of apoplexy at the age of 65, a presentiment for the future.

A Roman pavement had now been put in front of the ark and a new warden, Frederick Davis, made a munificent gift to the Synagogue of twenty-five marble columns. These enhanced an already attractive building. The Synagogue was also provided with electric light at this juncture. There was always a need for additional accoutrements for the Synagogue. Another example came in 1873 when Sir David Salomons gave the silver bells and a pointer for a Sefer Torah, which were described as "of exceptional beauty, elegant workmanship and extremely large." Unhappily Sir David died in July of that year.

He had been a major figure in the community for many years. Features of his life included being elected to the House of Commons and trying to take his seat, without saying the Christian oath. This resulted in his being ejected from the chamber and fined £500 for his presumption. In business, he was largely responsible for the creation of the High Street banks, founding the London & Westminster, but the bankers showed little gratitude and over the next century seldom appointed Jewish directors.

Sir David Salomons was a devoted member of the Central and his hearse paused outside the Synagogue on its way to the cemetery.

The United Synagogue Visitation Committee met at the shul in 1874. Nathan Joseph, another member of the family, was in the chair. The committee was in serious need of more financial support and where its likely expenditure in the year was £600, it had only managed to raise £370 towards the outgoings. It was a worthy charity and, in a year, looked after 10 Jews who had been discharged from asylums, 25 from prisons and 250 from hospital. The Chief Rabbi, Hermann Adler and Aaron Levy Green promised to appeal on the charity's behalf from the pulpit.

The Board of Guardians was able to report in 1875 that the number of appeals they had considered had dropped to 1,800 from the 2,072 of the previous year. This was the smallest number since 1859 but it still illustrated the poverty which afflicted so many in the community.

The Synagogue was becoming increasingly popular, not just for services but also for meetings of Jewish organisations. Among others using the Council Room in 1876 were the Anglo-Jewish Association, the General Council of the United Synagogue, the Society for the Study of Hebrew Literature and the United Synagogue Training Ministers Committee.

Many members wanted to make the Synagogue even more attractive. At Shavuot in 1876, for example, Lucy Cohen, a Rothschild, sent what were reported as "exotica" to decorate the shul. There were only minor grievances with which to deal. One discussed at the annual meeting of the United Synagogue that year was the money in the Central accounts used to pay for minyan men. When it could not be guaranteed that there would be ten men to make up the quorum for morning and evening prayers, it was quite common to pay a few poor Jews to attend the services to achieve the right number. Otherwise, prayers for the dead could not be said by the congregation.

It was, however, the view of some members of the United Synagogue Council that if a Synagogue couldn't produce its own minyan, it would be better to be shut. On a snowy January evening, for instance though, it would have been an unreasonable rationale as generalising from an exception. The view also ignored the fees paid to poor choir boys and choristers. Why should minyan men be different? The United Synagogue chair settled the discussion by agreeing to write to the member Synagogues and ask their Board of Management to consider the subject. It was the Victorian version of the back burner.

Aaron Levy Green's sermons were highly regarded. To mark the collections made for Hospital Sunday in 1876 the *Jewish Chronicle* printed the text of sermons given by each section of the community; Sephardim, United Synagogue and Secessionist. It was Aaron Levy Green's lengthy address which was chosen to represent the United Synagogue.

Another contentious issue came up when some seat holders objected to not being admitted to the marriage of Leopold de Rothschild to Marie Perugia in 1881 and wrote to the *Jewish Chronicle* to ask if this restriction was permissible. Maria Perugia came from a distinguished Jewish family in Trieste. The Editor of the *Chronicle* said that it did raise questions, but it would be discourteous to insist on attending if only the family were invited. In fact, no Jew can be prevented from entering a Synagogue.

As could have been expected, when two leading families were involved, the wedding was sumptuous. Nearly 1,000 people attended and the choir consisted of the best voices that the Central, Great and New could provide. The Synagogue was decorated with palms, camelias and azaleas, and the almemar was "profusely decorated with banks of flowers". The floor of the Synagogue was covered in crimson cloth and Sir Albert Sassoon, a notable immigrant from India and another friend of the Prince of Wales, lent a Gobelin tapestry. When the bride entered, flowers were strewn at her feet, and her bridegroom wore:

> a silk tallith exquisitely embroidered in massive gold at each of the four corners with his monogram encircled by a wreath of bridal flowers terminating in true lovers' knots.

The Emperor of Brazil may have been the first royalty to visit the synagogue, but the Prince of Wales came to the wedding of Leopold de Rothschild and Marie Perugia as well. He proposed the health of the bride and groom at the Dinner at Arthur Sassoon's house and he came again in 1898 for the memorial service for Ferdinand de Rothschild. The health of the prince at the wedding was proposed by Benjamin Disraeli shortly before he died. It was not surprising that a journalist writing about a wedding at the Central at the time used the headline "Marriage among Millionaires".

The community had had one large problem in the mid-1870's. Benjamin Disraeli was the prime minister and there was a great deal of criticism, accusing him of putting Jewish interests in the Balkans ahead of British. Certainly, Disraeli always spoke up for the Jews, even though he had been converted to Christianity when he was thirteen, after his father had fallen out with the Mahamad at Bevis Marks,

The international situation had become difficult for some years as Britain, Russia, Germany and Turkey argued over the independence of Balkan countries. Disraeli was also trying to enhance Britain's reputation abroad in foreign affairs. William Gladstone, the leader of the Liberal opposition was unhappy about Jewish support for their own distressed communities in the Balkan nations, and criticising the Jews for this was an item in his manifesto. After what was called the Midlothian campaign,

William Gladstone was returned to power. Ironically, much of the finance for his electioneering came from a Central member, Hannah Rothschild. The daughter of Mayer de Rothschild, when he died in 1874, she inherited and became the richest woman in Britain. She married the Earl of Rosebery in 1878, marrying out of the faith against the wishes of the family, many of whom didn't attend the wedding. Hannah Rothschild was a very good wife to Lord Rosebery but she was not a great beauty and Rosebery was a noted wit. He once wrote to a friend that he was going to Dieppe over the weekend and "Hannah and the heavy baggage" were coming on later. Unhappily, Hannah Rothschild died young. Lord Rothschild had wished her to be buried in the family vault in Scotland, but she had left clear instructions that she was to be buried in Willesden and her wishes were followed.

The Jews had originally supported the Liberal party because the Liberals had canvassed hard for the Oath Act. There was now a move by many Jews to the ranks of the Conservatives, and the Central members split between the parties. For instance, Henry de Worms and Lionel Louis Cohen of the United Synagogue, became Conservative MPs.

The change in allegiance came about because the Liberal leader, William Gladstone, had attacked the treatment of Christian congregations in the Balkans by the Turks. This was totally justified, but the Christians had been responsible, in their turn, for many attacks on local Jewish communities. British Jews and Gladstone were, therefore, at odds on the subject. This was just one reason why many changed allegiance to the Conservatives under Disraeli.

Within the British Jewish community one of the effects of the popularity and convenience of the Central was that it made the growth of the Secessionist movement less attractive. Apart from a new congregation in Bradford in 1873, which catered for a largely German Jewish community of immigrants, there would be no new Reform communities until the Settlement Synagogue in 1919. On the other hand, cooperation between the congregations was improving. In 1880 Professor David Marks, the Reform minister at Upper Berkeley Street, was invited to address the congregation in Liverpool Old Synagogue, which is unlikely to happen today.

High levels of membership did not always, however, make for large attendances. The Central was picked upon by the *Jewish Chronicle* at Simchat Torah in 1873. It noted the fine singing of Mr. Marks, the tenor, but criticised the number of empty seats, although many members were away.

The paper suggested that there were more Lulavim (a closed frond of the Date Palm tree, used at the festival of Succot) at Synagogues in North London than at the Central. Succot is a joyous festival and very unlike a Church service. Samuel Pepys, the Stuart diarist, had attended the Simchas Torah Succot service at Bevis Marks and found it much too noisy for his taste. It was a typical reaction of non-Jewish visitors when Succot came round. Succot was a very popular festival though. When the Sephardim only had a small Synagogue in the early Stuart days, police had to be called to control the crowds.

Aaron Levy Green was by now a highly respected minister in the national community. When the Melbourne congregation in Australia needed a minister in 1875, the Chief Rabbi, the Haham and Aaron Levy Green constituted the committee to judge the nominees. Aaron Levy Green was his own man, though, and not all his sermons were popular. In 1878, for instance, he presented a series on 'miracles' and aroused a great deal of adverse comment. Indeed, there were meetings to express public indignation with the content. His cordial relations with the Secessionist Synagogue were also the subject of much disapproval.

A number of the ministers were criticised by senior members of the community at the time. One Board of Management reader of the *Jewish Chronicle* decided to respond to a letter they had published in which the ministers had been said to "sing and chirrup their lives away and play cards all night." The writer spelt out their responsibilities in rebuttal:

> The ministers are bound to be up at early morn to officiate in the Synagogue, many of them are at their desk nearly all day....are often collecting Synagogue accounts....and again at the Synagogue for the Afternoon Service....They must attend funerals and the setting of tombstones....but must be back again to the Synagogue or their absence reported....visit asylums, prisons, workhouses and hospitals, are frequently called up in the middle of the night, then they must attend at the house of mourners at all hours, no matter how late.

It wasn't surprising that so many of them came from poor families so that their income was less insufficient than their relatives, but their selfless devotion to their congregants was even more admirable.

It wasn't just Jewish charities that gained the support of the Central members. In 1877 the Chief Rabbi instructed all his Synagogues to raise money for the Indian Famine Relief and the Central sent £190 to the fund. The Jessel family gave a similar sum to the Synagogue that year when Sir

George Jessel's daughter was married, and Sir George acted as warden in the Shabbot service preceding the nuptials. That year also saw two major gifts to the synagogue; a set of mourners' chairs, given by Asher Isaacs and a splendid Sefer Torah, the gift of Charles Wertheimer, (1842-1911), a noted art dealer, Charles Wertheimer was then a comparatively young man and probably picked up the Sefer Torah at a sale.

Edwin Samuel, (1826-1877) the elder brother of Montagu Samuel and a former president of the Central in 1874, died in 1877. Like his sibling he had devoted much of his life to the interests of the community, serving on the Board of Deputies and the Council of the United Synagogue. He was unlucky in that the problem in Victorian times was that there was no cure for so many diseases.

In the Spring of 1879, the Board of Management at the Central met to again discuss changes in the ritual on Sabbaths and Festivals. Aaron Levy Green, was not at the meeting which the minutes cover, and there is no evidence that the 15 recommendations proposed had his approval. Changes he did want made were also not always on the Board's list. He was still in favour, for example, of the three-year cycle for reading the sections from the sefer torah on Shabbat, but this was not one of the proposals of the Board of Management. He made up for his absence by more lengthy letters as Nemo in the *Jewish Chronicle,* notably several columns long in December 1880.

It was still unwarranted interference in the authority of the chief rabbi. On Nathan Marcus Adler's appointment in 1845 all spiritual matters were declared to be his responsibility as the chief rabbi. The same applied in the 1870 constitution of the United Synagogue, but in the 1879 proposals of the Central Board of Management there was this radical attempt to change what had been readily agreed.

The 1870 proposals, which had been passed by a meeting of United Synagogue Delegates under the chairmanship of the Central's Lionel Louis Cohen, were revived and the 15 points in the minutes were not merely suggestions. The Board asked that "The necessary steps be taken for carrying them into effect." What is more, the Board attempted to gain support from all the other major London Synagogues by seeking "a combined representation".

Furthermore, to gain even more support, the Central had again said that any recommendations the Chief Rabbi approved would have to be submitted to the Synagogue seat holders for their agreement. This was total arrogance.

Nevertheless, there was a conference convened at the Central in October 1879, four months later, to consider alterations, to which the

Strictly Private and Confidential.]

ק"ק כנסת ישראל

UNITED SYNAGOGUE.

Central Synagogue.

Extract from the Minutes of the Meeting of the Board of Management of the Central Synagogue held on the 23rd June, 1879.

The Board of Management are of opinion that the following alterations (*a* to *p*) on Sabbaths and Festivals are desirable, and unanimously recommend that the necessary steps be taken for carrying them into effect.

(*a.*) That the interval between the parts of the Morning Service be abolished, so that the Service be continuous.

(*b.*) That the Service commence at 15 minutes past 9 o'clock.

(*c.*) That the extra פִּיּוּטִים of שַׁחֲרִית and of מוּסָף be omitted, also אַקְדָּמוֹת and יָצִיב פִּתְגָם on שָׁבֻעוֹת, but that the portions of טַל and גֶּשֶׁם, and the portions of פִּיּוּט now said in מוּסָף שָׁבֻעוֹת, be retained.

(*d.*) That the reading in Synagogue of the מְגִלּוֹת on the Festivals be discontinued.

(*e.*) That the Reader commence שׁוֹכֵן עַד about 5 minutes to 10 o'clock.

(*f.*) That the repetition of the עֲמִידָה of שַׁחֲרִית be discontinued, and that the Reader read aloud from הָאֵל בְּרוּךְ till הַקָּדוֹשׁ; that the intermediate parts until אֱלֹהֵינוּ before רְצֵה, be read in silence; after which the Reader is to continue reading aloud till the end of the עֲמִידָה, as is the custom in the Portuguese Synagogue with respect to the מוּסָף Service.

(*g.*) That the singing of the 84th Psalm be omitted.

(*h.*) That the Reader intone אֵין כָּמוֹךְ at 15 minutes past 10 o'clock, and the Choir sing the אַב הָרַחֲמִים immediately following.

(*i.*) That when more than one סֵפֶר is taken out, the Choir is to sing וְזֹאת הַתּוֹרָה once only, namely, to the first סֵפֶר.

(*k.*) That יְקוּם פּוּרְקָן be omitted.

(*l.*) That אַשְׁרֵי be intoned, verse by verse, by the Reader and Choir.

4. Extract of minutes from 1879

London synagogues, except the Hambro and the New sent delegates. No ministers were invited to attend. Detailed recommendations were then sent to the Chief Rabbi, including a request by the Central to have a mixed choir. A second meeting set up a sub-committee to make official representations and Aaron Green did sit on this body. On the other hand, Rev. Marcus Hast, the renowned reader at the Great, the Chief Rabbi's synagogue, quite rightly declined an offer to join them.

The Central had reduced the time between the two shabbat morning services to five minutes with the intention of giving the members less excuse for not being present in the early morning and there were long articles in the press on the historical origins of the rules about the saying of the *shema*. The subject was contentious and the views of the members differed considerably.

When the committee had concluded their discussions, they wrote to the Chief Rabbi with their requests in April 1880. Many members had views and it probably resulted in far more interest being taken in the Synagogue elections at the time. Instead of members being elected because of their "social position and suavity of bearing" there was considerable "political electioneering". Indeed, one of the candidates at the Central took an advertisement in the *Jewish Chronicle* to set out his views.

The Chief Rabbi replied to the delegates in late May but made it very clear that he was only prepared to consider changes which did not go counter to the laws in the Shulchan Aruch (code of Jewish laws) and thus "impair the integrity of the Book of Daily Prayer." He would not give his assent to a mixed choir either.

The *Jewish Chronicle* commented that the committee:

> could not consistently have persisted with proposals of which the Chief Rabbi had expressed disapproval.

Even though they considered that the committee might regard Adler's decisions on their requests:

> reduced to proportions which to them who made them may well have seemed insignificant.

For example, the committee had wanted the Sabbath service to start later. Adler turned this down because of the prayers which had to be said early in the day. The opposition subsided. The standing of Nathan Marcus Adler after 35 years in office was such that it would not be an exaggeration to say he was revered. When he reviewed the recommendations and said he wasn't going to adopt most of them, his decisions were readily accepted by the community as a whole. The provincial congregations would, in any event, not have wanted interference from London in their rituals.

Although Aaron Levy Green was nearly 20 years older than Hermann Adler, it was Adler who was elected Delegate Chief Rabbi when his father had to take life easier and retired to Brighton in 1879. Aaron Levy Green's articles as Nemo in the *Jewish Chronicle* in the future often disagreed with Hermann Adler's views.

Why the attempt to undermine the Chief Rabbi's authority though? In 1879 Adler's doctors had told him to retire or risk dying. It was agreed by the United Synagogue that Adler's son, Hermann, should be appointed Delegate Chief Rabbi.

Now, on the one hand Hermann Adler had semicha and had served 16 years as the minister of the Bayswater. On the other hand, Aaron Levy Green was nearly 20 years older, an equally good preacher, and Talmudically self-taught to a high degree. In 1879 Adler was 41 and Green 58. Nathan Marcus Adler, however, had always intended Hermann to succeed him – there had been Adler rabbis for 500 years – and the United Synagogue had no difficulty in approving his appointment - they considered no other candidates. It would, in any case, have been very strange to appoint a Delegate Chief Rabbi who did not have semicha.

Logically, the Central Board of Management should have known that the Chief Rabbi would reject their recommendations. Was it arrogance to believe that laymen could replace the authority of the Chief Rabbi, or was it annoyance that their minister had been chosen over the younger man at the neighbouring Synagogue?

On a happier note, Aaron Levy Green started Sabbath morning children's religion classes in the same year. On Sabbath afternoons he conducted a children's service to which about 80 youngsters came. It lasted half an hour and was deliberately informal. Aaron Levy Green did not wear his canonicals and gave his talks in very simple terms. For the first three services he chose as his topics which religion should be chosen, why be religious at all and which were the best books to read.

As far as the adult members were concerned, there were lectures every Sunday morning from October 1879–May 1880 on aspects of Hebrew Literature. Aaron Levy Green gave the last on the *Philosophy of Thought in Judea in the First and Second Centuries*, which illustrated the academic progress he had made since those early days at the Great Synagogue.

There was a large attendance and the chair at his meeting was taken by Rabbi Solomon Schiller-Szenessy, who had attempted to set up a District Chief Rabbi office in Manchester in the 1850s, which would have undermined Nathan Marcus Adler's position. He was eventually unsuccessful and retired to an academic post in Cambridge, but he was still a good friend of Aaron Levy Green and accepted his invitation to preside at the meeting, even though it was generally known that he was persona non grata with Nathan Marcus Adler and Sir Moses Montefiore.

One of the wardens from 1881 to 1883 was Joseph Benjamin, but his main interest was in the Jewish Institute Concerts which he would organise for nearly 40 years. Besides his interest in music, he did not neglect the education of the older members. In the winter, there was a monthly lecture as part of the Study of Hebrew Literature.

Aaron Levy Green gave the first in 1880 on Maimonides and was introduced by a very senior member of the community, Arthur Cohen, MP; the barrister nephew of Sir Moses Montefiore had just been elected MP for Southwark and would go on to be president of the Board of Deputies. He had been the fifth wrangler at Cambridge and president of the Cambridge Union, so it was not surprising that a large audience of members came to the evening.

The minister did not only choose subjects for his sermons from the past. In September 1881, for instance, he spoke of the recent assassination of United States President James A. Garfield, and compared it to the assassination of Gedaliah in the Bible. The only fast in Judaism which commemorates a political assassination is that of Gedaliah on the third day of Tishri, immediately after Rosh Hashonah. The minister pointed out the revulsion with which Judaism regarded political assassination.

The generosity of members of the synagogue was exemplified by the will of Gabriel Benedict Worms, in which he left the synagogue £2,000, which would be at least £200,000 today. The interest on this large sum was to be paid to poor families at the rate of £5 each.

Ferdinand de Rothschild (1839-1898) also passed away. He was far more than a warden at the Central. He was also the Liberal MP for Aylesbury from 1885–1898 and was still responsible for the formation of the Unionist Conservative Alliance. He also gave £100,000 to the Evelina Hospital for Sick Children, which he had created in memory of his wife, who had died in 1866 with her premature baby. It is still part of St. Thomas' Hospital.

He made a large number of other bequests, including £2,000 to help create the Army Reservists Home. A trustee of the British Museum from

1896, Ferdinand de Rothschild left the Museum his plate, enamels, bijouterie, carving in boxwood, glass, arms and armour. It had all been at his home, Waddesden Manor, and the value was estimated at £300,000, which today would be about £34 million.

On occasions there were less welcome visitors to the Synagogue. On Yom Kippur in 1881 a converted Jew came to the Synagogue and decided to shout out "Believe in Jesus Christ". He was removed and handed over to the police. The magistrate fined him £10, which was about £1000 in today's money.

It was in the 1880s that pogroms started in Eastern Europe and hundreds of thousands of Jews emigrated to get away from the terror. They came to London and most went on to America, though over 100,000 would stay in the East End over the next fifty years. As a result, the established Jewish community was faced with a serious dilemma.

On the one hand they wanted to support their poorer brethren, and on the other they wanted to protect their image as loyal British subjects. On occasions the two objectives were incompatible. They soon divided into the East End Jews who had their own lifestyle and rituals and the West End Jews, of which the Central members were a part.

Aaron Levy Green addressed the contretemps in 1883 and pointed out that the Jews had always quarreled among themselves; Jacob and Esau, Joseph and his brothers, etc. He appealed for unity, but the community was now entering a period of conflict between distinct traditions; the East End Jews were more Orthodox than the majority of the original members of the earlier community and soon formed the Federation of Synagogues which particularly argued with the chief rabbi on the quality of kashrut supervision. The relations with the Secessionists were less divisive but the two were still different in their approach.

The East End Jews naturally resented their inferior financial position in their new country and the superior attitude of so many of the West End Jews towards them. The best way of counteracting this was to establish their own religious superiority and to point out how much more observant was their lifestyle; complaints about kashrut supervision were often an element in this. A number of the complaints were justified.

Aaron Levy Green wanted to heal the rifts with all the other sections of the community. When the Synagogue was closed for some time for repairs, he would walk every Sabbath to the Secessionist Synagogue and worship with his friend, the minister, David Woolf Marks. When asked what he thought of their service, Aaron Levy Green replied:

Well Marks, I have been thinking not so much of what your Synagogue has done as of what it has not done.

The Central was settling down very well. On the list of Synagogue donors to the Metropolitan Hospital Sunday Fund, the Central came third with just under £200. (£20,000 today). There was still the problem of the cost of the Minyan men, which in 1882 had come to £175. The annual United Synagogue meeting questioned the expenditure but had no alternative suggestions for regularly possessing a minyan for weekday services.

On Sunday, March 11, 1883, the Synagogue suddenly received a severe blow. Aaron Levy Green had officiated that morning at the setting of the tombstone of his old friend, Ephraim Alex, one of the founders of the Synagogue and first president of the Board of Guardians. Ephraim Alex was also, for many years, the Overseer of the Poor for the organisation.

In the afternoon Aaron Levy Green went to a public meeting at the Jewish Working Men's Club in aid of the Building Fund for the Jews' Free School, where it was reported "he made a most effective speech, full of characteristic witticisms." As he was walking home, though, he suffered an apoplectic fit, what we now call a stroke, and died. He had officiated at the Central for twenty-eight years. As the *Jewish Chronicle* wrote:

> The life of Mr. Green was coincident with a remarkable change in the position of the Jewish clergyman in England - a change cujus pars maxima fuit. He strove, and strove successfully, to raise his profession from the position in which it was placed half-a-century ago.

This was somewhat of an exaggeration. Aaron Levy Green still hadn't even been invited to be a member of the Central's Board of Management. Neither would his successors for the best part of 100 years. The advertisement for his replacement offered a salary of £300 a year, tax free and with a free home. Candidates would not be considered if they were over 40 years of age. The Chief Rabbi's salary, by comparison, was £2,000 a year but that was truly exceptional. The dayanim were paid so little that Lord Rothschild gave them each an extra £50 a year to enable them to make both ends meet.

The year 1883 also saw the death of Morris Oppenheim, (1824-1883) who had been a warden since 1881. He was the son of the secretary of the Great Synagogue and was a highly respected barrister. In 1868 when the Chief Rabbi was sued in Schott vs Adler over a butcher's licence, Morris Oppenheim had been part of the Chief Rabbi's defence team.

It was a case which established the chief rabbi's authority in matters of kashrus. Because there were a number of kosher butchers in the Whitechapel district, the chief rabbi wouldn't approve of another. He said that competition between them would be too severe. His ruling was part of the Din but he was sued as a result. In the event the magistrate upheld his ruling.

David Woolf Marks, the Reform minister, was called as a witness for the butcher, but he confirmed that the Chief Rabbi was acting within the Din. Nathan Marcus Adler had, in fact, offered the butcher an alternative location but this had been turned down.

Morris Oppenheim was a member of the Board of Deputies, worked hard on the Law and Parliamentary committee and was assiduous in his attendance. He was at the Board's meeting in 1882 when only nine deputies in all found the time. Unhappily, he suffered from depression and committed suicide.

The necessity now was to find a successor to Aaron Levy Green. There was a great deal of competition and much lobbying. One of seven candidates was Aaron Levy Green's nephew, Aaron Asher Green, who would become the Hampstead Synagogue minister for many years. He

5. Edwardian Chuppah

reported calling on a Central member to solicit his support for his candidature and being left in the hall. Eventually the member appeared and told him:

> I'm awfully sorry Mr. Green, but I have the Rev .... in the library and the Rev.... in the drawing room, and I expect the Rev.... in ten minutes. If you would not mind walking round the square for a little while, I should be glad to have a chat with you then.

The *Jewish Chronicle* would also have to find a replacement for Nemo. There were plenty of letters in the years to come, but nobody effectively replaced the Central minister.

5

Emanuel Spero, David Fay and Michael Adler

In the twelve months between 1883 and 1884, the Chief Rabbi presided over three memorial services at the Central. The first was for Sir George Jessel, (1824-1883), the Master of the Rolls and the first Jew to be appointed to such a high legal position. He was a very good lawyer and was remembered for recalling that his largest fee was 800 guineas (£840) in a case before the House of Lords where he only said "I wish to withdraw the appeal." His advice before the case was worth the fee. Aaron Levy Green's memorial service was followed by that of Baroness Charlotte de Rothschild, (1818-1884) whose charitable efforts gained her a well-deserved high reputation.

It wasn't going to be at all easy to replace Aaron Levy Green. At one time there was a suggestion that Hermann Adler and Simeon Singer should take the pulpit on alternate weeks, but this solution was eventually decided to be full of problems. The members of the synagogues involved were not in favour. The Central members were offered three alternatives but only 66 voted and split 22-22-22.

In the end the decision was made to divide the appointment in two and Emanuel Spero was appointed Reader in 1884 and David Fay preacher in 1885, after he had given three sermons. Although he had been the minister for two provincial communities, the Central Board of Management assessed his competence very carefully.

Aaron Levy Green's tombstone was set in the Willesden cemetery in December 1883, with Emanuel Spero, his colleague for 29 years, conducting the service. The family did not accept the offer of a monument and the stone was of simple Aberdeen granite. It was ironic that Emanuel Spero stood on the spot where Aaron Levy Green had conducted the burial service for Ephraim Alex on the day they both died. There is a memorial poem in the Book of Jewish Verse.

Now dimly thro' our tears we see his face,
And treasure up his mem'ry in our hearts
He stood in front a model Priest and Man,
Grand with a righteous energy for good,
Resplendent with a love for all his kind;
But most of all his great love for his race,
No work too hard - no cause that wanted help,
But he, the foremost one in doing good.
Honesty and Manliness and Truth,
A trinity of virtues joined in him.
Too soon for us - but not too soon for him
Has he been taken into Rest and Life.
For that perfection which he sought in us
He now has found in Immortality.
Dry up our tears - our God hath taken him,
He knoweth best. And when we go to rest
May it be found his bright example made
Us worthy of joining him on High.

Emanuel Spero was known as the silver voiced chazan and when he died in 1928 he had only been retired for three years, after 41 years in office at the Central. He was more than a chazan. When Aaron Levy Green died he conducted the services very competently for six months. He was in the tradition of Myer Lyon, known as Michael Leoni, who had been an opera singer at Covent Garden and was the chazan at the Great from 1767.

It was Lyon's singing of Yigdal which was heard by the Methodist, Thomas Olivers, and used for the English hymn, "The God of Abraham Praise". In *Hymns Ancient and Modern*, Leoni's contribution is still acknowledged. The Methodist annual conference in 2021 passed a resolution to support the banning of importing Israeli products, so the relations would appear to have soured a little over the 250 years.

Emanuel Spero was born in Denmark and came from a family of rabbis. His father had served during his career as the minister in Swansea, Wolverhampton, Penzance, Leeds, Liverpool and Glasgow. His son was discreet, but made his views on the Synagogue services very clear in an interview he gave on his retirement:

Our services are far too long....I believe that a shortening of the service would make for far more decorum and more devotion.

David Fay (1854-1907), who succeeded Aaron Levy Green, is long forgotten. In the histories of the synagogue, he is only listed as D. Fay, but for 18 years he served the congregation with the utmost dedication and at the expense of his health. He was educated at the Jews' Free School and when he grew up he became a teacher there for some time. His ambition, however, was to be a minister and in 1877 he was appointed to the Hull community.

From there he went on to Bristol in 1880, following predecessors like Aaron Levy Green. He spent a lot of time as Hon. Sec. of the Committee of Visitors among the Jewish Poor, and of the Jewish Religious Education Board for sixteen years from 1887-1902. So, he was well qualified to be the successful candidate out of seven for the position of preacher at the Central; after three years he was appointed secretary. The process of his selection was unusual in that the synagogue members were asked to say in which order they would vote for the candidates.

David Fay cast his net wide in his choice of topics for sermons in 1884. He devoted one of those he gave to gain his selection to the vacant post, to the Belgian priest, Father Damien. The cleric had ministered to lepers in Hawaii when they were banished to an island, and eventually he died of leprosy as well in 1889. He would be beatified in 1995. It was a fine example of self-sacrifice which David Fay applauded from the pulpit.

With the arrival of so many refugees in the East End of London, the inequality and intimidation of women in parts of society and in a number of legal areas became a problem to be tackled at long last. It may not have affected the lady members of the Central, who could stand their ground if necessary, but their support for their poorer coreligionists was now coming to be organised.

In 1885 Constance Rothschild, Sir Anthony's daughter, formed the Jewish Association for the Protection of Girls and Women and the JAPGW did sterling work in tackling criminal activity, like white slavery, in which several East End Jews played an infamous part, and cases of abuse.

The eminence of a number of the members was now a widely agreed aspect of the Synagogue. It was typical that when Rev. Simeon Singer came to preach at the Central in 1886 he took as his theme the responsibility of wealth. This could have been a reaction to the fact that in the past four years the memorial tablet in the Synagogue had only had one name added as remembering the Synagogue in a will. Ten years later Nathan Laski, Haham Moses Gaster's son-in-law, would write from Manchester that Central members did not support the poor enough but he set a very high standard.

The United Synagogue remained the authority with the right to approve all expenditure on the Synagogue and at a meeting in 1886 even found the time to authorise an additional £30 to the previous agreed figure. It was two-way traffic; in the same year Baron Henry de Worms MP, a member of the Central, complained about the way his appointment to the government had been handled in the United Synagogue's annual report. He didn't consider it sufficiently effusive.

The competition in the City between Lord Rothschild and Samuel Montagu was already to be. found reflected in the proceedings of a special meeting of the United Synagogue at the Central in 1886, called to examine the body's finances.

Comments from delegates like "setting class against class" and "endeavouring to buy cheap popularity" were gleefully reported in the press.

Only a few years after the death of Aaron Levy Green, the synagogue lost Rev. Samuel Lyons in 1887 at the early age of 57. He had retired in 1884 and died in 1887. He had been the second reader at the synagogue for thirty-two years. He was born in the Jews' Hospital and Orphan Asylum after his father died. He became the second reader of the Branch Synagogue in 1855 and served in that capacity until he fell ill in 1887. Like so many other ministers at the time, he was only considered a member of the staff. As his obituary recorded:

> Mr. Lyons endeavoured to compensate for the lack of any great intellectual capacity by a painstaking zeal in the discharge of his official duties, and he enjoyed the respect of his congregation, as well as the esteem of the various Wardens under whom he served.

"Under whom he served". Unfortunately, it summed up the status of synagogue ministers for many years.

The year 1887 also saw the death of Lionel Louis Cohen MP, a stalwart of the Synagogue. He too passed away at the early age of 55. He was a banker and for some years the Manager of the London Stock Exchange. He sat as the Conservative MP for Paddington North when most of the community still supported the Liberals. Although he was a vice president of the United Synagogue, he remained a member of the Central Board of Management.

Within the community Lionel Louis Cohen was a prime mover in the creation of the Board of Guardians charity and worked hard to see the United Synagogue Act placed on the statute book. He eventually presided over the first meeting of the United Synagogue Council and became a Vice President. In 1881 he had also created the first fund for the relief of the Jews in Russia.

Lionel Louis Cohen was very highly respected in his lifetime but the attendance at the memorial service at the Central was not as large as it should have been. It was fitting, therefore, that memorial windows were created in his memory.

The new Synagogue attracted journalists, and one from the *Graphic* came to the Shabbat service in 1889. He reported that the synagogue was "a somewhat plainly decorated long room" but was struck by:

> the great truth that much of the English church worship, more especially its order and regularity, is derived from the Elder church.

In 1889 the first warden, Barnett Meyers, (1814-1889) died. He had been a warden from 1870-1877 and the community lost one of its most benevolent philanthropists. Born in Aldgate, Meyers started work when he was thirteen and became a highly successful businessman. Happily married and retired, there were no children and Barnett Meyers devoted the rest of his life to Jewish charities.

Among other gifts, he bought eight acres of land for the Jewish Orphan Society, which combined with the Jewish Hospital to create the Norwood Orphanage. He also was one of those who were instrumental in the creation of the Willesden cemetery and helped to supervise the layout and planting of the ground.

There were few charities which did not receive his help and he was typical of the support many richer Jews gave to their poor brethren in the East End. He was president of the Borough Jewish Schools, vice president of the Jewish hospital, and gave one of the first scholarships to students at Jews' College. It was recorded that he was one of the kindest, gentlest, most sympathetic of spirits....prosperity did not spoil him.

Both Hermann Adler and David Fay were concerned about the education of girls and at the Central, David Fay started special confirmation services for them in 1896. There were also classes for anybody in the congregation who wanted to improve their knowledge of Hebrew and Judaism. It was hard going because there was a tendency at the time for the nation to become more secular. and less religious. Attendances at the synagogue were "less fashionable than in former years". Hermann Adler, by then the Chief Rabbi, wasn't even sure that Confirmation Services should be offered for girls.

The Upper Berkeley Street Synagogue had introduced them and David Fay followed suit. The fact that the Orthodox Synagogue was following in the footsteps of the Progressives was not a problem for the Central at the time. Hermann Adler had started them at Bayswater but the idea was later abandoned. Aaron Levy Green, writing as Nemo in the Jewish Chronicle, had dismissed them as "fashionable displays of millinery". David Fay instituted them anyway. *The Jewish Chronicle* was very impressed and commented:

> It will go hard indeed if the earnest exhortation publicly addressed to them by the minister does not live imperishably in their hearts.

David Fay had held three of these special services by 1899 but wanted to hold them annually or at least biannually. He was so sure of the support of the wardens and the Board of Management that, without consulting them, he wrote to the *Chronicle* to invite the superintendents of other London synagogues to send their pupils to him for training. The standard he set was rigorous. The girls had to pass an exam to be invited to the service, but the truth was that the children needed to be amalgamated, as the Central didn't have that many girls between thirteen and sixteen.

When David Fay took over the Central classes in 1886, there were 23 pupils and two years later this had increased to a total of 55. Mrs. Fay had been brought in to teach the juniors. The attendances were considered praiseworthy. David Fay was then invited to take over the office of supervisor at the Jewish Religious Education Board from his brother-in-law Morris Joseph, who would go over to the Upper Berkeley Street Reform synagogue. The defection occurred when Hermann Adler, as the Chief Rabbi, refused to accept Morris Joseph's nomination as minister of the Hampstead synagogue which caused outrage in that congregation.

David Fay was a determined character. Over the years of his involvement, the number of Jewish children on the JREB roll, went up from a handful to 8,000. In 1892 he also started Chanukah Military Services and these continued until after the Great War. The Central had been one of the first congregations to hold Batmitzvah services and when the Hampstead Synagogue consulted the Chief Rabbi about the practice in 1889, it was told the service should follow the example of the Central.

It was during David Fay's time that Hannah Rothschild (1859-1890) started a Jewish Working Girls Club in the East End. Although she married Lord Rosebery, who would become the prime minister, she remained a member of the Central and often attended the services. She was particularly noticed when she came to shul after the birth of each of her four children: Margaret, Sybil, Harry and Neil. Of course, halachically, all four were

Jewish, which made the 6th Earl Rosebery a Jew, but there is no record that he was a member of the Central!

When she died at only 39 it was noted that by Hannah Rothschild's bed was a beautiful mezuzah with some Passover afikomen (matzo) which had been given to her by Sir Moses Montefiore. On the wall in Hebrew were the words "May the Lord bless you and keep you." David Fay and Emanuel Spero conducted the funeral service at Willesden and Lord Rothschild and Leopold Rothschild said kaddish (the memorial prayer). To mark her passing Lord Rosebery gave the Central 100 guineas. (£105 – today £12,000). Both Lord Rosebery and William Gladstone came to the service.

In 1893 Samuel Moss had been in the box for ten years and would serve for a further eleven. He was celebrating his silver wedding that year and marked it by taking the choir to Brighton for the day. The relations between Hermann Adler, the Chief Rabbi, and the Central were now very warm. In 1897 he accepted invitations to preach in the synagogue on three occasions. Now the Chief Rabbi after the death of his father in 1890, it was contentious that at Succot he had commented unfavourably on the Zionist conference proceedings in Basle. He was not in favour of Zionism and in thanking him for his address, it was the view of the warden that his sentiments "would be approved by most of the members of the English Jewish community."

Zionism was a concept that would split British Jewry for the next fifty years. Both Joseph Herman Hertz, the choice for chief rabbi after Hermann Adler died, and Haham Moses Gaster were keen Zionists but Lord Rothschild, the lay head of the United Synagogue and Chief Rabbi Hermann Adler were very much on the other side in the early days.

Raising money for charity depended a good deal on the Honorary Officers. The Central Branch of the Orphan Aid Society was particularly fortunate to have as its secretary Edith Jacob. In 1896 she collected weekly contributions from 55 subscribers out of a splendid total of 215. Presiding over the society was David Fay and there were also nine life governors who in two years brought in 110 guineas (Today £13,550.)

In 1897 Frederick Davis and his wife celebrated their Golden Wedding. He was a successful art dealer in New Bond Street and a past warden at the shul. A large number of charities benefited from the anniversary, totalling donations of over £400. (About £50,000 today). In addition the Davis' gave a dinner for the nursing staff at the Evelina Children's Hospital, and 100 parcels of groceries for the pensioners at the Aged Needy Society. It took four days to entertain 1,400 pupils at the Jews' Free School and in return the children gave them silver salt dishes. The childrens' contributions were limited to ½p and the list of presents from their friends probably matched their own generosity.

In 1898 a Jewish Educational Conference was held at the Synagogue and was notable for an address by Dr. Gustave Schorstein, an expert on phthisis, a form of tuberculosis, which was a serious killer at the time. In a paper called "masterly and pathetic", Dr. Schorstein condemned the high volume of work in the curriculum of East End Jewish schools, many of whose pupils were his patients. Dr. Schorstein was very highly regarded in the community but died at 43 from diabetes.

The ability of the East End refugees to acclimatise to English culture was a matter of continuous concern to the leaders of the community. To help them and to combat the conversion societies who were trying to win them over as well, in 1900 Dayan Feldman suggested creating a number of Jewish Institutes. These would be Reading Rooms in many parts of the country and would enable the refugees to associate with people from their own background. It needed financial support, of course, and the Chief Rabbi asked all his ministers to preach to that effect in May 1907. Michael Adler made a powerful appeal at the Central and the Jewish Institutes continued to be useful bases for intellectual study and social gatherings for many decades to come.

Another family who had served the Synagogue well was the Beddingtons but in 1900 Alfred, the Financial Representative 25 years before, died suddenly.

> His sound common-sense, his unerring judgement, his practical advice, his instinct for what made for the best interests of the place of worship he had loved so well, had always been at the disposal of its management, and no matter, however trivial and however drastic, had been arrived at the deliberation of the executive body without having been sifted and scrutinised and weighed against, at the bar of his judgment.

The turn of the century saw the outbreak of the Boer War and over 2,000 Jews volunteered; 116 of them died serving their country. They were particularly remembered at the Military Service in 1901, organised by Francis Lyon Cohen, which was the 9th to be held at the Central over the years. It was honoured by the attendance of the Lord Mayor and his wife, the Lord Lieutenant, the Duke of Bedford, and the Chief Rabbi.

Jews from both the army and the navy were represented and the commanding officer for the service was Lieutenant Colonel David de Lara

Cohen, who was the Officer Commanding the 1st London Division, a Territorial Army body; David de Lara Cohen was a stockbroker and accountant with a particular fondness for military service. He had been made a sub-lieutenant in 1876 and was steadily promoted over the years till he reached the rank of Lieutenant Colonel.

The Boer War came at a particularly sensitive time for the Jewish community in Britain. Because of the pogroms in Russia, over 100,000 Jews had fled to Britain and a considerable proportion had made homes for themselves in the East End. They were soon accused of undercutting the wages of the native workers and, as a result, antisemitic incidents increased.

Many of the original community, who belonged to Synagogues like the Central, tried to help the newcomers to assimilate, but the size of the problem made it very difficult for organisations like the charitable Board of Guardians to cope. In addition, when the war was over, the number of British forces casualties was far greater than ever expected; 22,000 died and a further 23,000 were wounded.

The inquest on the war not surprisingly looked for scapegoats for it breaking out. One proposed reason was the economic disputes in South Africa over control of the diamond and gold trades. A number of the companies involved had been founded by Jewish immigrants and antisemites blamed the Jews for initiating the conflict to protect their interests. In fact, the war was primarily delayed revenge for the British defeats in the first Boer War some fifteen years earlier. Following their centuries old tradition, the South African Jews had found a hole in the market.

The Boer War concentrated minds and was said to explain the indifference of the community to United Synagogue elections in 1900. At the Central only 30 out of 350 members turned up to vote, which was dismissed as "insuperable apathy". There seemed to be more interest in seeking municipal office than in serving as a parnas. But the Central was making a profit and the members had the excuse of the war. The *Jewish Chronicle* commented:

> We do not think that an intelligent interest in Lord Robert's campaign is incompatible with an equally intelligent interest in the administration of the House of Worship.

In the middle of the Boer War Queen Victoria died and Edward VII's coronation was scheduled for a Thursday in June 1902. Unfortunately, the

King developed appendicitis the night before the ceremony and the coronation had to be postponed until a Saturday in August.

The Chief Rabbi was invited to the installation at Westminster Abbey, and solved the problem of the conflict with Shabbot, by attending an early service at the Western Synagogue, and then walking to the Abbey with a police escort. Things had improved since the coronation of Richard the Lionheart, when 30 Jews were killed by an antisemitic crowd.

Lord Rothschild, Sir Anthony's nephew, was also present at the Coronation as a great friend of the King from university days. As Edward was profligate in overspending his income, he was particularly indebted to Lord Rothschild, who arranged a £100,000 mortgage for him on the Sandringham estate. (£11 million today). Edward had made him Lord Lieutenant of Buckinghamshire in 1889; the first Jew to be so honoured.

David Fay's responsibilities and activities had a devastating effect on his health. He suffered from sleeplessness and diabetes. At this distance in time it is impossible to diagnose the cause for the sleeplessness. It could well have been stress but, for whatever reason, David Fay had to take a lengthy leave of absence from the Central and eventually resigned in 1902. The Central seat holders had the greatest sympathy for him. They passed a resolution:

> That the general meeting of seat holders of the Central Synagogue has learnt with the deepest regret that owing to continued ill health, the Rev. David Fay has found it imperative to resign the office of Minister of the Congregation. The meeting desires to put on record the high appreciation of his zealous service and devoted labours over a period of 18 years, and tenders the warmest sympathy in his enforced retirement, with the expression of its earnest hope that the cessation of his congregational and communal work will, by Divine Grace, be the means of sparing him to his family and friends for many years in renewed health and strength.

It was not to be. David Fay died five years later, at the early age of 53, and reference was made in his obituary to his terrible suffering. The Chief Rabbi wrote:

> When he was called upon to occupy the pulpit....of so significant and popular a minister as the Rev. A.L.Green, there appeared no prospect of his attaining the position which his lamented predecessor

had achieved by his oratorical talent, his geneality, many sidedness and great capacity for work. Yet gradually David Fay won for himself the regard and love of his congregants by his untiring devotion to duty, his unvarying courtesy and his acting up to the conviction that neither the pulpit, nor the reading desk, nor the congregation, exhaust the rightful claims upon a minister's time and thought. The writer gratefully records the sound advice and sympathetic ear that he at all times received at the hands of this truly loyal friend.

David Fay definitely deserved to be remembered, but that is why we have statues, memorials and plaques. Without any of these, history books become something of a last resort.

Within a short space of time at the end of the century, the Synagogue lost both Ferdinand de Rothschild, (1839-1898) and a stalwart former honorary officer in the death of Frederick Davis. (1845-1900). The Rothschilds all came to Ferdinand de Rothschild's memorial service and to the happier occasion of Evelyn de Rothschild's barmitzvah. The Chief Rabbi gave sermons at both. Ferdinand was such a public figure that at his death the London cab drivers tied black ribbons to their whips and the *Jewish Chronicle* devoted no less than four and a half pages to his obituary.

At the time Frederick Davis had been a warden for twelve years and in addition had found the time to represent the Synagogue on the Board of Deputies and the Council of the United Synagogue, besides sitting as a JP. Another long-serving warden, Joseph Pyke, a prominent financier and a great character, stood down in 1901 after being run over by a hansom and severely injured at an advanced age.

Joseph Pyke was well taken care of in hospital, which fully justified the support the Synagogue gave to the Metropolitan Hospital Sunday Fund, to which all the London Synagogues contributed. The Great collected £254 but, on the list of contributors, the Central came a respectable fourth with £74. There was no Jewish Hospital until after the First World War, because even with something apparently as uncontentious as hospitals, there was disagreement.

The Chief Rabbi supported King Edward VII's Hospital Fund and considered that health should be a national, rather than an ethnic minority concern. For Orthodox Jews, however, the provision of kosher food and rituals like laying tephillin could lead to mockery by non-Jewish patients in a secular hospital, and the Din would be easier to observe in a Jewish hospital. The attempt to build a Jewish hospital was supported by Haham Moses Gaster, whose brother, Anghel, was the charity's treasurer for many years and eventually one was opened.

Over the years some of the United Synagogues were in surplus, some broke even and some were subsidised by the richer communities. Many of the poorer Synagogues did not want to acknowledge that they needed what were, in effect, charitable donations to balance their budgets. The United Synagogue officers were normally, therefore, not enthusiastic about everybody knowing how the annual income was distributed.

In 1901 the Central representatives proposed that a return be made regularly, identifying how much the Council provided to the costs of running the United from the annual contribution agreed with each Synagogue, and how much came from the richer Synagogues to supplement any shortfall.

It was not surprising that only the Central was in favour of such openness and the motion was not approved. In later years the accounts would include items of over a million pounds listed under the heading of Miscellaneous Expenses. There was no suggestion that money was being spent fraudulently, but supervision of those responsible for the expenditure was made far more difficult by the figures being left vague or not available at all.

The rule today is that as charities, accounts must be registered with the Charities Commission, but professional accountants might well welcome more detail.

The Central also asked the 1901 meeting to agree to abandon the restriction on the synagogue to not spending more than £80 a year on the religious classes. This was agreed.

One of the charities the United Synagogue supported was Jews' College, where Sir Adolph Tuck had become treasurer in 1903 and chair of the College Council in later years. He became a warden at the Central in 1910 and sat in the box for the next sixteen.

The honour of being elected a warden was taken seriously. In 1903, for instance, when Edward Pinder Davis was elected, he was escorted to the box at the Friday evening service by the two wardens, Samuel Moss and Arthur Isaacs, together with the retiring warden Joseph Trenner.

In 1903 Rev Michael Adler was appointed to take David Fay's place and only retired in 1934. This time there was an advisory committee to consider applications and the members weren't consulted. Like his predecessors, Michael Adler came from a poor East End family where his father was a Polish tailor and his mother Dutch, in a family with eight children. He went to Jews' College and University College London, getting his BA, before being appointed in 1890 as the first minister of the new Hammersmith Synagogue at the age of 22.

All his life Michael Adler made things happen. He would persevere, on many occasions against considerable odds, and always worked for the disadvantaged. In 1893 he became the chaplain at Wormwood Scrubs prison. The park was newly developed. The prison had only been built by convict labour in 1874 and Michael Adler was able to work to ameliorate the harsh conditions under which convicts were kept.

Michael Adler was also the senior Hebrew master at the Jews' Free School. As such he wrote *Elements of Hebrew Grammar* in 1897, which warranted a second edition in 1899. In the same year he published the *Student Hebrew Grammar* and set a new standard in the relationship between the students and their teachers. He was particularly anxious to improve the teaching of the children in the community. He had the support of the Haham, Moses Gaster, who had said:

> Daily study and daily prayer went hand in hand, but study was considered superior. A Beth ha-medresh enjoined greater respect and greater sanctity than Beth ha-keneset - the school stood higher than the Synagogue, One may sell a Synagogue to build a school, but one may not sell a school to build a Synagogue.

Of course, the newcomers from Eastern Europe had been brought up to know Hebrew and speak Yiddish. As late as 1906 the report of the Children's Chanukah service at the Synagogue made the point that the sermon by the visiting Rabbi, was in English.

The United Synagogue approved the idea of an advisory committee to help the Board of Management at their Synagogues choose a candidate for a ministry vacancy. That was the new system adopted by the Central when appointing Michael Adler and in future it would be followed. The advisory committee was ten strong, so there was plenty of advice.

The United Synagogue Visitation Committee had lobbied the War Office to have Jewish soldiers recognised as a distinct group, and as a result, in 1892, the first Jewish Chaplain to the Forces was approved. Rev. Francis Lyon Cohen was appointed and when he retired in 1904, Michael Adler took his place. He could soon be found on Salisbury Plain, taking services at the summer camps, and officiating during Chanukah. It was agreed that the Magen Dovid should be the emblem on his cap rather than the normal Chaplain's cross.

In 1907 the United Synagogue decided to study the way in which Jews' College was operating and there was a heated discussion on the composition of the committee which would look into its curriculum. Sir Adolph wanted those who supported the college to serve on the reporting committee, but a number of the United Synagogue council wanted more who had shown in the past that they were critical of its operation.

The core of the argument was whether the students should be taught primarily rabbinical studies or whether they should be taught to be trained bureaucrats when they took up their posts on graduation. The United Synagogue wanted bureaucrats and the officers of Jews' College were determined to produce Talmudic scholars. Over the years the Jews' College principals stuck to their guns.

Jews' College was usually in financial difficulties as the result of its attitude to the knowledge of its graduates. It simply didn't get adequate support from the United Synagogue. This was in spite of the fact that most of the United Synagogue ministers were eventually graduates of the college.

The fact remained that in 1902 no less than thirty students received their Jews' College Preliminary Grade Teacher certificates and of those, thirteen were women. The financial situation would deteriorate when the Great War broke out as dividends from investments declined. It became patriotic to invest in War Bonds instead of local charities.

A particularly serious loss was the £1,000 that the Sephardim gave to the college each year. Most of this came from the Imperial Continental Gas Company which Sir Moses Montefiore had founded to light city streets. It was in Chief Rabbi Nathan Marcus Adler's time as Chief Rabbi of Hanover that the city benefited. Their electrical plant was destroyed by the Germans, however, and the Sephardim couldn't provide the money again until after the war.

Sir Adolph appealed to the United Synagogue for more support, but they recommended reducing the number of the college staff instead. Sir Adolph was furious:

> That the Spanish and Portuguese body are satisfied that their annual outlay of £1,000 is a good investment for the Jewish community as a whole, is well evidenced by the fact that one of their leading Elders, as Chairman of Jews' College, as well as various other gentlemen from that body, on the Council of the College, have had every opportunity of thoroughly acquainting themselves with the work of the college at first hand. The Executive of the United Synagogue,

unless they wilfully shut their eyes, possess the same knowledge and assurance.

It did no good. The staff at Jews' College had to pull in their belts still further and what happened to money provided by members of Synagogues would be a subject raised on many occasions in the future.

In the early days, a large percentage of the Central members were also apathetic about the United Synagogue elections, but there were still a considerable number, like Alfred Beddington, who were prepared to take a great deal of trouble to keep the Synagogue on the right road.

In 1903 Emmeline Pankhurst founded her British Women's Social and Political Union with the objective of getting Votes for Women. The suffragette movement would become a major national issue, and one of its earliest supporters was the Central Synagogue warden, Alderman Joseph Trenner, who had a business manufacturing artistic designs.

At the annual meeting of the Synagogue, he put forward a motion to give the vote to women seat holders, equally with the male members. It shows what an uphill struggle Mrs. Pankhurst was to have, that there was not even a seconder for the motion. Joseph Trenner tried again at the annual meeting of the United Synagogue that year and again there was no seconder. In 1912 the Jewish Union of Women's Suffrage was formed and started to campaign themselves.

Chief Rabbi Hertz would support the women's right to a say in Synagogue management, but the reaction of the men was that they would be "driven out" of their Synagogues by "irrational and emotional women". It would not be until 1927 that the United Synagogue finally gave way, and then it was against considerable opposition. The motion was finally only passed by 66 votes to 54.

Victorian women were not allowed to vote or hold office in synagogues, though if they were members, they had to pay their dues. British democracy is the result of the Civil War in the 17th century and it was the King's refusal to call parliament into session that led to the war. The rallying cry of the parliamentarians was "No taxation without representation" and it could well have been used by Jewish ladies when they sought the same rights as the men in the United Synagogue.

The Jewish press described the suffragettes as "Blackguards in Bonnets" and when they demonstrated at Synagogues, they were forcibly removed and then force fed if they were imprisoned and went on hunger strike in their cells. It was barbaric but it went on for years.

Another complaint about the way the United Synagogue was run referred to the results of elections. It was the practice to announce the winners but not to give the votes cast for each candidate. This practice was still being questioned a hundred years later by candidates who had failed to be elected.

The objective of the antisemites was to have an Aliens Act passed to halt Jewish immigration and Lord Rothschild and the Chief Rabbi worked tirelessly to prevent this happening. It didn't help that Arthur Balfour, the prime minister, had said in the House of Commons that the problem with immigration was, primarily, the number. of Jews coming into the country.

The main attack of the antisemites was on the possibility of dual loyalty; that Jews had a loyalty to the Jewish community as well as a loyalty to Britain. There needed to be pro-Jewish public relations and a ceremony to remember those Jews who had died in the war was, therefore, very appropriate. A bronze and marble tablet in memory of the fallen was placed on the wall of the facade of the Synagogue and was unveiled by Field Marshall, Earl Roberts, in March 1905. The Field Marshall had come to one of the Chanukah Military services in 1902 and the support of the most popular soldier in the country was very welcome.

The address by the warden, Edward Pinder Davis, emphasised this:

> This memorial stands here in eloquent testimony to the fact that British Jews are inspired by a love of King and country no less enthusiastic and no less devoted than that which animates their fellow subjects.

It was significant that the ceremony was held in the Central rather than the Great Synagogue. Certainly, during the. Napoleonic Wars, two royal Dukes visited the Great and there would have been no alternative to the Great when remembering the Crimean War. Now that so many of the senior members had moved to the Central, however, the Great would have become more of a heritage site than the setting for such occasions.

When remembering the casualties in the Boer War, there was also among the congregation Sir Marcus Samuel, the founder of Shell and now the Lord Mayor of London. Sir Marcus' father had a gift shop in London and jewellery using elaborate shells was very fashionable. Very good ones were to be found in Japan and Marcus Samuel was sent to Tokyo to set up a business buying them. He also discovered, however, that the Japanese lacked oil and, with the opening of the Suez Canal, shipping it from the

Middle East had become feasible. So Marcus Samuel started to trade in oil and called his business Shell.

In 1904 the Sukkah at the Synagogue was enhanced by a gift of flowers from Sir Marcus and Lady Samuel, which had just won second prize at the Royal Horticultural Show. It was at the end of the High Holidays which had seen the Chief Rabbi coming on the first day of the festival. This was a custom that lasted at least until the middle of the century. What was also notable was the hiring of a nearby hall for free Yom Kippur services, where 1,000 occasional worshippers, gathered and the excellent decorum was particularly noted. The report specified, however, that the service was for men, which suggests that the ladies were still not treated properly.

The meeting rooms at the Synagogue were still popular and in March 1904 the Board of Deputies met there. Alfred Alvarez and Joseph Freedman represented the Central and the agenda covered many problems the communities faced, not only in Britain but in countries like Russia and Romania as well, where there were still pogroms.

The Board were also concerned with Sunday Trading and the Aliens Act. When the businesses of Orthodox Jews were closed on Shabbot, the enforced additional closure on Sunday left them with a five-day week trading, and efforts were made for many years to give them dispensation to open on Sunday. Christian bakers certainly had an advantage, as the Sunday Baking Act 1822 prohibited baking on Sunday and when the emigrants arrived in the East End, Jewish Orthodox bakers were adversely affected. The situation wouldn't really change until 1936.

When elections were to be held, the Central Board of Management now sent to members an account of the number of occasions on which each member attended the meetings. When this disclosed that some didn't attend at all there was a suggestion that other Synagogues did the same thing, but the idea was not universally adopted.

What was recognised was the 80th birthday of Phillip Valentine in June 1904 who:

> Continues to perform his duties with wonderful activity and zeal at the Synagogue at which he has been the most familiar personality for the past 53 years.

Meeting at the Central now gave additional status to new organisations. One such was the Jewish Territorial Organisation, which Israel Zangwill and Lucien Wolf formed to promote the idea of a Jewish National Home in Uganda rather than the Holy Land. This was highly contentious and would be rejected by delegates to the Zionist Conference in 1905. Prior to that meeting the JTA held a meeting at the Central to formalise their position. The organisation was only disbanded in 1925.

Minutiae were also not neglected. The Lord Chancellor had concerns that Jewish MPs taking the loyal oath, had been asked to swear on the name of Jehovah rather than G-d. This was strictly against the Din where the former name was never used, and the Lord Chancellor promised to see that it didn't happen again.

The Chanukah Military Service had brought the Synagogue to the attention of the armed forces and, at Passover in 1907, a considerable number of men attended the service in the Synagogue, having been given the time off to do so. Representatives of two warships and more than a dozen army regiments were made very welcome.

The standing of the Synagogue now led to some wild exaggeration. Repairs to the building brought reports of "multitudinous scaffolding", and by December 1907 a wedding took place which was again described as a "Marriage among Millionaires." The canopy was stated to be of white satin supported by gold poles. The account was corrected by pointing out that the poles were twisted brass and the white satin canopy was, in fact, purple velvet, but the headline remained in the memory.

Events at the Central always made for thorough coverage in the media but the services didn't alter in the slightest as Michael Adler ensured that they were strictly observed.

Maintaining the traditions of the Synagogue were the two wardens in 1907, Robert Waley Cohen and Edward Pinder Davis. In both cases they were following in the footsteps of their relatives, Edward Davis being the son of Frederick Davis and Robert Waley Cohen the grandson of Jacob Waley and the son of Nathaniel Cohen.

The Chanukah Military Service continued for many years. It was reinstated in 1919 but the attendance was not as great as before the war. Colonel de Lara Cohen had returned to his civilian occupation of stockbroking and accounting and died in 1937 in his eighties. Dayan Gollop arranged another service in 1926 at the Bayswater but the annual gathering, which still occurs, is now the responsibility of the Association of Jewish Ex-Servicemen and Women.

The creation of the Jewish Ex-servicemen's Legion provided an opportunity for another annual event, which was the gathering in 1930 at Horseguards Parade in the same month as Remembrance Day. After the Second World War, Chanukah Military Services were held at the Hampstead shul in 1947 and the New West End in 1948 and 1949. The

Legion's gathering still takes place every year at Horseguards Parade and the service of Remembrance at the Royal Albert Hall in 2020 saw the Jewish chaplain, Rabbi Major Reuben Livingstone, given the honour of carrying the Bible during the proceedings.

6

The Michael Adler years

One of Michael Adler's earliest objectives was to create a Jewish Working Men's Club in the Soho district of London. His poorer Jewish brethren didn't only live in the East End and enabling them to belong to a local social club in their own district was a worthy objective. Rents were heavy, however, and Michael Adler had to raise donations of over £1,000 to get the West Central Jewish Working Men's Club off and running. He managed it though, forming a committee in September 1903 with many members from the Central.

At the end of 1904 the Board of Deputies gave £100 to the Great Synagogue to run Shabbat afternoon services for the poor East End working Jews and their children. It was specified that the services were for the poor, and it was noted that previous services had attracted congregations in their hundreds. At the same time, it was recognised that the weather could affect attendances and more would come if the sermons were in Yiddish or German, rather than English.

This division in the community between the West End and the East End was now accepted without question and the use of the Great to teach English to poor immigrants on Shabbat afternoon left the original members to attend the morning service with their class distinctions intact.

The year 1903 saw a Russian pogrom in Kishinev, when 50 Jews were killed and the Jewish community was heavily persecuted. There was worldwide condemnation, but this did not influence the Russian government at all. Michael Adler, like many other ministers, preached a powerful sermon, but the event which undermined the Czar was the Russian defeat in the Russo-Japanese War in 1904-5. The Japanese were able to take on the enormous Russian Empire because Kuhn-Loeb, the American Jewish bank, raised $250 million to finance the Japanese armed forces.

Samuel Moss died in 1904 soon after resigning as a warden. He had been in the Box for 21 years and was best known as a peacekeeper. He was also on the council of the United Synagogue and fulsome tributes were made to his work on behalf of the organisation.

Praising Samuel Moss was certainly not contentious, but Michael Adler had a much more difficult task that year when it came to an obituary for Theodor Herzl, the Zionist leader, who had been a very controversial character in his lifetime. Michael Adler knew there was plenty of opposition to Zionism in his new community. There were supporters, like Haham Moses Gaster in the Sephardi congregation, though the Haham was opposed by most of the Sephardi Mahamad, the lay leaders. Michael Adler was, therefore, very diplomatic in the pulpit:

> The cause Dr. Herzl set before him was a noble one, to rescue his coreligionists from the disabilities and persecution from which they still suffered in many lands. He was a born leader of men and possessed the magic power of being able to impress others with his own enthusiasm. Though one might not approve of his scheme, one could not but admire his wondrous energy, his unselfish devotion to his people and the ideal character of his striving. Judaism was broad enough to encourage every phase of opening in its midst, if only the object was pure and sincere, and for that reason all Jews felt the loss of the Zionist leader with the keenest of a personal grief.

Herzl's objective was to gather the Jews together in the Holy Land. The objective of the antisemites was to stop Jews coming to Britain. The pressure for an Aliens Act now increased after the Boer War. An organisation called the British Brothers League gathered some support and led the way, although when the Aliens Act was passed in 1905, it was the result of a host of misapprehensions.

The accusation was made that immigrants were flooding into the country and creating unemployment. An official report in 1895, however, had quoted a figure of 24,700 immigrants a year between 1891 and 1893, and a figure for emigrants of 164,000; America, Canada and Australia seemed to offer far better prospects.

The East End was also in no way typical of the country overall, or even London. Large parts of the country still had no Jewish inhabitants at all. Then it was stated by antisemites that with an Aliens Act, British workers would no longer have their income undercut by immigrants prepared to work for lower wages. Speaking generally, the claim wasn't true as Jews mostly sought work in the growing tailoring trades and very few were to be found, for example, among the dock workers.

Support for an Aliens Act would have been expected to be found by the leaders of the workers. In fact, Keir Hardie, the founder of the Labour Party, opposed the bill. His grounds were that its clause, making a contract to work an essential for an immigrant, would just make it easier for unscrupulous employers to bring in such workers by providing the contracts.

It would have been assumed that the Jewish community would be against the bill but when it came before the House of Commons the four Conservative Jewish MPs all voted in favour of the legislation. One Jewish Liberal MP abstained and the other three voted against.

The community remained badly split. Foreign Jewish immigrants, arriving in the East End, were still tending to spoil the community's desired image of loyal British Jews. Many Jews who had moved to the West End after a lifetime of hard work, wanted the reward of a positive image. On the other hand, there were still many who continued to have immigrant relatives in the East End. and were only a generation away from being newcomers themselves. As a consequence, they were even more inclined to protect the interests of their kinfolk.

An Aliens Act could obviously prevent a Jew's persecuted relatives from finding freedom in Britain. Those who had assimilated were likely to approve of the bill and those who still had links with the East End were likely to oppose it. There was also the perfectly genuine aim for many of helping their poorer brethren in every way they could, with the possible exception of having them arrive in the country in the first place!

The Board of Guardians, in particular, had for years been struggling with the need for financial support for an increasing number of East End Jews. The amount of money needed was hard to find. As a consequence, with the Board's actual cooperation, the Aliens Act resulted in many potential immigrants being deported to their original countries. These poor cases individually received little publicity but involved terrible hardship on very many occasions.

The introduction of the Zionist movement only complicated matters, because the Zionists were proclaiming the Jews to be a nation, which strengthened the antisemitic dual loyalty argument. It was not only the Chief Rabbi, Hermann Adler, who was very much anti-Zionist; the movement recruited very limited support in the community as a whole. On the other hand, Michael Adler was the son of a poor East End family of immigrants and would have felt for the plight of those who wanted to stay in Britain. He knew of the distress of those who were expelled.

The position of the main political protagonists was complicated as well. Arthur Balfour, facing defeat in the next general election, needed as many vote-getters as possible for his manifesto. An Aliens Act might only result in a small number of extra votes in all, but it was likely to be a step in the right direction. Arthur Balfour sat for a Manchester constituency, though, and the chair of the local party was Jewish, a relation of the Frenchman Alfred Dreyfus, and a keen Zionist. Keeping everybody happy was extremely difficult and the eventual solution was to introduce the Act, but to make it possible for most potential immigrants to avoid its restrictions.

Even so, the passing of the Aliens Act did mean the bureaucracy for getting naturalised became both more extensive and expensive; the number of successful applicants duly fell. In September 1905, for example, there were only 68 applications to the Home Office and, apart from Russia, who provided 23 of them, another 13 countries made up the rest. It was only as the East End families grew, that the total number of Jews increased as a whole.

In 1904 Francis Lyon Cohen, the first Jewish Chaplain to the Forces, resigned and Michael Adler took his place. The office of the Jewish chaplaincy was now located in the Central and Michael Adler had a lot of additional work to do. He even employed an Hon. Military Secretary in Jerrold Annenberg. Michael Adler had not wanted the position when it was first offered to him and only agreed to run the Chanukah service because it would be cancelled otherwise. He then became enthusiastic about the work and was officially appointed by the Army in 1905 and the Navy in 1906. He asked the authorities for a job specification and was told he had:

> authority to act as spiritual adviser to all troops of that communion in the United Kingdom. No expense to the public has been contemplated in the appointment.

It wasn't a paying proposition but there were probably about 500 Jews in the army and there was a Synagogue in Aldershot. A considerable number of enlisted men came to the Central for Passover and Leopold de Rothschild provided funds to entertain them.

There were many anomalies with which to deal. One of the problems with Jewish recruits in the coming war was to have their religion registered correctly. When they enlisted, they were often put down as Church of England which made getting leave for Jewish festivals a difficulty. Many also changed their names to fit in better, as they saw it, with their Christian comrades. One such was the future Jewish VC, Issa Smith, who was Australian and whose real name was Ishroulch Shmeilowitz. He also won the French Croix de Guerre and its Russian equivalent. Another Jewish VC in the First World War was Jack White, who was born Jacob Weiss. He joined up again in the Second World War but was demobilised when it was discovered that he wasn't born in Britain. He died at 53 in 1949.

A royal marine, Isaac Cohen, was registered as Church of England because the interviewer taking particulars said "C of E?" and Isaac Cohen thought he had said "Civvy" and agreed. Michael Adler got him permission to take time off for the High Holydays. Isaac Cohen served throughout the First World War and joined up for the Second. He was killed at Dunkirk.

In 1905 the Central was able to hold a Silver Jubilee service and Chief Rabbi Hermann Adler delivered the sermon. Philip Vallentine resigned after 50 years as Secretary and gave the congregation a Sefer Torah, which is an expensive present. His sons presented the synagogue with a silver crown for the scroll. There was a service to mark his 50 years as Beadle and the Chief Rabbi, Stuart Samuel MP, and Michael Friedlander from Jews' College all spoke warmly of his efforts. Unhappily, a little later on, Philip Vallentine died of syncope, a drop in blood that flows to the brain, at the age of 81. The Beadle left £6,000 though. (over half a million today).

This was because there were effectively two Philip Valentines. He was the devoted Beadle and also the major publisher of Jewish books in the City. His father was a prominent figure in the East End and Philip Vallentine grew up to be the foremost retailer of Jewish books. He published Vallentine's Almanack, which had been an essential reference book for the community since Isaac Vallentine first produced it in 1848.

Among the gifts in his estate was an annual present to the Jews' Free School of the five-volume set of *Pentateuch and Sabbath Services* which he had also published. There was obviously a widespread belief that it was going to be hard to find another Philip Vallentine.

Phillip Vallentine was typical of the Jews who had been born in the East End but had moved upmarket to the West End. For fifty-three years he dispensed "courtesy and old-world politeness" to everybody who came to pray at the Central and he was so highly regarded that the Chief Rabbi and a host of luminaries came to his funeral.

It is said, though, that the good die young and 1906 also saw the death at the early age of 60 of Rev. Simeon Singer, still known for what became called the Singer Prayer Book.

The community honoured him in the traditional way. At the Willesden cemetery, like all Jewish cemeteries, the graves nearest the chapel are reserved for the wisest and not for the wealthiest. The nearest grave to the Willesden chapel is that of Simeon Singer. The Chief Rabbi cut short his holiday in Germany to be at the funeral.

Phillip Vallentine, as Beadle, was succeeded temporarily by
L.J.Solomon, the Secretary. He appealed for an increase in salary, as he had
to undertake the additional duties of the Beadle in the Synagogue and, with
some reluctance the United Synagogue approved an increase in salary for
six months of twenty pounds. (That would be over £2,000 today). In
December 1906 Max Schulman was appointed Beadle and served for the
next twenty years.

With Michael Adler's coaxing, the Central now had a Ladies'
Needlework Guild, the Literary and Debating Society and the Working
Men's Club in Tottenham Court Road, the brainchild of the minister,
Leopold de Rothschild and Felix Davis. The Synagogue was still ready to
help its poorer brethren. It was in 1905 that the South Hackney Synagogue
learned of six stained glass windows which the Central hadn't eventually
used and asked for them for their own congregation. This was readily
agreed.

The Synagogue also supported the Visiting Committee of the Hebrew
Congregations. This body took on the responsibility of visiting prisons,
asylums, workhouses and hospitals to try to help the Jewish inmates. In
1906 there were 68 Jewish prisoners, but 45 of them were serving sentences
of a month or less. It was significant that the Central was one of only three
congregations which financially supported the Committee.

Michael Adler continued the tradition of holding a Military Service at
Chanukah and tried to send an invitation to attend to all the Jewish
members of the armed forces. The army cooperated and, at the 1905 service,
the band of the East London Volunteer Engineers backed up the chazan.

The minister also became a key member of the appeal for funds for
Walter Webber, who had spent his fortune of £12,000 raising the Western
Province Mounted Rifles and an Ambulance Corps for the British side in
the Boer War. He called his forces the "Captain Webber Foreign Legion".
The government refused to compensate him after the war, however, and
questions were asked in the House of Commons in 1909 for an explanation,
which was not provided.

Supported by Michael Adler, three generals and 50 MPs, the appeal
enabled Walter Webber to recover financially and in later life he would head
a boycott of German goods when the Nazis came to power, forming the
"Chief Webber Boycott Association". One result was a march of 50,000 from
Stepney Green to Hyde Park but, once again, he paid too little attention to
his own interests and went bankrupt.

By now many of the main Jewish organisations held their meetings at
the Central. These included the monthly meetings of the Board of Deputies,

the meetings of the Board of Guardians and the Jewish Religious Education Board. The synagogue's own Literary Society attracted speakers like Haham Moses Gaster, and was quite prepared to examine non-literary subjects.

In November 1905 Canon Barker, the Rector of Marylebone, chose as his subject "Ought all citizens to take an active interest and part in politics?" Members of the synagogue had voted "yes" on many occasions, but recently, in Disraeli's time, this had aroused criticism that their interests were not necessarily those of the nation.

Societies come and go. In 1900, 18 Jewish Study Circles were created throughout the community, but by 1907 only a very few remained in existence. Indeed, the president of the London branch, speaking at the meeting at the Central, suggested dissolving the society, though he only had two votes in favour of the suggestion.

In 1911 the Conference of Jewish Minsters was held at the Central and a number of concerns were discussed. The Bishop of Winchester was prominent in the societies devoted to converting the Jews, and his efforts were assisted by the fact that an estimated 10,000 Jewish children in Stepney were getting no religious education at their schools. There was a good deal of criticism of his activities.

The ministers also wanted to meet with the United Synagogue to discuss religious matters and, in general, there was a good deal of unrest, which reflected the state of the nation at that time. Michael Adler participated, and he enjoyed a busy year. He had also agreed to be president of the Association of Jewish Students and introduced their programme with a lecture on *The Monuments and the Bible*.

It is unusual for any association not to have an opposition party and the Central was no different. At the annual meeting of the United Synagogue a letter from the Central asked that Synagogue officers should only serve for a maximum of four years. Asher Isaacs had already served twelve years as an Honorary Officer at the Central and there wasn't another officer who would be immediately affected by such a resolution. The chair brought the letter to the attention of the meeting and it was agreed that it would be minuted. Which meant that nothing would happen.

Asher Isaacs had, in fact, been a member of the Central Board of Management since 1875, and when he died in 1913 he had been the Financial Representative for 20 years. In his last year the synagogue's income had reached its highest level of £4,211 and had been able to contribute £1,681 to the United Synagogue for its communal purposes. Asher Isaacs could always rely on the charity of the members. This generosity was particularly noticeable at Succot in 1914 when 800 children were taken through the Succah and given sweets, cakes and fruit. On Simchas Torah the same gifts were given to 1,000 children.

Financial Representatives have the responsibility of advising the synagogue whether to adopt the proposals of members, and that can create animosity if they fail to recommend acceptance. Asher Isaacs always tried to maintain harmony and it was sad that he died in the year he celebrated his golden wedding.

When it was necessary to replace David Fay as secretary in 1902, L.J. Solomons was appointed Assistant Secretary and then Acting Secretary in 1903. He was made secretary at a salary of £600 a year for a probationary period of six months in 1906 and filled the role until 1913. He also served as Secretary of the Home and Hospital for Jewish Incurables for several years.

The United Synagogue officers insisted on making decisions on matters which should have been the concern of the Central Board of Management. For example in 1909 Max Shulman wanted a living room for his accommodation, as his was three metres below the ground at the Central. There was such a room, but Michael Adler wanted it for his drawing room and the United Synagogue gave their approval to that arrangement. The letters page of the *Jewish Chronicle* devoted columns to criticising the US officials, but their decisions were final.

From 1906-1910 one of the wardens was Lionel Louis Cohen's nephew, Robert Waley-Cohen, (1877-1952). Waley-Cohen would effectively run the United Synagogue from his election as Vice President in February 1918, because the President, Lionel de Rothschild, was for many years largely a figurehead. Robert Waley Cohen's connection with the Central reflected the synagogue's standing.

When he was made a warden in May 1906, according to the Central's tradition, he was inducted on a Friday evening and escorted to his seat in the Warden's box.

Robert Waley Cohen would prove to be the 'Curate's egg' writ large. He did a very good job in expanding the organisation. By 1940 the number of United Synagogues had increased from 16 to 40. He had also transformed the finances of the organisation by the sale of the New Synagogue for £135,000, which is about £20 million today. He had been to the right school – Clifton's Jewish Boarding House at Bristol – he spoke with the right accent, he had all the right connections within the Cousinhood, and he had a very healthy bank balance. The Chazan, Emanuel Spero, said of him:

> It was always a pleasure to him to give unstinted praise to and appreciation of a minister's service, He had a gentle and fatherly

manner and one could not but feel that there was true goodness and sincere friendship in his advice,

He had initially accepted the senior positions in the community out of respect for his father, Natty, a very successful city businessman who had invented Labour Exchanges and the Cambridge University Appointments Board. Natty was born Nathaniel Cohen, but he married Elizabeth Waley and their children became Waley Cohens. Robert Waley Cohen joined his cousin, Marcus Samuel at Shell, and he rose to be No 3 in the organisation. During the war he would do excellent work to ensure supplies of petrol were sufficient for the armed forces and he was knighted as a result. He also found a great deal of time to work for the United Synagogue.

The downside of Robert Waley Cohen was that, like his father, he had a terrible temper. If his will was not obeyed, he lost his cool time and again. He also had a mother who taught the classes at the Reform synagogue and all his life, Robert Waley Cohen tried to bring the United Synagogue and the Reform back together. He wasn't observant himself. As a Cohen he had the privilege and responsibility of blessing the congregation on Festivals, but when he bought a farm in Somerset, he would drive up to the synagogue to do so, which is against the Din and a terrible example for the less Orthodox.

Robert Waley Cohen had been brought up to rule – he loved power, and seriously disliked dissent once he had made up his mind. From 1911-1945, however, the Chief Rabbi was Joseph Herman Hertz, and he was equally determined to get his own way. One of his ministers, Ephy Levine, said of the Chief Rabbi that he never chose a peaceful solution until all else had failed! As a consequence, the two fell out on many occasions. Both had strong groups of supporters, but the Chief Rabbi had the greater authority, because all religious decisions were ultimately within his compass.

It is indicative of the trouble Waley-Cohen gave Hertz that he wrote to him in 1928, when he was vice president of the United Synagogue, and told him:

> I do not think you will ever find the Anglo-Jewish community willing to submit to the unquestioned authority of anyone in any matter other than questions of pure 'din'. I certainly am not. I count it as a great blessing that it has always been the practice in our community for the leaders – lay and clerical – to take counsel together and to reach a common agreement and work together in the interests of the community and we should all be only too

delighted if you would do that with us. I do not think pontifical authority could be justified, and I should very much regret it if you finally decided that it is essential to your self-respect.

It was widely recognised that Waley Cohen wanted to define what was "pure Din" and that the "common agreements" would be what he wanted. It was the constitution of the United Synagogue that gave the Chief Rabbi his authority and his status should not be likened to that of the Pope. It was not, however, the self-respect of Hertz that was in question, but his responsibility for keeping the community strictly Orthodox, which Waley Cohen wanted to alter. Waley Cohen met his match with the Chief Rabbi. Hertz, like the Adlers, was not about to sacrifice his authority to any lay leader.

A less contentious member of the Waley Cohen family was Dorothea his sister, (1882-1964), who devoted much of her time to the religion classes at the Synagogue.

The Synagogue was extensively repaired in July 1907. As one commentator put it:

> Has anyone seen the Central Synagogue of late? It is hardly recognisable. The stately building is hardly to be discerned by reason of the multitudinous scaffolding that fill it. I have never seen the Synagogue so full before. If they could only keep it up on ordinary Sabbaths after the reopening.

Michael Adler continued to be concerned about the poverty to be found in the poorer parts of the West End. In 1908 he formed the West Central Aid Society, to raise funds for the Board of Guardians and was elected president with Joseph Trenner as vice president. Like other United Synagogue ministers he also preached for funds for the Jewish Institute, which provided reading rooms for immigrant Jews in the East End. Similar facilities were provided by Christian Conversionist societies and the West End Jews were active in opposing their efforts.

Of course, not all the members were equally involved. At the AGM in 1907, for instance, only 38 attended and the rest of the members were obviously content to let the Board of Management run the Synagogue on a day-to-day basis. There were discussions on subjects as diverse as different methods of shnodering (giving to charity) and cheaper seats for Jews living in the poorer parts of Soho, but there were few decisions except to pass the annual report.

In 1909 Nathan Solomon Joseph died at the age of 75. He had been a tireless worker for Jewish charities and was particularly noted for his architectural work. In addition to building the Central, he had been the architect of the Bayswater and the New West End synagogues. He was the United Synagogue's architect as well.

Perhaps his best work was as the architect for the Rothschild's Four Per Cent Industrial Dwellings Company. Offering a slightly larger dividend than the government's Consols (Gilt Edged), the Rothschilds in 1885 set about building decent housing for the poor in the East End. Nathan Solomon Joseph supervised the construction of 6,000 buildings in all.

In December 1910, the memorial service at the Central for Michael Friedländer, the long-time head of Jews' College, saw all the major religious leaders of the London community mourning his passing. The college had expanded and grown in stature under his aegis, and he had set an example for his successors which they all followed diligently. Students at the College continued to have a Talmudic curriculum throughout the future years. Michael Friedländer was also a member. of the Central Board of Management.

Distinguished public figures continued to join the synagogue. One of the most famous solicitors in the City was Sir George Lewis, (1833-1911) whose cases included some of the most notorious of the age. He had prosecuted the directors of Overend & Gurney, who had caused the financial collapse of 200 companies in 1866. They were, in fact, only found guilty of a grave error of judgment, but the case made Lewis even more famous in the courts. One of the results of the Overend & Girney debacle was that interest rates rose to an almost unprecedented 10% for 10 months.

Sir George was also well known in the theatrical and literary world. The marriage of his daughter at the Central in 1902 had involved large numbers of guests and columns of publicity in the media. The reports included full descriptions of the costumes of the principal attendees and an enormous list of the presents given to the young couple; from the umbrella stand of Mr. and Mrs. J. Waley Cohen to the silver vase of Mr. Justice and Lady Bingham. Children gave each attendee at the synagogue a spray of white flowers when they arrived and Mrs. J. M. Barrie and Arthur Pinero were there as well.

When George Lewis died in 1911, 100 floral tributes were sent to the Central and the memorial service in the synagogue saw the full range of Jewish nobility coming to pay tribute. The most notable events in the London community were now held for the most part in the Central.

The most serious event affecting the Jews in 1911 was the only recorded pogrom in British history. It happened in Tredegar in Wales which was going through very difficult economic times. Jewish companies were said to be operating the Truck System by which the wages of employees could only be spent in company shops where the prices were inflated. Rioting broke out in August over a weekend and many Jewish families were offered security in the homes of non-Jewish neighbours.

Unlike similar situations in Russia or Eastern Europe the Tredegar magistrate went into the street and read the Riot Act. The police charged the rioters with such violence that the riot leaders complained of brutality. The Worcestershire regiment was called in from Cardiff and the whole unpleasant event was over in a couple of days. Winston Churchill, the Home Secretary, refused to intervene when some of the riot leaders received prison sentences.

The reaction of the community was mixed. Lord Rothschild condemned the Jewish community in Tredegar as being "a bad lot" and L.J.Solomons, the secretary at the Central denied that Tredegar was an antisemitic outbreak because the Jews weren't physically attacked. The counter argument, of course, was that antisemitic acts include many which are non-violent; books, plays, speeches etc.

There were local problems as well. When the United Synagogue had a surplus, most of it continued to go to the central body and they spent it as they saw fit. David Alexander was the president of the Board of Deputies and the Central's representative on the United Synagogue. He objected strongly at the AGM to the paucity of support for the religion classes at the Central. The needs of the community as a whole and the individual Synagogues's local bodies would continue to be a cause of aggravation.

Michael Adler (no relation to the Chief Rabbi's family), settled down well at the Central. He had married Sophie Eckersdorff, (1869-1912) who was German, and they had four children. Unfortunately, she died of heart trouble when she was only 43 years old. She had founded the Girls' Club and Home and was founder and president of the Hammersmith and Central Synagogue Guilds. A vivacious lady, there was a great deal of sympathy for the family.

Renewed attention was given to the religion classes and a professional lady convenor was retained to increase the attendance. As a result the numbers went up from an initial 78 to 95 in 1913, but one critic said that the newcomers were all from the Soho Synagogue and not the children of Central members. Of course, a lot of the Central children would have had

Hebrew teachers at their homes; going to classes was not as prestigious as home tutors.

The Great War presented a problem for everybody – from the royal family to the latest Jewish immigrant from Germany or Austria; their names were now the names of the enemy. Prince Louis of Battenberg had to resign as First Sea Lord in 1914 and the royal family changed their name from Saxe Coburg to Windsor in 1917. Within the Central Synagogue many followed suit. A number had already, as an English name made their continental origins more obscure.

A Jew's Hebrew name doesn't have a surname. It is the child's name followed by the father's, Joseph ben Moshe, for instance. When it became the custom to take a surname, it was often their occupation – Taylor, Goldman – or the town where they were born like Hamburg, Frankfurt. They also took religious names – Cohen, Levy, Abraham, Jacob. Comparatively few Central members kept their birth names.

When war broke out Michael Adler considered it his duty to serve on the Western Front in France. Rev. Benjamin Michelson (1873-1957) and Rev. Mendel Zeffert (1892-1958) took his place temporarily. Mendel Zeffert was not a West End rabbi. He was brought up in the East End and spent most of his life there.

After the war he became the minister of the East London Synagogue, noted for its long-time minister Joseph Stern, known locally as the Bishop of Stepney. When he retired in 1928, Mendel Zeffert took over and served until 1958. Jews' College continued to produce British ministers. In 1916 a student at the College preached the sermon at the Central, and this was the first time Israel Brodie, the future Chief Rabbi, spoke at the Synagogue.

The United Synagogue officially approved Michael Adler's absence from the Central, but the chaplain gave most of his salary from the Central to Mendel Zeffert and Benjamin Michelson. As a major and an army chaplain he would have earned £300 a year, but without much to spend it on except his family.

The poorer Jews in the West End had created the West End Talmud Torah in Dean Street, Soho and many were in need. In 1915 the Central supported a fund to provide clothing and footwear for "the Jewish poor in the district" and in 1918 a "Distress and Loan Fund". Leopold de Rothschild turned 70 in 1915 and had been associated with the Central since 1883. He considered it hardly appropriate in wartime to have lavish celebrations, and instead letters of congratulation were sent by the Central Board of Management and many communal charities.

The permanency of the Central Synagogue was settled in 1916 when a 999-year lease was agreed with the landlords. There was a premium to pay of £5,000 and an annual ground rent of £235. £5,000 in 1916 is about £340,000 today.

In 1917 the synagogue basement was turned into an official air-raid shelter and the congregation donated a YMCA hut for erection on the Western Front. Zeppelin raids in London did not affect Hallam Street, and the most damage in the West End was caused by the discarded British shells after they had been aimed at the incoming bombers. There were a number of fatalities in Maida Vale, which led the Haham, Moses Gaster, to take the family to Brighton, but this was not a common practice, as it would be in the Second World War. It was one of the public reasons for Moses Gaster being made to resign his office in 1918.

The most important event for the community during the war was the Balfour Declaration, promising a National Home for the Jews in Palestine. In 1916 the war was not going well for the Allies and the government hoped desperately that the Americans would come in on their side. Arthur Balfour, the former Conservative prime minister, was now Foreign Secretary and delegated Sir Mark Sykes to find out what Zionism was all about. When David Alexander, the president of the Board of Deputies and Claude Montefiore, the president of the Anglo-Jewish Association heard of the potential plan, they wrote to *The Times* in May 1917 to say that the community didn't want a National Home. Claude Montefiore had also created the Liberal Synagogue movement and was very much a maverick in the community. The Chief Rabbi and Lord Rothschild wrote a response and said the community supported the idea of a National Home.

The Chief Rabbi, Joseph Hermann Hertz, had been a staunch supporter of the Zionists in South Africa and Lord Rothschild had just succeeded his dead father and didn't intend anyone to take his leading position from him. Eventually in 1917 the government issued the Balfour Declaration and the Board of Deputies met to consider the letter their president had written. By a small majority the Board rejected the letter and the president, David Alexander, had to resign.

The defeat by 56 votes to 51 was primarily because the provincial delegates voted against the president by 36-4. The London delegates all voted in favour of the president and that support included Joseph Freedman and another Central delegate. It was not surprising; David Alexander had first been appointed to the Board of Deputies in 1877 as a Central Synagogue representative and had served the organisation with devotion for 40 years. The community was still bitterly divided on the question of Zionism.

In helping to fight the war, there was no obligation for Michael Adler to volunteer. There was no conscription until 1917 and there had never been a Jewish chaplain to the forces during a war. It was also obviously going to be very dangerous. Indeed, the War Office initially rejected the move, but after Michael Adler had sent in a report on the Jewish soldiers he had visited independently in France, it was agreed in January 1915 that he be promoted from his Captain's rank to Major and allowed to serve on the battlefields. He was initially given the title of Temporary Chaplain but soon proved his worth.

After the war he wrote a 10,000-word article for the *Jewish Guardian* on his experiences. He was, of course, originally the only Jewish chaplain at the time and was soon complaining that the 1,200 Jewish soldiers might not have a service for months, where soldiers normally attended a weekly church parade. By the end of the war there were eight Jewish chaplains, including Vivian Simmons, the minister at Upper Berkeley Street, and Arthur Barnett, the minister at the Western. Dayan Mark Gollop was with the troops at the ill-fated Dardanelles campaign.

Michael Adler was very active. He gathered support from the Jewish communities in Paris, Havre, Rouen, Versailles and Boulogne. He would arrange services before battles, notably one at Yom Kippur before the battle of Loos in 1915. He wrote a *Soldiers Prayer Book,* which Chief Rabbi Hertz expanded into *A Book of Jewish Thoughts,* and which served as a model for the *American Military Prayer Book* when one was needed later in the war.

At the end of June 1915, the Chief Rabbi came to the Western Front and Michael Adler helped him conduct a service with enemy shells punctuating the prayers. The army headquarters were always helpful and cooperative, as were the Christian chaplains. Michael Adler was provided with lists of Jewish soldiers he could inform of services. This was a privilege not given to other chaplains.

He wrote his notes in Hebrew in case they fell into the hands of the enemy, though some of the Christian chaplains spoke and understood Hebrew quite well. He noted that, among the Jewish soldiers, it was those from the provinces who had a greater knowledge of Hebrew than the Londoners. He was still deeply concerned about the correct teaching of Hebrew.

There were problems, of course. He translated the burial service into English and had copies sent to the Christian chaplains. He arranged to have photographs of the graves of dead Jewish soldiers sent to their families. He also agreed with the War Office that the graves be marked with a Magen David rather than the usual cross. He arranged for matzo to be made for Pesach, but it was wrongly delivered and stored in a warehouse for some months. It was a stressful life he could have avoided but didn't. Among all the chaplains to the forces in the First World War, 172 died, and in the second World War, 96 British chaplains died in addition to 38 more from the Commonwealth.

There was only one mitzvah Michael Adler could not keep; he had to ride on Shabbat so that he could conduct two services; one in the morning and one in the afternoon. The congregations of soldiers might be many miles apart on the extended front line. So, he would travel from one location to another with a Magen David fixed to the bonnet of his car. The area he had to cover was 50 kilometers from Ypres. As he wrote:

> I had often to travel long distances for these meetings, but all labour in connection with their organisation was more than amply repaid by the large number of men thus being enabled to meet other Jewish lads and to take part in some form of Jewish religious service under the peculiar conditions in which they lived. On the second day of Rosh Hashonah in 1916, at the town of Albert where the battle was still raging, [the old barn] was filled by a congregation drawn from men who had come direct from the trenches and who begged me to come again on the Day of Atonement.

One problem he didn't find was antisemitism. He said:

> I say without the slightest hesitation that whatever indication of ill-feeling towards the Jew was so small as to be entirely negligible...
> .the general conduct of the Jewish soldier won for him an excellent record throughout the Army, and tended in every way to reflect credit upon the Jewish name.

Services were held in many different settings; sometimes in barns in ruined buildings, sometimes in the open air, disused churches, monasteries, cornfields and army clubs. Michael Adler became very well known, with a selection of nicknames, such as the Wandering Jew, and OC (Officer Commanding) Jews. Writing to him, the post would be delivered if it was simply addressed to the "Jewish Chaplain France".

Of course, it was dangerous, particularly when aircraft were added to the German military weapons and regularly bombed allied positions:

It was not a pleasant experience to hear bombs exploding around one with no other protection than that afforded by a canvas or tin roof.

His presence at the Western Front was an inspiration though. As one Canadian soldier told him:

> I was delighted to see a Jewish chaplain so close to the line conducting religious services for the men, as I was under the impression that you lived at the base, where alone Jewish soldiers received your ministrations.

Michael Adler was constantly moved by his reception. At his first Yom Kippur service, men marched in fully equipped straight from the lines, special orders having been issued to allow them to do so. There were about 200 in the congregation. Many of them fell in action a few days later when they went into battle and:

> the knowledge that a fierce struggle was shortly about to take place seemed to add an air of solemnity to our prayers which no words of mine can adequately depict.

He would move his base to be nearer the front and travelled long distances to conduct funerals. He recalled that on one occasion the mourners all wore their tin hats during the ceremony at the graveside, as they were under continuous shellfire.

> I had frequently to journey to the front area where the battle was still swaying, in order to keep in touch with our soldiers whenever possible and to bury those of our men who had fallen.

As the years passed the congregations grew, with American and Empire troops coming to the services as well. Lorries were provided to bring men from long distances and by the High Holydays in 1917, over 1,500 men gathered together. The Wandering Jew became chaplain to the American forces as well.

Jews were involved in many aspects of the war. One of Michael Adler's friends was Lieutenant Colonel Solomon J. Solomon RA, who was responsible for the painting of tanks, a new weapon at the time. All kinds of talents were to be found. At one Rosh Hashonah service at the Western

Front the shofar was blown by a soldier from a London regiment who had been a bugler in the Jewish Lads Brigade.

There were many casualties among the families of the Central members. One member who served many years as a warden was Edward Pinder Davis; he sat in the box from 1907-1920 and was also chair of the Marylebone magistrates. His eldest son, Second Lieutenant Herbert Pinder Davis, was killed in 1916. In all, over 2,000 British Jewish service personnel were killed in the First World War and nearly 7,000 were wounded.

All five of Rev. Spero's sons served in the army in the war and three were wounded. In 1919 Emanual Spero's contract at the Central ended, but the Board of Management agreed with the United Synagogue to extend it for a further five years. Michael Adler married again in 1920 and his second wife, Bertha, who was of the Lorie family, survived him.

The Synagogue settled back into its normal way of life. Among the 1919 weddings was that of Major Thomas Sebag Montefiore to Irene Cohen. The Major was a regular soldier and had won the DSO and the MC in action. He would become a Lieutenant Colonel and commandant of the First Regiment of the Royal Horse Artillery. His wife had played her part as well. She was the Commandant of the London nurses 140 VAD. It was a very elegant wedding conducted by two of the Sephardi ministers.

Michael Adler found the situation at the Central very different though from that he had experienced at the Western Front. Soon after he renewed his office at the Synagogue, he was complaining of the empty seats he found at the services for much of the year, He said:

> The rising generation are becoming entirely lost to the synagogue. Less and less does the synagogue play any part whatever in the thoughts and progression of life and further and further they stray from the fold.

The war had also adversely affected organisations like the Jewish Lads Brigade. Meeting at the Central in 1919, the commandant, Colonel Sir Frederick L. Nathan, pointed to the shortage of officers. Of the 35 London officers at the outbreak of war, no less than 19 had died on active service.

Michael Adler would set out to restore the pre-war situation, but few recognised at the time that 1914 was the end of an era. Many of those of the rising generation who had fought in the war also had their faith at least temporarily undermined by their experiences.

It had been a terrible war. Many stately homes were sold off as their pre-war staff had so often died at the Western Front. British women had proved their worth, manning munitions factories and working as nurses. One who was shot by the Germans as a spy was Edith Cavell, whose statue was unveiled by Queen Alexandra in 1920. Sir George Frampton was the sculptor but would accept no payment for it. The 1920s would be the days of the Flappers, as the young women became liberated from their traditional subordination. It would eventually change the minds of the United Synagogue Council.

The members of the Central were now often associated with the garment industry but this was only part of the story. For example, one member who held his seat for forty years, served on the Board of Management and died in 1917 at 62, was John Jacobs. At one time he controlled eighteen sailing ships and pioneered the carrying of molasses and oil on them. A bachelor, he was the founder and chair of the Institute of Ship Brokers and also served on the Board of Deputies.

The community was developing and society was changing too. The Labour party would take office for the first time in January 1924, Sir Robert Waley Cohen would often be at daggers drawn with the Chief Rabbi, but the traditions of the Central would not alter as a pillar of the United Synagogue.

7

Between the wars

In 1918 after three years in the trenches, Michael Adler's health broke down and he had to rest. He said afterwards that a colleague had recalled that "after I left the Front, all went well!" Humour has its place in most circumstances, but Michael Adler would have needed nerves of steel to avoid a breakdown in the world of the Western front. Comforting gravely wounded soldiers in field hospitals, watching them die of horrendous wounds, conducting any number of funerals and trying to keep up their spirits under fire, were enormous challenges. It was also a continuous effort for, unlike the soldiers, the chaplains were needed all the time and could be ill spared to be withdrawn from the front and to take a rest.

Michael Adler was awarded the DSO for his efforts. The decoration is normally given to officers who have distinguished themselves in battle, so it was particularly complimentary that it should have been given to a Jewish chaplain. Arthur Barnett, from the Western Synagogue, took over as senior chaplain to the Jewish forces.

When he was recovering, Michael Adler turned his attention at home to arguing with Synagogue wardens that they should encourage their ministers to volunteer for active service as chaplains, as more were always needed. The response was not what he would have wished and there were few newcomers. It only emphasises the devotion of men like Michael Adler.

He was welcomed back to the Central after the war ended and was sufficiently restored to health to address the boys at the annual Chanukah service in December 1919. He was soon advancing some contentious opinions about the Synagogue ritual, like Aaron Levy Green. In 1920 he joined with Hermann Gollancz, (1852-1930), the minister at the Bayswater, and Aaron Asher Green (1860-1933), the minister at the Hampstead, in advocating the three-year cycle of reading the Pentateuch.

This was not an individual opinion by a minister but a recommendation by three very senior clerics. Hermann Gollancz had reached retirement age at Bayswater in 1918, but his term of service was readily extended by five years. In 1923 he would be the first rabbi to be knighted and Aaron Asher

Green was also highly regarded. Nevertheless, Chief Rabbi Hertz, like his predecessors, turned the idea down.

The only effect of altering this decision would have been to shorten the service and to reduce the time it took to prepare in advance the reading of the weekly portion of the Pentateuch. That may have suited both the congregation and the minister, but Hertz, like the Adlers, believed it was a step in the wrong direction.

In the future the ritual of different branches of Judaism would differ considerably, but those congregations acknowledging the authority of the Chief Rabbi would keep to the traditional framework.

A notable anniversary occurred in 1920 when a special service was held to commemorate the Golden Jubilee of the consecration of the Synagogue and the Chief Rabbi preached the sermon. During the service Sir Adolph Tuck lit eighteen candles on the war memorial candelabrum in memory of the eighteen members of the congregation who had fallen in the war, and another candle was lit by the father of a departed officer. A record of the fallen was also unveiled. The names were on two tablets on either side of the Ark, given by a member who wished to remain anonymous.

The threat of an Aliens Act at the time of the Boer War memorial service had made the contribution of the community to the fighting a very positive factor in emphasising the communal patriotism. Now it was matched by a comparable problem facing the Jews in the country after the Great War, when immigration of all kinds was now strictly restricted, as there were insufficient jobs for a demobilised army. Philip Taylor, a future warden, was demobilised in 1920 when he was a quartermaster sergeant and was unable to get a job for four years.

It would be two years after the war before the full list of casualties was chronicled. There would be no specific memorial after the Second World War when the horrors of the Holocaust made any other disaster infinitesimal by comparison.

It was significant that one of the scroll bearers at the Golden Jubilee Service was Moses Gaster. He had been the Haham of the Sephardi community for more than 30 years but had fallen out with the lay leaders and had resigned a year or so before. His invitation to carry a scroll was an indication of the esteem in which he was still held by the general community, and for the last twenty years of his life he was often invited to preach in Ashkenazi as well as Sephardi Synagogues

The candelabrum itself was designed by Percy Macquoid (1852–1925) who was by profession a theatrical designer. It is, technically, in the form of a classical tripod supporting a boldly gadrooned [notched] bowl, with a flat cupola-shaped cover, rising to a golden flame. Where the cover joins the bowl is a board, on which rest the nineteen cup nozzles, each containing a thick, orange-coloured wax candle. The flat and fluted legs are covered with gilt and there are finely modelled lions' masks. They end in gilt lions' paws feet, connected with a fillet (a band separating the moulding) decorated in a fine wave moulding.

The base on which the candelabrum stands is of Verde antique marble and altogether stands over five feet high. The execution of this work of art may sound complicated, but it is an admirable design; the change of the metal, in conjunction with its fine colour and beautiful proportion are quite remarkable. Nothing was too much trouble. Only the very best would do to commemorate those who made the ultimate sacrifice. The nineteen candles are still lit every Yom Kippur.

Members of the synagogue continued to gain national honours. Robert Waley Cohen was knighted in 1920, Marcus Samuel was promoted to the House of Lords in 1921 and in the same year Samuel Instone and Bernard Oppenheimer received knighthoods.

Samuel Instone (1878-1937) was the son of a German refugee and started the Instone Airline with his two brothers. He was always innovative and made the first telephone call to an aircraft in flight. He also introduced uniforms for his aircrew, the first non-military organisation to do so. His contribution to the development of airlines was considerable, but his fame was transitory and the Instone Airline is long forgotten.

His brother, Captain Alfred Instone, (1883-1957) served on the Central Board of Management for many years and was a playwright, as well as the Mayor of Paddington in 1927-1928, and a past master of the Worshipful Company of Loriners. A loriner makes bits, spurs and small metal objects.

Sir Bernard Oppenheim (1866-1921) died soon after he received his knighthood when he was only 55 years old. He was a diamond merchant and during the first world war started a business, training disabled soldiers to be diamond cutters. At its peak the company trained 2,000 veterans. Bernard Oppenheim deserves to be remembered as well.

The Honorary Officers did not neglect their poorer brethren. The free Yom Kippur service was held in a nearby hall as usual in 1922, and Adolph Tuck and Sir Robert Waley Cohen duly attended the Minchah service. Adolph Tuck read Maftir and Sir Robert talked to the congregation. Even if the congregation only came to shul on this one occasion in the year, they were still made very welcome.

The Welfare Committee of the United Synagogue worked hard to provide services on the High Holydays. The Great Synagogue assembly hall could take many thousands of worshippers and twenty different East End school centres were used for children's services. Benjamin Michelson undertook to organise the assemblies.

The Prime Minister had said his objective was to create a land fit for heroes and the achievements of the army gave anything to do with them a high status. It reflected in the growing popularity of the Jewish Lads Brigade, and one of their events in 1922 was a Chanukah service at the synagogue. It was attended by the First London Battalion and their regimental band took part in the service. As many as 400 congregants came to tea afterwards.

Michael Adler turned his attention to undertaking the mammoth task of listing all the Jewish soldiers who had served, won awards, been wounded and died in the Great War. There were 50,000 who had served in the British and Empire forces, and it involved him in taking enormous trouble and covering enlistment, Jewish hospitals, Jewish units and every aspect of their contribution.

He built up alphabetical lists of those killed in action and obtained letters of support from both Jews and non-Jews. The eventual result was the publication of the *British Jewry Book of Honour* in 1922. British Jews won five Victoria Crosses and hundreds of other awards. Of course, 100,000 Jews also served in the German army and of these, no less than 12,000 died. It was a Jewish platoon commander who recommended one of his soldiers for the Iron Cross; the recipient was Adolf Hitler! Before the Second World War Hitler gave him an emigration visa to America and ensured that he received his army pension throughout the conflict.

In 1923 Chief Rabbi Hertz came to the Synagogue on the first day of Succot, which had now become a tradition. On this occasion, however, he gave permission for his sermon to be broadcast on the new radio service. Although the Chief Rabbi was born in Hungary and brought up in New York, he spoke with a light Scottish burr to his voice and was very impressive in all he did. He was popular all over the Empire and raised funds for innumerable charities; in 1924 at the Central he appealed on behalf of the Bayswater Jewish Schools.

During 1923 the "Slaughter of Animals Bill" was introduced in parliament to avoid unnecessary cruelty to animals, but shechita was acknowledged to be acceptable. Michael Adler did not allow his literary work to intrude on his ministerial responsibilities. In 1924, for example, he brought to the attention of the educational authorities a book which was on the prize list but contained an offensive Jewish caricature. It was withdrawn.

The Aliens Act had been passed in 1904 to reduce Jewish immigration. In 1924 the problem of refugees from Europe came before the Aliens Committee of the Board of Deputies, meeting at the Central. Immigration had been severely curtailed after the war, partly because there was widespread unemployment and immigrants might take jobs from British workers. Partly because a lot of the refugees were coming from Russia and might well be Bolsheviks, aiming to overthrow the state.

Jewish immigrants on their way to America, influenced the United States to pass its own legislation to discourage them. The result was that many were deported to England and housed in a building put up by the shipping companies on the site of today's Southampton Airport. Atlantic Park in Eastleigh could accommodate over 3,000 people, but they couldn't move on from it until their cases were sorted out. For example, children of aliens had to register when they were 16 years old, but many failed to do so because they simply didn't know they had to.

For the 500 or so Jewish inhabitants, Atlantic Park was known as the Jews' Temporary Shelter, a charity which had started in 1879 to help the homeless and would continue to support Jewish refugees until long after the Second World War. Atlantic Park was closed in 1931 when the last 176 Jews were allowed to stay in the country, as the Board agreed that they would personally ensure that they weren't a burden on the state.

It took years to settle the problems of Deportation, Registration and Naturalisation and William Joynson-Hicks, the Home Secretary, was not helpful. As many as 980 Jews were deported from Ellis Island, and only when Lady Swaythling negotiated with the American State Department, were most of them admitted. It was another example of the wealthier Jews being very prepared to try to help their poorer brethren.

In 1925 Albert Woolf and Robert Waley Cohen were elected wardens but only four months later Albert Woolf died. He had been involved in the synagogue for many years and was particularly noted for his work among the poor of the community.

The Ladies' Guild was established in 1925 and had an immediate problem with the marriage of Louis Gluckstein, the son of one of the founders of Lyons, the major catering company at the time. The difficulty was that Louis Gluckstein was two metres tall and couldn't get under the chupah, which had to be raised for the ceremony. In future years he would become Sir Louis Gluckstein and he became chair of the Greater London Council.

The congregation mourned the death of Sir Adolph Tuck in 1926. His son, Desmond Tuck, served as a warden from 1927 to 1948. They were originally a Silesian family and Raphael Tuck, the father, was a carpenter. His eventual success was a remarkable story of innovative thinking. When he emigrated to London, he started a small shop in the City selling prints and frames. When, however, the cost of postage was reduced in the 1870s Tuck decided to start selling inexpensive Christmas cards.

It was not the custom at the time to send Christmas cards, but Queen Victoria and Prince Albert had initiated the practice of dispatching them to their aristocratic friends and Raphael Tuck built on that foundation. To gain the habit more publicity he then offered 500 guineas (£525 – £50,000 today) for the best Christmas card designs, with a panel of judges from the Royal Academy, who included Sir John Millais. When you come to think of it, here is a poor immigrant workman who became a brilliant marketing man and was in no way abashed by the company he chose to keep.

The resulting publicity created a national pastime. Raphael Tuck moved on to picture postcards in 1894 and created another national habit, producing no less than 40,000 different choices. His sons were no less imaginative and after he died, they created jigsaw puzzles and Valentine cards. Adolph Tuck and his son, Desmond, still found time to look after the Central and when Adolph Tuck turned 70 in 1924, the synagogue gave him a gold Chanukah menorah as a "thank you", but he died in 1926. As the vote of condolence said:

> His long period of office had been marked by wisdom and gentleness, tact and discrimination, and would always serve as an inspiration and example of how a man, encompassed by the cares of a busy life, could yet devote himself so wholeheartedly and effectively to the needs of his Synagogue and his Religion.

The Board of Management decided to leave the Warden's office vacant for a year as a mark of respect and affection. Adolph Tuck had served many Jewish charities with distinction. He was typical of the advance of Central members from poverty in the East End to a comfortable life in the West End. He was educated at the Jews' Free School which was for poor children, but went on to Breslau Yeshiva. He became the head of the family business when his father died. The Tucks were an observant family and Sir Adolph made his mark in the printing trade by founding the Association of Card Manufacturers. He was made a baronet in 1910.

When he died, he was cremated and buried at Willesden cemetery. Cremation is against the Din and it certainly defiles dead bodies. Maimonides and the Shulchan Aruch both condemn it, but Nathan Marcus

Adler had agreed that the ashes could be buried in the cemetery, though the wish of the deceased to be cremated did not have to be honoured.

Willesden was originally created on 12 acres of land purchased from All Souls, Oxford in 1872 and it had been extended in 1890, 1906 and between the years 1925-1935. A considerable percentage of the most eminent members of the community were buried there.

In 1924 Emanuel Spero retired after forty years as the Central's chazan. He was made Emeritus Reader at a meagre salary of £100 a year, but died in 1927, mourned by the congregation, his wife and nine children. His successor was Aron Stoutsker from the Great Synagogue in Amsterdam. Finding the right man had been a difficult task, as Emanuel Spero had naturally been highly regarded. A selection committee of twenty-three was appointed in the Spring to find the best choice and there were twenty-seven applicants for the post.

The warden making the report to the Board of Management said they were all in favour of Aron Stoutsker, whose wife was "a cultured English lady". In the end, a large attendance voted unanimously to confirm the committee's choice and Aron Stoutsker would be the Central's chazan for the next twenty-five years; it was a fortunate move for the Cantor because the congregants at his former Synagogue in Amsterdam would die in the Holocaust. When the Nazis announced their deportation, the Amsterdam dockers went on strike and today there is a heart-warming statue outside the Synagogue of a docker standing, with arms akimbo, in defence of the community.

Marcus Samuel (1853-1927), had become Lord Bearsted in 1925 and just before he died in 1928 presented a splendid marble Almemar to the synagogue in memory of his parents. The synagogue had to be closed for two months, but its decor was much enhanced by the Almemar. The old almemar went to the Margate synagogue. The family put in a lot of communal work as well as being very generous. When his brother, Samuel Samuel MP (1855-1934) died, the Soup Kitchen for the Jewish Poor lost its president and a memorial service was held at the shul. Like his sibling, Samuel Samuel had been very philanthropic, besides being a major figure in the family bank and Shell.

He won the Putney seat in the 1922 general election, in the face of much antisemitic opposition and strengthened the representation of Jews in the House of Commons in commercial matters. For years, on the evening of the Budget he would give a Dinner at the House for bankers and industry leaders and he presided over the 12th International Parliamentary Commercial Conference in 1926. Over thirty nations sent representatives.

Another very welcome gift at the time was £2,000 from warden, Joseph Jacobs, to create a Minister's Augmentation Fund. In all he sat in the Warden's box from 1920-1938 and Joseph Jacobs did not restrict his generosity to Jewish causes. In the same year he gave St. Bartholomew's hospital a 200 Kilovolt X Ray Therapy Support for the Radiological Department which was very welcome.

Joseph Jacobs also supported other non-Jewish as well as Jewish causes. He was the son of a cargo ship owner and passionate about Britain as a maritime nation. Over the years he bought at auction a number of Nelson memorabilia, including the Admiral's writing desk, dining table, sideboard and armchair, which he then donated to the nation. Equally though, when the Home for Jewish Incurables was in financial difficulties during the war, he gave them a very welcome £100. (At least £7,000 today).

In 1925 there was a conference of Anglo-Jewish preachers where the papers were of a high standard, There was one, however, which created a degree of discord. Michael Adler gave an address prior to the conference and took the opportunity to castigate political Zionists – those to whom the aim for a national home immediately, was even more important than the Biblical promise of a return when the Messiah came.

Michael Adler condemned such thinking, calling the political Zionists:

> Godless and irreligious Jews to whom our faith is of no consequence and with whom the Jewish creed and practice involve no obligation.

He was condemned in the press as intensely anti-Zionist, but changed his mind when he went to Palestine in June 1929. There was a reception to mark his return at the nearby exclusive Langham Hotel. After so many years Michael Adler was publicly treated as a communal notable. In the first of the Sherlock Holmes stories, his antagonist, Irene Adler, was portrayed as staying at the Langham.

In December 1928 the silver jubilee of Michael Adler as the minister of the Central was marked by the gift of a menorah and a testimonial on a Sunday afternoon. There was no major celebration, but the anniversary coincided with the beginning of the Slump and members were pulling in their horns.

Michael Adler, in the lecture at the Langham, was ready to admit that he had not been a convinced Zionist until he went to Palestine, but had been quite won over.

He found himself in a country with over 800,000 non-Jews and only 160,000 Jews, 100,000 of whom had come since the war. In that time the number of Jewish villages had increased from 45 to 145. He was particularly pleased to find that all the commercial transactions in Tel Aviv were conducted in Hebrew. Michael Adler conveyed to the audience the plea of the Hebrew University that funds should be raised for a chair in Jewish History.

The attendees also heard an address by Sir Meyer Spielman, the president of the United Synagogue Central Keren Hayesod Committee which raised a lot of money for Palestine. The president still found it appropriate to say that he "did not actually call himself a Zionist today". Most of the community was still anxious to avoid any evidence of double loyalty.

The chair of Keren Hayesod was, however, Simon Marks, of Marks & Spencer, and he certainly was a Zionist. The community could support the Mandate without too much difficulty, but Zionism and the National Home created more dissension, even after the Balfour Declaration.

It was only shortly after the reception, however, that riots broke out in Palestine in the August, resulting in a large number of casualties. The views of the members on Zionism differed, but the riots in Palestine in 1929 were so severe that a Palestine Emergency Fund was started and over £5,000 (£300,000 today) was collected by the Central members.

Non-Jewish charities continued to be supported by the members. The Financial Representative of the Synagogue from 1914-1921 was Edmund Phillips, a Bond Street jeweller, and his was one of the shops which collected gifts of jewellery for the Elizabeth Garrett Anderson Hospital appeal, but not on Saturday, when it was the only shop in Bond Street to be closed.

In 1929 the American Rabbi Harold Reinhart became the minister at the Reform Synagogue in Upper Berkeley Street. He had very strong views. At home, for example, he had refused to have the Stars and Stripes flag in his Synagogue when America came into the First World War, because he was a confirmed pacifist. There had been continuous efforts over the last ninety years to heal the breach between the Orthodox and the Secessionists, but it was Harold Reinhart who decided the differences were too great to be resolved.

He now persuaded a small gathering of Upper Berkeley Street members to allow him to join the World Union of Progressive Judaism and guided his community to disassociate themselves from Orthodox practice on far more radical lines than ever before. Of the 1,250 members of the synagogue, only sixty attended the meeting which approved the move. The motion was passed by 39-6. On such a small vote the community joined a body where Claude Montefiore, the founder of the even more left-wing Liberal movement, was president. From now on the breach would be impossible to mend.

The annual meeting of the Central in 1929 was a mixture of good and bad news. The Synagogue had the largest surplus ever, but few members bothered to attend the gathering. The congregations on Shabbat were unsatisfactory and Chazan Stoutsker placed part of the blame on the fact that the Synagogue had a mixed choir, when his male choir in his former ministry in Amsterdam had just won first prize in the choir competition. Desmond Tuck, who presided, agreed to get the Board of Management to look into the question, but it was not a subject that created much interest among the members,

Although the Synagogue was in surplus, it still accepted a donation of £100 from the Union of Hebrew and Religious Classes which seemed to many unnecessary with such a wealthy congregation. The St. Georges Hall had not been available for overflow services, due to them falling on a Sunday that year, and the nearby Drill Hall had not been as popular. The same would happen in 1930 and, therefore, it was agreed once again not to make a charge for attendance.

Joseph Jacobs, the long-serving warden, was always ready to help the classes. For some years he laid on charabancs to take the 80 or so pupils and teachers to his country home in Chesham Bois for tea, games, rambles and sports. The prizes were presented to the successful children by Lady Tuck.

Another member who died in 1930 was Lucien Wolf (1857-1930), one of the most prominent journalists and Anglo-Jewish historians in his day. A wide variety of Jewish communal organisations sent representatives to Willesden for the funeral, with Dayan Lazarus and Rev. Stoutsker officiating. As the Synagogue was being redecorated, however, the memorial service was held at Upper Berkeley Street. The Orthodox and the Reform would split in the years to come.

Lucien Wolf came from a father who had fled Germany after 1848 and a Viennese mother. He was another East End Jew who moved to the West End, and he was known for his middle-class aspirations. All his life he defended Jewish communities throughout the world and tributes came from as far afield as America and Poland.

He was, however, very anti-Zionist and after the Balfour Declaration he founded the League of British Jews to oppose it. He received considerable support in the Synagogue. In his younger days he was also the first president of the Jewish Historical Society of England and he had been the Foreign Editor of the *Daily Graphic*. A stout opponent of the Czar, he was pro-German in 1914 and his reputation came under fire as a result. To the end of his days, however, he was a voice to be listened to on a range of subjects, including opposition to the Sunday Closing regulations.

Apart from the work of elected officers, the voluntary work carried out by ordinary members is often forgotten as the years go by. For example, one of the families who were prominent supporters of the United Synagogue were the Freedmans. The doyen was Joseph Freedman, (1860-1949), who had started his business life as a pedlar in the Welsh valleys but had made a fortune with a furniture company offering hire purchase when it was a new idea.

Joseph Freedman rose to become the Honorary Officer responsible for the United Synagogue buildings, and used the United's finances to expand the number of Synagogues in London. He joined the Board of Management at the Central and became an Elder at the United Synagogue. It was his nephew, Josie Freedman who served as a warden from 1940-1947, during the difficult Woburn House years.

Joseph Freedman was not only a supporter of Jewish education, gratefully acknowledged by Rabbi Dr. Solomon Schonfeld, but underwrote the Hertz Chumash, enabling it to be sold as a much-reduced price. His grandson-in-law, Philip Taylor, took over as financial representative and then warden after the war. Joseph Freedman was very observant and would stand for the whole of the Yom Kippur service, 14 hours out of the 25. When he became too old to manage this, he delegated the responsibility to Philip Taylor, who was not best pleased to be selected.

The year 1929 saw the. beginning of the Great Depression and by 1932 over 3.5 million people in Britain were unemployed. Naturally, the businesses of many of the Central members were badly affected, but even in such terrible times, some prospered. For instance, the popularity of Hire Purchase grew, as people were able to pay for their furniture over a period of years instead of having to find the total cost at the outset.

Joseph Freedman's business was one of the beneficiaries and it was family folklore that in those dreadful years he went on record as saying, "The day profits fall below 200% we'll all be ruined"! As he was in charge of the development of United Synagogues, he was the kind of executive who was much appreciated.

Like many other members, Joseph Freedman didn't confine his charitable work to his own community and the United Synagogue. In his case, he was very much involved in the Bethnal Green & Shoreditch Jewish Benevolent Society which had been created to raise funds for the poor at Passover. In 1932 £870 (£53,000 today) had been raised and expenses had been kept to £3, which was remarkably efficient.

He also worked for the Board of Deputies, being responsible for the disused cemeteries in Sheerness and Penzance. He represented the Sheerness community on the Board of Deputies and voted for the president at the famous meeting after the Balfour Declaration. No part of the Jewish heritage in Britain was neglected by the Board. Joseph Freedman was always willing to help.

When he died in 1949 he left £2 million and one of his grandsons won the Derby with *Reference Point* in 1987. Louis Freedman was both a member of the Central Board of Management and Senior Steward at the Jockey Club. He also had much to do with the creation of the Race Relations Board but, from the Central's point of view, the family disintegrated over the next fifty years and was lost to Jewry. As has always been the case with the Central, others took their place.

The Central was always prepared to help worthy causes. Successful as the West Central Jewish Club had been, the members drifted away when they grew up and in June 1933 the West Central Old Boys Club was formed to maintain their association. Lacking anywhere to meet, the Central gave them free use of part of the building and were gratified to see that the membership doubled within a year. Isaac Wolfson, the father of the future president of the United Synagogue, made one of his earlier charitable donations, renovating and reconstructing the club rooms in 1937.

The Union of Jewish Women also held services at the Central to mark the conclusion of courses for girls in Judaism and Hebrew. The UJW did much good work. For instance, it sent clothing to Palestine for those made homeless in the riots which took place in 1929.

One prominent member of the community died in 1930 and though he wasn't a member of the Central, it was fully expected that Michael Adler would mourn his passing from the pulpit which he did. This was Rabbi Victor Schonfeld, (1880-1930), the minister of a small Orthodox congregation in North London and one of the foremost defenders of Orthodoxy in the country. It was Victor Schonfeld who started the school which eventually became the Hasmonean School under his son, Solomon Schonfeld.

At Chanukah in 1931 the 28th Chanukah Military Service was held with representatives of all the armed forces attending, past and present. There was a Dinner dance afterwards and Viscount Bearsted presided. It would have given Michael Adler much pleasure that the battles were still recalled.

The AGM in 1932 only attracted 16 members, though the senior warden attributed this to satisfaction at the way the Synagogue was run, rather than the members' apathy. There were no contests for the offices. Income exceeded expenditure by over £2,000, but after the United Synagogue finances had been duly supported, the surplus was reduced to £85. What was noteworthy was a gift for the religious classes of fifty guineas (£52.50) from Ralph Specterman, which in today's money is £3,500. A Jewish Museum was established that year and the Synagogue donated seven pairs of bells and a pointer to the exhibits.

The free Yom Kippur service moved in 1932 to the Adolph Tuck Hall which was especially fitted out for the occasion. Henry Jacobs provided the Ark and the curtain in front of it, and Desmond Tuck came to read the book of Jonah in the afternoon. Senior members of the congregation acted as wardens and there was a large attendance.

A congregant who was lost in 1932 was Joseph Cowen, (1868-1932), one of the most prominent Zionists in the country and an early supporter of Theodor Herzl. He was a founder of the British Zionist Federation and director of the Jewish Colonial Trust. There were two memorial services: one in the Synagogue after the funeral and one by the Zionists. Although many of the most prominent leaders of the community came to the Central Memorial Service, the community as a whole, continued to be divided over the concept of the National Home.

Michael Adler had now become a Zionist supporter. He recognised Joseph Cowan's fidelity to the cause and said in his sermon at the service:

> G-d buries his workers but continues the work. Until from Zion shall go forth the law and the word of G-d from Jerusalem, the work must go on, however many of the workers and whosoever they be, that fall by the wayside. For the work is greater than the worker.

Aaron Levy Green's nephew, Rev. Aaron Asher Green, (1860-1933), the minister at the Hampstead synagogue from 1892-1930, passed away in 1933. By contrast with Joseph Cowan, Aaron Asher Green had decided that Zionism was against the best interests of Judaism, but he was very much in the family tradition of non-conformity of opinion. He had been roundly condemned for agreeing to teach the New Testament to those students at his religious classes who asked for the information.

The religion classes continued to receive priority at the Synagogue. In 1933 Michael Adler was able to report at the 48th annual meeting that there were now 96 children registered and the average attendance was eighty.

Overall, the economic problems brought by the Slump put an even greater burden on those members who were prepared to give up their time for the Synagogue. In November 1932 some unwelcome visitors with a duplicate key stole into the synagogue at night and took silver balls and a pointer from the sefer torah in the ark.

By 1934 the Nazi persecution of their Jewish community was only too easy to recognise, though Hitler was well regarded in some British circles. The Chief Rabbi came to the Central on the seventh day of Passover and spoke on behalf of the Central Fund for German Jewry. He told the congregation that this was no time for denunciation and lamentation. Instead, practical help was needed in large amounts:

> Blessed be the man who will give tangible expression to his solidarity with our suffering brethren.

Many members of the Synagogue were also members of the Zionist Federation. As the situation in German deteriorated, the University Zionist Federation met at the Synagogue to hear lectures on Zionist history. The German Zionist Federation's need for financial support became even more urgent when they signed the Haavara agreement with the Nazis in August 1933. This enabled German Jews to emigrate to Palestine if they left most of their assets in Germany to be looted by the government.

As a result of the Haavara agreement fifty thousand German Jews escaped the Holocaust between 1933 and the outbreak of the Final Solution, but those who came to Britain often had to adjust to poverty after affluence in Germany. It had been agreed with the British government that the Jewish community in Britain would ensure that the refugees did not become a burden on the state, which had millions of their own unemployed to look after first. The community donated £3 million over the years, (some £200 million today) but even this generosity could not provide the standard of living for many of the refugees that they had enjoyed at home.

A number of Germans who had become immigrants in Britain over the years did build good careers. One of the Central members who passed away in 1934 was Julien Wylie (originally Julien Ulrich Samuelson Metzenberg) whose parents had come from Prussia. Wylie became a Southport accountant and then a theatrical agent. He became so well known for producing over 100 pantomimes that he was known as the King of Pantomime. He was a member of the Central for 20 years, but he was only 56 when he died. One of his friends remembered him fondly and said "He never took to drink. He took to ice cream – buckets of it."

There was always room at the Synagogue for eccentrics and one member of the Board of Management who died in 1935 was Charles Stone, who owned a shop in Regent Street. It was Charles Stone's habit to give highly unusual Dinners which might be themed around such concepts as a circus, a police court or a rodeo. The invitations were much prized.

By 1935 the possibility of war with Nazi Germany was growing more likely. The annual Chanukah Military service at the Synagogue was now organised by the H.M. Forces committee of the Board of Deputies and at the dinner after the service, an appeal was made for volunteers to join the territorial army, which would be called upon if war did break out. The impoverishment of the German Jewish community by antisemitic Nazi legislation also led to a third fund raising campaign being launched for them during the year as well.

That there was antisemitism in Britain could not be denied. The owners of houses in Glasgow refused to give a tenancy to an applicant because he was a Jew and their behaviour was denounced in parliament, after which they had to retract their objections. Their behaviour was compared to the increasing volume of antisemitic legislation in Germany.

On a lighter note, the 1930s saw the growing popularity of dinner dancing. Many Jewish musicians formed their own bands; among them were Geraldo (Gerald Bright), Ambrose (Bert Ambrose), Harry Roy, Sid Phillips and Joe Loss, who married his wife, Mildred, at the Central in 1938. The wedding was a massive event covered by the newsreels. Joe Loss was the son of Russian immigrants in the East End and was typically educated at the Jews' Free School. He formed his band when he was 20 and became the youngest bandleader in the country. Another example of finding the hole in the market.

Michael Adler had turned his attention to the Jewish Historical Society of England where he edited their Transactions and became president from 1934-1936. He enjoyed history and produced a biography of *Aaron of York*. The oldest stone house in the country is that of Aaron of York in Lincoln. He was the richest man in the country in the time of Henry II. It is no easy task writing about the early Middle Ages as the written records are in Old English, which is difficult to decipher and unlike modern English usage. Michael Adler was up to the task. In recent times a new community was started in Lincoln on the probable site of the mediaeval synagogue, and their motto was "Heimsche since 1159."

Michael Adler also wrote a notable study of the *Domus Conversorum*. This was a house in London where converted Jews could live and enjoy free maintenance in mediaeval times. His presidential address in November 1935 was on the *Domus Conversorum* and he was in distinguished company, as the vote of thanks came from the old Haham, Moses Gaster, a noted academic, and was seconded by the foremost Anglo-Jewish historian, Cecil Roth.

The Jewish Historical Society of England was the original idea of Sir Isidore Spielman who set up the Jewish Historical Exhibition in the spring of 1887. Designed to present the community in the best possible light, the society followed on from the exhibition. By the time Michael Adler was elected president, there were 650 members and its meetings were very popular. Applications for 1,000 tickets were sent for the Lucien Wolf Memorial lecture which was delivered by Sir Marcus Samuel later that month.

Of course, Michael Adler's election coincided with the growth of Nazism. This meant that the JHSE had a role to play in establishing the long-term traditions of Jewish participation in British history. Between the wars he spent a lot of time on research and his history of the Domus Conversorum was a notable addition to our knowledge of the Jews after their expulsion in 1290.

Henry III had set up the Domus Conversorum in 1232 on a site which became the Public Record Office in Chancery Lane. By 1280, shortly before the Jews were expelled, there were 97 inhabitants. Several of the converts achieved offices of state and although the numbers naturally declined after the expulsion, the last convert to enter the house was in 1609 and the organisation was only abolished in 1891. The first wardens of the Domus Conversorum were all originally Normans until 1394 which, again, linked them to the original Jewish immigrants in the time of William the Conqueror.

As Michael Adler wrote:

> The smallness of the number of the names of the Domus, forty-eight in a period of 319 years, is in itself an eloquent testimony to the fidelity with which Jews, as a whole, adhered to their ancestral faith, in spite of royal bounties, and in the face of incessant persecution. Driven from one land to the other, they possessed that stern stuff that makes heroes of men and that renders their memory a source of pride to those that come after them.

The book clarifies a number of previously obscure points. First, that the keeper of the Domus Conversorum was known as the Master of the Rolls. It was a royal not a legal title. Michael Adler established that Thomas Cromwell, Henry VIII's successor to Cardinal Wolsey, lived there for some years. He also made a sound case for the apparent inconsistency that both

Marlowe's *Jew of Malta* and Shakespeare's *Merchant of Venice* had much accurately to say in their plays about conversion and Jewish practice, even though the Jews were not allowed to live in Britain. How could they be so knowledgeable?

Both the Globe and Blackfriars theatres were near the Domus. One of the converted Jews in the home was Nathaniel Menda. In 1577 he was publicly converted and read aloud in Spanish a statement of the reasons that led him to embrace Christianity. This was translated into English, printed and widely distributed. It was highly likely that both Marlowe and Shakespeare learned of Jewish practices from it.

Successive monarchs took a keen interest in the home and many converts took the names of the kings and queens. Although there were so few inhabitants, the home had two chaplains and the crown paid all the costs, which included pensions for the converts. In spite of the fact that there were no converts after the time of James I, the Master of the Rolls as late as 1851 was granted for life "the custody of the house or Hospital of Converts, for the habitation of the Keeper or Master of the Rolls, Books, Writs and Records of the High Court of Chancery". It was only in 1891 that this ended.

Michael Adler retired in 1934 and was made the Emeritus Minister in recognition of his many years of devoted attention to the interests of the Synagogue. A testimonial was raised which enabled him to receive a cheque for £1,000. (About £70,000 today). He died in a Bournemouth nursing home in September 1944 at the age of 76. In 1939 he was still hard at work and published *The Jews of Mediaeval England*.

The book had involved him in large amounts of research. It had 384 pages and was printed by the University of Pennsylvania. He paid particular attention to the Jews of Bristol and Canterbury. He was another notable Central Synagogue cleric whose pioneering work still benefits the community and the state. The book is still available for instance, in the National Library of Australia.

The memorial service was held at Woburn House where the congregation held its Sabbath and Festival services after the Synagogue was destroyed in the Blitz. The Chief Rabbi read the memorial prayer and Cecil Roth, the foremost Jewish historian of his time, said:

> If genius has been defined as an infinite capacity for taking pains, then Michael Adler can be said to have possessed it in no small measure. Where the rest of us often boggled at the mass of material, he confronted it with the same persistence that he showed in all his

other work, spending day after day in the Public Records Office, going through the original sources, deciphering the most cramped hands, working through volume after volume of the least tractable materials. The result of his labours was not an article but a monograph.

Roth was himself an expert on mediaeval British Jewry but commented:

The last word had now been said, in most cases. Nothing remained to be added, and another corner of Anglo-Jewish history had been finally and investigated. His monographs on medieval Exeter and Canterbury secured him a reputation among the local historians. His biography of Aaron of York, the most prominent of medieval Anglo-Jewish financiers, is a contribution to the reign of Henry III in its wider sense. His history of the *Domus Conversorum* put the study of the Middle Period in Anglo-Jewish history on a new basis. [All these papers with the exception of that in Exeter are included in his volume of essays, 'The Jews of Medieval England.'] There was an interruption in his historical work for a while when he was at the height of his activity as Minister and Chaplain, but when he returned to it he showed the same vigour as ever, and after his retirement it became his principal solace and occupation. He now acted, moreover, as editor of the publications for the Jewish Historical Society and its more recent volumes showed on every page traces of his meticulous care. Even during his last illness, before he entered the nursing home, he wrote asking me for some work to take with him. The community can ill spare such men, who as they pass are not, alas, replaced. So far as the Jewish Historical Society goes, I fear that it will be unable to survive further losses, such as it has suffered by the deaths during the past few years, of which that of Michael Adler, the latest, is by no means the least.

In fact, the Jewish Historical Society is still with us and has grown considerably in membership and academic work.

8

The Second World War

Michael Adler's successor was Philip Cohen, a Manchester man and a graduate of Jews' College. He was inducted by the Chief Rabbi in September 1934. Philip Cohen was a sound educator and he had set up a Children's synagogue at the Hampstead shul before coming to the Central. In addition to his other responsibilities, he became the headmaster of the shul's religion classes and was able to report at the 55th annual prize giving in June 1939 that 100 children attended on Wednesday and Sunday.

Religious studies on a Sunday were a typical part of the school week, but to raise those numbers on a Wednesday was an achievement. It was not surprising that a plea was made for him to be relieved of some of his secretarial work at the synagogue, so that he could spend more time on the classes. This was agreed.

To be employed in the Slump was an end in itself, but a United Synagogue minister was not well rewarded. Statistics show that in 1934 the average annual wage in the country was £840. The starting salary for the Minister at the Central was £650, which was set by the US, rising over the years to a maximum of £750, less rent on the minister's home. Honoraria for weddings, barmitzvahs and funerals would have made the total income more respectable, but it was not surprising that most ministers still came originally from poor homes. Wealthy families continued to have more remunerative occupations planned for their sons.

In January 1935 the synagogue was the natural setting for a memorial service for Lady Alice Waley Cohen who had died in a motor accident in Jerusalem. She was there with Sir Robert for the opening of the Iraq Oil Pipeline, which was his initiative; they had been married for over thirty years. Lady Waley Cohen was a Beddington and a great supporter of the Central, where her husband had, of course, been a warden before becoming a major force in the United Synagogue.

There were no contested elections that year and the Board included Isaac Wolfson, whose son and grandson would have a major role to play in the running of the Synagogue in future years. The Chair at the meeting announced a third appeal for German Jewry and also thanked the ladies' guild for their efforts. It reflected the continuing unsatisfactory status of the women that he singled out their hard work in keeping the Synagogue vestments clean. Their role was still confined to wifely occupations and there were still no ladies on the Board of Management.

There were female exceptions who refused to fill the role designated for them. Marie Rothschild, for example, was a formidable personality in charitable circles until she died in 1937. She had married at the Central in 1881 and although she had lost her husband in 1917 and her son, Evelyn, who died on active service in Palestine, Marie was such a well-known and independent character that the family received letters of condolence from George VI, Queen Elizabeth and Queen Mary on her passing.

That October, Samuel Samuel MP (1855-1934) also died, and a memorial service was held at the Synagogue. Samuel Samuel was Lord Bearsted's brother, a partner in Marcus Samuel and one of the founders of Shell. He had been MP for Wandsworth from 1913-1918 and won a strongly contested election for Putney in 1922. In that election there was a good deal of antisemitism to be overcome on the hustings, but he had ended up with a majority of 8,500, which showed, not for the last time, that as far as electoral manifestos were concerned, antisemitism was not a popular policy in Britain.

Samuel Samuel was also a director of Lloyds Bank when Jewish directors of High Street banks were a rarity. He was so well regarded that he was invited to preside over the 12th International Commercial Conference in London in 1926.

Samuel Samuel ended his life as the oldest member of the House of Commons, but he added to his parliamentary duties a great deal of charitable work. He naturally had a great many friends and one of them, Gustave Tuck, remembered him publicly as the soul of generosity.

The 39th Naval, Military and Air Force Chanukah service was held at the Synagogue in December 1935, organised at this point by H.M. Forces Committee of the United Synagogue. The officer commanding was now Col. Robin Joseph DSO, of the Royal Engineers and Dayan Mark Gollop gave the sermon. It was appropriate that, even after 20 years, some families were still mourning relatives who had died in the Great War. Lieutenant Oliver Emanuel of the Wiltshire Regiment was just one who was still fondly remembered in the columns of the *Jewish Chronicle* every year.

The annual meeting of the Union of Hebrew and Religion Classes also took place at the Synagogue in 1935 with Dr. Jacob Snowman, the famous mohel, presiding. Isaac Wolfson had agreed to be Vice President and there was regret at the death of one of their senior members, Rabbi Arnold Mishcon, the father of the future Lord Mishcon. The Union had given grants of over £1,700 to a number of Synagogues. It seems very little, but in today's money it is over £100,000. The annual exams were to be held in the Great Hall at University College; the status of Jewish education was carefully maintained.

In 1936 The West Central Old Boys Club was now to be found headquartered in the basement of the Synagogue and Isaac Wolfson, the son, generously agreed to finance the enlarging, improving and modernisation of the space. Those who were too old for the religion classes were offered a wide range of activities, from draughts to wrestling and the club was now very popular.

The Honorary Officers were not the only executives to be almost permanently in post. Joseph Jacobs was a warden from 1920 to 1938 and Desmond Tuck from 1927 to 1948, while the Board of Management in the 1930s continued to be supported by such familiar names as Sir Robert Waley Cohen and Sir Anthony de Rothschild.

One of the Jewish charities with a very long history was the Jewish Hospital and Orphan Society, which as far back as 1890 looked after 55 children who had lost their parents. In 1937 several members decided to form a Central Synagogue Orphan Aid Society and in their first year were able to donate £250 (£15,000 today), to the cause. There was another organisation with problems which came to the attention of the Synagogue at the same time. The West Central Jewish Lads Club were in need of somewhere to meet and the Central generously offered them space in the building, which saved the club from going out of existence.

The contribution of individual members to the charitable needs of the community was epitomised by the life of Sir Leonard Cohen (1858-1938) who served as a warden of the synagogue from 1889-1893. The son of the MP for North Paddington, he was a successful stockbroker, on the Council of the Stock Exchange for many years and retired in his forties to devote his time to the Board of Guardians.

He became their president in 1900 and served as such for twenty years. It was Sir Leonard who organised the Jubilee Dinner in 1909, when £25,000 (£2.5 million today) was raised for the poor. He helped non-Jewish charities as well, and in 1938 the Duke of Kent sent condolences on his demise on behalf of the King Edward Hospital Fund.

Antisemitic legislation was increasing in many parts of Europe. In Haham Moses Gaster's Romania a law was passed making it compulsory to employ 75% Romanian clerical workers, with heavy fines if firms didn't apply the ruling. Furthermore, cut price shops started to undermine Jewish enterprises in Bucharest. The Anschluss in Austria showed much support for the Nazis and Jews were expelled from legal and medical occupations in Poland. The British community made massive efforts to help refugees from these countries and the Central members played a full part. They also sent representatives to Willesden when Lord Rothschild died in September. It was a bad year for the Rothschilds as Leopold had died in April.

With war on the horizon, the attraction of Baden Powell's Scouts and Girl Guides became greater. The headquarters for the 24th St. Marylebone troop was the Central and Jack Peters was the highly regarded scoutmaster for many years. The Jewish Girl Guides had held their first annual service in 1924 and in May 1939 the 15th service was held at the Central. More than 300 attended. Some synagogues still have Girl Guide troops today, like the Sixth Stanmore Guides.

There were still outbreaks of violence in Palestine and a Royal Commission produced what was known as the Peel Report in 1937, advocating partition for the holy places into three segments: Arab, Jewish, and Neutral. Rabbi Shlomo Fisch, preaching at the Central, said that it would neither satisfy the Jews' economic needs, nor their spiritual aspirations, comparing what was suggested with the lands promised to them in the Bible.

Another distinguished lecturer that year was Cantor Shlomo Pincasovich, (1886-1951) one of the finest chazans in the international community. A large audience of 350 people came to his lecture to the Literary and Social Society in 1938 on the origin and historical development of Chanukah. During his lifetime he made 300 recordings, many of which were played during the evening. It was the Cantor who developed the first systematic course on chazanut at Jews' College after the war.

One of the last connections with the early days of the synagogue came to an end in 1939 when Michael Green, (1852-1939), Aaron Levy Green's third son, died at the age of 87. A stalwart of the Board of Guardians for over 50 years, (Hon. Sec.1894-1902, Vice President 1905-1912), Michael Green carried on the good work of his father in many areas of the community. A stockbroker, he was known on the Exchange as The Rabbi, but his religious position was different to his father; he became a founder of the Liberal Synagogue.

Over the years, the cause of equal rights for women was still well supported at the Central, even if they didn't sit on the Board of Management. A memorial service was held for one of its most determined advocates when Constance Hostier (1865-1939) died in June. Mrs. Hostier had founded one of the most famous secretarial colleges in the country and was said to have trained 30,000 pupils in her lifetime. She was also very active in both Jewish and non-Jewish women's organisations and was the first woman to be elected to the London Chamber of Commerce. A Vice President of the International Council of Women, Constance Hostier was a formidable petitioner.

Women were now to be found in the choir at the Central, even if this remained a contentious subject in the community. Good voices were hard to find, however, and it was necessary in 1938 to advertise for sopranos and tenors to strengthen the team.

The Synagogue was still supporting the young people. The West Central Old Boys' Club continued to meet at the Synagogue and took pride in winning the AJY Debates Cup in 1939. Isaac Wolfson had paid for two shower baths to be built in the Synagogue area allocated to the club. Many members joined up when the war came and there were casualties.

When the second world war finally broke out, the need for Jewish chaplains to the forces was again a problem to be solved. Most of the British community ministers were now graduates of Jews' College and the question was raised whether they would be competent on distant battlefields, or whether their Talmudic training at the college had made them religiously knowledgeable, but likely to fail in their bureaucratic duties. The ministers, in fact, rose to the challenge admirably.

They certainly had major new responsibilities. There was, for example, a small Synagogue in the West End, the Dean Street Talmud Torah, with a minister called Rabbi Moshe Lew. When he volunteered to become a Chaplain, he was attached to the army and found that his designated area of responsibility was the whole of India. He did a fine job, as did his colleagues.

The Synagogue's religion classes lost their headmaster when Philip Cohen also volunteered to be a chaplain and served throughout the war. In 1940 he officiated at a number of Synagogues in Leeds during the High Holydays and his sermons impressed the congregations, who presented him with a silver tea service for his efforts,

Although his decision to be a chaplain had the full approval of the Central congregation, the war changed Philip Cohen's views on orthodoxy. When the war ended he resigned from the Central in 1946, after only three months, and instead became the assistant minister at the Liberal Synagogue from 1946-1958. He was still to be seen, however, at the Bayswater on the second day of festivals, as this is not a part of the Liberal ritual. As a Cohen, he also took part in blessing the congregation.

He then moved on to be the minister at the North West Reform Synagogue in Alyth Gardens from 1958-1972 before retiring. He died at 78 in 1985. Philip Cohen served as chaplain to the Mayor of Haringey and did a great deal to build up Alyth Gardens Synagogue, including the construction of a youth centre. At the launch of the project the attendees included the local MP, Margaret Thatcher. It was a nice touch that two non-Jewish councillors carried sifrei torah in the service, wearing appropriate tallesim.

Philip Cohen is the only British minister who has held posts in Orthodox, Reform and Liberal communities, He was very popular and known as a great cricket lover. In his memory a window was mounted at Alyth Gardens where a panel shows a cricket ball heading for the stumps.

When Philip Cohen went off to war, Rabbi Benjamin Michelson (1875-1957) took his place. It was his second stint at the Central as he had replaced Michael Adler during the First World War. Although he was always known as Rev. B.N. Michelson, he had been awarded his semicha at Jews' College in 1899. At that time, however, the title of rabbi was still restricted to the Chief Rabbi.

Benjamin Michelson was very highly regarded for his work in the East End, though Chief Rabbi Brodie remembered his address to him in Newcastle when he celebrated his barmitzvah. He was an elderly man when he agreed to step into the breach at the Central again and he lived to be 82 before dying in 1957.

Benjamin Michelson shared the responsibility at the Central with Rev. Emil Nemeth, who went on to the Highgate synagogue after the war in 1947. Emil Nemeth had worked very hard during the Blitz to help those made homeless by the bombing. He also held services in air raid shelters. After it ended, he served the Highgate congregation with distinction for 21 years. and obtained semicha in 1963. He was very diplomatic, although his task wasn't easy. A scholarly word, an erudite quotation calmed the turbulence which from time to time disturbs communal life. He died on Kol Nidre night in 1968 at the early age of 57. There was a very large memorial service.

There was great suffering in the Blitz and in 1940 the Synagogue volunteered to house 400 non-Jews who had lost their homes in Poplar. They were also fed by the Synagogue, whose members wanted to play their part in helping their fellow citizens. The BBC headquarters near the Synagogue was one of the targets of the Luftwaffe and was nearly hit in April. The Synagogue was designated an official air raid shelter.

The blitz on London was eventually disastrous for many Synagogues. The Bayswater, the Borough, Hampstead, Hackney and Brondesbury all suffered damage. The Great was destroyed and on Saturday, 10 May 1941 the Central was also bombed and flattened. It had been used as an assembly centre for people whose homes had been destroyed in the Blitz, but they were safe in the basement.

Over 500 bombers dropped more than 700 tons of high explosive bombs and 86,000 incendiary bombs on London on 10 May. Only a single incendiary bomb hit the synagogue, but it caused a raging fire. It fell on the North Western tower, setting fire to the gas pipes in the gallery. It was described at the time as. "a furnace of blue-white incandescent light." Everybody did their best to help. Air Raid Warden Ita Ekpenyon, originally from Nigeria, rescued one woman from the debris and reportedly sang a stirring spiritual to calm the locals. Emil Nemeth was in the building at the time and had a narrow escape.

As dawn broke, Hallam Street was a shambles of broken bricks, smoking embers and partially demolished houses. The Synagogue had been completely gutted. The fire engines had only been able to reach the area at five o'clock in the morning. The ruins of the Synagogue remained an unstable structure for a month. The police reported that:

> Debris from the Synagogue in Great Portland Street has recently fallen into the street – the road is already blocked. There is no danger.

Well, except for the work of a doctor in Hallam Street who had been experimenting with poison gas, of which there were samples on his roof. Luckily, they were not affected by the bomb and were quickly removed to nearby University College Hospital.

Among the treasures destroyed was the memorial to the men who had died in the Boer War, and a replica was made after the war and placed in the chapel at the Willesden cemetery. Aron Stoutzker's flat was also hit but not too badly. When the family came down from their temporary home in Watford to survey the damage, they saw their grand piano in the middle of the street. It was the most important thing Aron Stoutzker saved. Fortunately, most of the ritual appurtenances had been stored elsewhere and the clothing survived.

Ed Murrow, (1908-1965), reporting for CBS, the radio broadcasting company in America, lived in Hallam Street during the war and broadcast his experiences that night. It was powerful support for the case for America to come into the war on the allied side.

Now a new venue for the congregation had to be found. By the following Friday it had been decided to hold services at Woburn House near Euston Station, which was a folly of Sir Robert Waley Cohen. He had wanted to join Jews' College and the United Synagogue and promoted the new building which he hoped would lead to savings on administrative costs.

The additional rent for the large new structure he had built was supposed to be partially financed by it being hired out for functions and lectures, but there was never sufficient demand to make the building financially viable. It was, therefore, an unlikely solution to the problem that the Central congregation found themselves needing a new venue, with the resulting income helping to reduce the deficit.

The members had much further to walk, but Rev. Nemeth was a good preacher and although the Adolph Tuck Hall at Woburn House did not have the grandeur of a Synagogue, all the usual Sabbath and Festival services were held there. Daily services were still conducted in the remains of Hallam Street. Weddings and Barmitzvahs continued in the somewhat anonymous Woburn House setting, with the wardens still in top hats.

Emil Nemeth didn't confine his activities to the Synagogue. He joined the Marylebone Shelter Council to help look after people who had been bombed out. When people are asked to help in the face of danger, it often brings out the best in them.

The prayer books and tallesim in the boxes below the seats of the old synagogue were presumably destroyed with everything else, but spares were soon found. The services were as dignified as ever. On one Sabbath in Woburn House, the son of the magnate Charles Clore was barmitzvah, but Clore had recently experienced marital problems and spent most of the service in quiet tears. Diplomatically, nobody would have commented.

There was one additional problem which was who was going to negotiate with the government after Germany had surrendered? After all, the destroyed and damaged Synagogues were entitled to the war damage reparations, like the other victims of the Blitz. The government didn't care if the Synagogue had been United, Federation or Reform; they just wanted one organisation with which to deal, and it was not until 1943 that a Synagogues' War Damages Committee was set up for that purpose.

The Blitz claimed many victims, but there were also many acts of heroism. One of the most notable fell to Harry Errington, who was Chair of the West Central Old Boys Club from its foundation in 1932 and the Athletics Youth Leader at the Central's Youth Club. He was the son of Polish immigrants, Solomon and Bella Ehrengott. During the war Harry Errington joined the Fire Brigade and during a raid courageously risked his life to save two comrades who were trapped in the basement of a blazing building.

Twenty people had been killed but Harry Errington could have escaped without difficulty. Instead, he dug out one colleague, carried him out of the building and then went back into the building for another trapped fireman. For his heroism he was given the George Cross, which is the highest civilian honour awarded, and the equivalent of the military Victoria Cross. He was the only London fireman to be so honoured.

Harry Errington was a very modest man and became an excellent Savile Row tailor after the war. He lived to be 94 and received a well-deserved obituary in the *Guardian.*

There was naturally a great deal of stress because of the Blitz; Joseph Freedman was still on the Board, now over eighty, and a widower living in a hotel. During the night of one raid, a bomb shattered all the windows in his room, and he was found walking on the glass on the floor and murmuring "I'm alive I am."

The Freedmans provided Honorary Officers for several United Synagogues and the Joseph Freedman Hall at Dunstan Road Synagogue was named in his honour. They were practical businessmen, but Joseph Freedman was sufficiently involved in the Central to be asked to speak at the prize giving of the religion classes.

There were an abundance of businessmen like the Freedmans. One day during the disastrous Slump, a Director of his large business called the Chairman and said "We've got to fire the manager in Cardiff. He's fiddling the books." Joseph Freedman said "Nonsense." "No" said the Director, "I can prove he's fiddling the books." The Chairman sighed. "You don't understand", he said "I know he's fiddling the books. He's been fiddling the books for years. But we're making a profit in Cardiff!" It went into the family folklore, and it illustrates the practical skills of members of the Board of Management, available to the synagogue.

There were other Freedmans; Sonny Freedman was his great nephew and the representative of the synagogue on the Welfare Committee of the United Synagogue. Sonny Freedman also sat on the Board of Management and for many years read the book of Jonah at the afternoon service on Yom Kippur.

The Board of Management was meeting again by May 25th after the bombing because life had to go on. The Central family were involved in different ways. The Chazan's son, Sylvan, became a composer and had his first march composition played on Remembrance Sunday in 1942. He changed his name to Stout-Kerr and had written the march while a schoolboy at Harrow, in memory of a pilot friend who had been killed in the Battle of Britain. On the community front, it was in 1942 that Sir Robert Waley Cohen was elected president of the United Synagogue, a position he had effectively already held for many years.

The Beadle, Morris Roth, had taken on the responsibility of Scoutmaster and on one occasion handed out no less than 26 cub badges at the Synagogue. The Central's Habonim group also met there every Sunday afternoon. By the beginning of the war it had thousands of members around the world.

Habonim is a Jewish youth organisation and it prepares its members for Aliyah (emigration) to Israel. It was founded by the housemaster at the Jewish boarding house at the Perse School in Cambridge, Wellesley Aron, and was organised like the Perse School Scout group which was one of the earliest in the country.

There was no doubt that there were difficulties with Woburn House which had nothing like the aura of a Synagogue. In 1944 Senior Warden Desmond Tuck chaired the Annual General Meeting and acknowledged that there were complaints. He asked the members to try to find an alternative venue, but it was never possible. Some members were holding services in their own homes.

Everybody did their best; Mr. Pestor, their old choirmaster had come out of retirement and Desmond Tuck congratulated him on his 80th birthday. The Western Synagogue had also been Blitzed and their congregation was now holding morning and evening services in the remnants of the Central, for which no rent was charged. Old differences were forgotten in wartime.

The latter years of the war were the days when the V1 flying bombs were raining down on London and were followed by the even more damaging V2 rockets. These only stopped when the invading allied armies captured the launching pads. It was impossible to blame members for a lack of attendance at services and classes. One had to adjust during the war, and this was especially true when the bulk of the Synagogue was no more. Three sons of members had died in action by 1944 and one of the common phrases which came to be very pertinent was "Grin and bear it".

In 1944 Michael Adler died and the memorial service at the Adolph Tuck Hall was led by the chief rabbi. Tribute was paid to Michael Adler's work as pastor and scholar and there was no doubt that an equally able minister would be hard to find.

After the war in 1946 a temporary synagogue was built in the basement of the old synagogue with 550 seats, consecrated by the Chief Rabbi in September 1948 and opened by Desmond Tuck. The senior warden had again agreed at previous AGMs that Woburn House was inadequate but always had to confirm that no better hall had been found.

The Synagogue still had a financial surplus in 1945 of £170 and, in passing, Desmond Tuck regretted the resignation of Philip Cohen which had obviously come out of the blue and was in no way expected by the members. One development to endeavour to improve attendances was the creation of a Central Synagogue Youth Fellowship which at least attracted a lot of youngsters to the inaugural meeting.

One Central Synagogue youngster who was making the grade was Rev. Stoutsker's daughter, Evelyn, who came third in a competition for producing a 'Come to Britain' poster. There were 862 entries. She was a student at the Architectural Association School. A lot of the children had been evacuated during the war and spent years away from the Synagogue. It was, therefore, recognised that new efforts would have to be made to bring them back into the Synagogue orbit.

In January 1946 Chief Rabbi Joseph Herman Hertz died at the age of 73. He had not experienced an easy time in his 33 years as Chief Rabbi. Apart from two world wars and the disaster of the Holocaust, he had to deal with a United Synagogue led by Sir Robert Waley Cohen, who questioned his authority on many occasions, to such an extent that in latter years the two could only communicate through intermediaries. The Board of Deputies was, however, absolutely right when they said:

> He raised the prestige of the Anglo-Jewish community by his learning and devotion to his people and by the dignity wherewith he performed his functions. He was a tower of strength for his brethren during many most difficult years.

There were other lesser absentees, and in 1946 the Synagogue was advertising for a choirmaster and choristers to fill the gaps. Good choirmasters were not, however, thick on the ground, and A.E.Mandel soldiered on as choirmaster until 1951 when he retired after serving from well before the war. It wasn't easy to keep the congregation together without a permanent Synagogue but in 1946 the warden, Desmond Tuck, was able to report another surplus in the accounts. He commented ironically at the AGM:

> Whether they enjoyed a surplus spiritually he would not care to say.

In 1950 the United Synagogue celebrated its 80th anniversary and it was particularly noteworthy and admirable that the wealthier communities, which included the Central, still helped the poorer congregations financially. By the anniversary more than 30,000 families were members of the organisation. The early principal officer, Lionel Louis Cohen, would have been pleased that his nephew, Robert Waley Cohen, was still the president of the organisation, which had now grown to 23 synagogues, plus 19 district synagogues and 31 affiliates. Members of the Central still played a major part in the deliberations of its committees and Robert Waley Cohen remained a member of the Central's Board of Management.

It was difficult to get a building licence for a new Synagogue, as there were blitzed buildings which had been hit by the Blitz with a higher priority than a place of worship. Licensing restrictions were not abolished until 1955. In 1956 the building of a new Synagogue on the old site was started and the building was consecrated in March 1958. As Cyril Shine recalled in later year:

> During the two years that elapsed before the completion of the new synagogue, the Sabbath and Festival services were once again held at the Adolph Tuck Hall in Woburn House. The High Festival services were held at the Dukes Hall of the Royal College of Music. Daily services were maintained at Hallam Street in the remaining part of the old building, as was the office administration and the Hebrew classes.

The Synagogue's connection with the Willesden cemetery came to an end in 1947 when a new burial ground was consecrated in Bushey. Burials at Willesden were now restricted to those who had already bought plots, although they were numerous, and burials are still taking place at Willesden seventy five years later.

In 1947 Isaac Wolfson, (1897-1991), the son of the old member of the Board of Management, was appointed a warden of the synagogue and in 1962 he became the President of the United Synagogue. He was the first to be elevated to that office from outside the magic circle of the Cousinhood. He came from a poor family in Glasgow but had transformed the fortunes of Great Universal Stores, a mail order company founded by the Rose family.

Isaac Wolfson had joined them in 1932 and became the joint managing director that year. When the Rose brothers stepped down he should have become chairman but he wasn't considered a big enough name for the City to accept. It wasn't until two figureheads had eventually disappeared that he was made chair in 1946.

He also broke the mould of United Synagogue chair and was the first man from a poverty-stricken immigrant family to hold that office, though his father had been successful in his endeavours and had given a great deal of support to the Synagogue. As the son had a major company to run, he was happy to leave the day-to-day supervision of the synagogue affairs to his co-warden, Philip Taylor, who only had a small business but was a very senior Freemason, and was actually promoted three times in Grand Lodge, which is exceptional. The two of them stayed in office from 1948-1963. Not until Eric Charles was in office from 1989-2011 did any future members of the congregation serve longer.

Isaac Wolfson was very Orthodox and a great philanthropist. He gave millions of pounds to support both Jewish and non-Jewish charities. He had his problems though, one of which led to him giving evidence to a government enquiry. When he left for the enquiry he had black hair, but when he returned his hair had gone white. Running a large company was not without exceptional demands and consequences.

In 1946 the United Synagogue had to institute a Religious Education Rate to support the London Board of Jewish Religious Education. The finances of the organisation were stretched, as Synagogues in the suburbs ran large deficits which even the Synagogues with a surplus could not underwrite. The Central played its part without complaint.

The cemetery at Willesden was augmented by a new burial ground at Bushey in September 1947. Over 300 graves had been destroyed or damaged by bombing in the war but the connection between the Synagogue and the cemetery had lasted for 75 years. The Willesden cemetery would become a heritage site in 2020.

In 1948 after opening the new temporary synagogue in the basement of the old building, which would be the members' home for the next eight years, Desmond Tuck retired from being a Warden after twenty-one years, ending the contribution of the family which had begun when his father, Sir Adolph Tuck became a warden in 1910. The contribution of the Tucks was typical of the families who supported the Synagogue from its inception. Desmond Tuck was also vice president of the Jewish Blind Society.

The same year saw the death of Gaskell Jacobs, (1877-1948) when he was 71. He had been the financial representative and then a warden from 1933–1947, working over the years with Adolph Tuck. He was a nephew of Joseph Freedman and after the war there were no less than six relatives of the Freedmans on the Board of Management.

Gaskell Jacobs could rightly be described as a pillar of the community. He conducted services, trained the choir on occasions, taught the children and acted as the Registrar for Marriages. If all that wasn't enough, he was also the founder and president of the South East London Synagogue and in his memory, his wife gave the Synagogue its ark, Almemar and furnishings. He served the Central community for forty years and as the new minister, Simmy Isaacs, said "Very few knew of the great amount of work he did behind the scenes."

Isaac Wolfson's son, Leonard, the future Lord Wolfson, was in his father's company too and chafed, as a young man, at playing second fiddle to his parent. He also sat on the Board of Management and at meetings would sometimes contradict his father, which was *lèse majesté*. At one meeting the subject of choir stands came up because the new synagogue didn't have any. "I'll get those," said Isaac. "I can get them cheaper," said Leonard. "No, I can get them cheaper" said Isaac." Leonard came back. "I can get them for nothing", he announced. Isaac smiled. "That" said his father "is cheap enough".

When the two wardens, Isaac Wolfson and Philip Taylor, had sat in the Box for 15 years, Leonard tried again. "You should stand down" he told his father "You've sat long enough". Isaac looked at his son with paternal affection. "Well" he said "It's regular work!".

It is very easy for a warden to fall out with a member, if the member doesn't get his own way. For example, one Shabbat a father came to Philip Taylor in the box and said "My son, aged 12, has learned the Haftorah and I'd like him to say it". Now for a boy to learn a Haftorah at 12 involves a great deal of hard work and deserves to be rewarded, but there was a problem. Philip Taylor told the father "I'm very sorry but a member has yahrzeit, (memorial prayers for a parent), and asked for the Haftorah three months ago, which we, of course, agreed. So he must say it."

The father broke the distressing news to the boy and on the Monday morning Philip Taylor received a letter from the father. "My son was so upset that he says he'll never go to synagogue again". Of course, the father should have asked for the Haftorah for the boy before he ever started learning the work. Philip Taylor replied: "I can quite understand your son's disappointment, but it's a bit hard to blame the Almighty for the sins of the Honorary Officers." It was said that the boy kept his word.

Where Philip Taylor tried on occasion to lighten disputes with a touch of humour, the decorum in the synagogue was not neglected. When memorial prayers are said at festivals, some members attend solely for that purpose and then leave immediately afterwards. To avoid such unseemly exits, the prayers in 1952 were put back to almost the end of the service before saying Aleinu.

Running a synagogue is a joint effort and many of the hardest workers are not even remembered as the years go by. As far as the ladies are concerned, it was taken for granted that the food and wine for the kiddushim would appear, as if by magic, after the sabbath service and also at communal meetings. Those who worked as part of the Ladies Guild often stayed well in the background.

One of the most hard working for many years was the daughter of Josey Freedman, the warden during the war. Rosie Randall was a power of strength for the Synagogue on the Ladies Guild. Josey Freedman died at 94 many years later. He contracted cancer in his seventies, but his doctor nephew pointed out that he was thin and old and correctly gave the cancer little chance. In his late eighties he was still walking to shul and remarked that he didn't know what Jews did on shabbat if they didn't go to Synagogue.

In 1950 the chazan, Aron Stoutzker (1882-1968) had retired and the Synagogue was still without a permanent home. Even so, Philip Taylor was able to announce at the AGM that there was now a waiting list for membership and there were increased attendances on Shabbat. Jack Harris, the Financial Representative, could point to a surplus in the accounts of £14. The religion classes had joined with the nearby Dean Street Talmud Torah, which had doubled the attendance. Even without a decent building, the Synagogue was in full operation. The only weakness appeared to be the need for "a bass immediately" for whom they advertised.

The Synagogue had, in fact, made significant progress since the war. The income had doubled since 1948 and the shul could now normally show a small profit at the end of the year. To mark the Queen's coronation, Desmond Tuck gave every child at the religion classes a prayer book and the annual elections returned the same Honorary Officers.

Aron Stoutzker had been appointed in 1925 and was 68 when he stepped down. He lived to be 86 but the hunt was now on for his successor. There were fifteen applicants for the position and it was agreed that each should be interviewed and his voice tested. Number two on the list was a young, emaciated chazan named Simon Hass. When he had sung his piece, Isaac Wolfson was so impressed that he closed the proceedings and said he didn't want to hear anybody else. Simon Hass (1927-2022) was inducted in April 1951 and became one of the shining lights of the community.

The new chazan was born and brought up in Poland and was a very young student at the Belza Yeshiva. When the war broke out Poland was divided between Germany and Russia and, as a thirteen-year-old Jew, Simon Hass was arrested and sent to a camp in Siberia. He was there for seven years, but it was finally agreed between the allies and the Russians after the war that the Poles would be repatriated.

Whilst in the camp he was appointed the chazan at the Great Synagogue in Irkutsk, Siberia, when he was only 17. It was typical of the Soviet regime that at one point he was sent to prison for four months for religious activities.

In spite of the massacre of millions of Jewish Poles in the Holocaust, there was still a great deal of antisemitism in Poland and those of the Hass family who had survived, moved on to Paris, where Simon Hass won a scholarship to the Conservatory after having studied at the Lodz Conservatoire. As a graduate he saw an advertisement for a chazan in Britain and after a short time there at the Hendon Synagogue, applied for the post at the Central. In 1992 he recalled:

> The first time I knew freedom was early in 1950, when at the age of 21, I arrived in this very special country. I had escaped from the tyranny of Nazi Germany and the despotism of Stalin, during my seven years in Siberia.

He didn't speak English well, but his tenor voice was absolutely excellent. His experiences in Siberia had been traumatic and he had lost family through Russian brutality. When he sang in the Central on Yom Kippur, he would name the concentration camps in which so many Jews had perished, and for that brief moment his voice would break and tears would come to his eyes. As he said once:

> Little did I dream 23 years ago when suffering under tyranny and persecution, that I would live to see this day in this great freedom loving country.

Simon Hass was asked in 1980 whether he had thought of accepting offers from abroad. He said:

> I love this country and the freedom is more than all the money ones offered. So I could have lived in New York, but after seven years with my parents, six brothers and four sisters in a Siberian camp, treated worse than animals, to me this country is so very special.

He was a very charitable man. He was asked how he managed it. He explained that, for example, when Sir John Cohen died, he left him £2,000 and that was where the charity came from. He donated the royalties from his records to the Ravenswood village for those with serious learning difficulties, the Tottenham Home for Jewish Incurables, and the Salvation Army. It was a busy life and he very much enjoyed helping others. As he once famously said:

> I have met so many millionaires. Not all, but many are as miserable as sin.

There were 50 to 60 weddings a year at the Central and Simon Hass took care of his voice; he had singing lessons twice a week to keep it up to scratch.

There was a notable event in 1951 when Lord Justice Lionel Cohen (1888-1973) entered the House of Lords, the first Cohen to do so. A member of the Central in his younger days, his grandfather was Lionel Louis Cohen. The family had come to Britain in 1780 from Holland and the Lord Justice had been a Captain at the front in the Great War and wounded in 1916. He was vice president of the Board of Deputies from 1934–1938 and president of the Board of Guardians from 1940-1947. His cousin was Edward Beddington, another stalwart of the Synagogue. The community was honoured.

After the war it took over sixty years to pay the national bills incurred for the conflict. Money was extremely tight and income tax rates rose to about 90% if you earned around £10,000. Even so, Philip Taylor was able to announce in 1951 that the Central members had supported fund raising for the Board of Guardians, the Joint Palestine Appeal, the Central British Fund, the Metropolitan Hospital Sunday Fund and the Home for Jewish Incurables. Philip Jacobs, the Secretary would have liked to be on the list of worthy causes as well. At the AGM he asked for support for his endeavour to get higher salaries for Secretaries from the United Synagogue.

In 1952 the Synagogue lamented the death of the architect, Morris Jacobs, at the very early age of 44. Philip Jacobs, the Secretary, resigned in 1954 and was replaced by Michael Stoller. The salary was still only £580 a year and the successful candidate would have to be under 45 years of age. At the time £10 a week was the starting salary of a university graduate of about 21.

Sir Robert Waley Cohen also died that year at the age of 75. He had devoted a vast amount of time to the United Synagogue and was the founder of the National Shechita Council. If he was not always an easy colleague – his business career was adversely affected by this – he was nevertheless an extremely hard worker, and the expansion of the United Synagogue was very much to his credit. He remained on the Central's Board of Management till the end and presided as president of the Jewish Memorial Council only a month before his passing.

It was now agreed that the younger members of the congregation should be represented on the Board of Management. The two logical choices were the sons of the two wardens and they were duly appointed to the Board. There was still no invitation for the minister or chazan. There was no election for the young men and as long as they remained on the Board they never faced one.

Support for Israel was now of greater importance and the Central branch of the Joint Palestine Appeal raised over £1,000 in 1952. (That's £30,000 today).

In 1953 Isaac Wolfson was able to announce that the Synagogue's income had doubled since 1948 and there were now 600 members. Jack Harris was able to report a surplus of £300. What was now needed was a new Synagogue.

Teaching the children was a task that demanded a great deal of hard work and in May 1955 a service of rededication was held at the Synagogue which recognised the teachers' efforts. The Chief Rabbi attended, along with the leader of the London County Council. and 150 teachers and their friends. The service was conducted by Rabbi Louis Jacobs and impressed the head of the LCC, who was very complimentary when he addressed the gathering.

There would be even more attention given to the members' children when the Morrison family financed the building of four new classrooms and a playground in memory of Max Morrison in 1958.

9

The Simeon Isaacs years

Philip Cohen's replacement in 1946 was Simeon Isaacs. A graduate of Etz Chaim yeshiva, though not a fully-fledged rabbi with semicha, he had been educated, like so many other ministers, at Jews' College and University College London. Before the war he had been appointed by the United Synagogue to look after their Boys' clubs and he also ministered at the South East London Synagogue.

Like Philip Cohen, he, too, had been a chaplain to the forces during the war, having volunteered in 1941. Unlike Philip Cohen his commitment to Orthodox Judaism was unaffected. Remembering the war years, he made light of the problems of active service, recalling the difficulty of becoming a vegetarian for so many years. Kosher meat was not available on battlefields. When he left the South East London Synagogue, he was replaced by a young refugee Rabbi in his twenties, Immanuel Jakobovits, who had escaped from Germany and of whom much more would be heard later.

Simeon Isaacs had a variety of postings in the army. He was appointed as the senior Jewish Chaplain to the Central Mediterranean Theatre of War and also served in Northern Ireland and India. He would have gone through all the traumas which had broken down Michael Adler's health in the First World War. Simeon Isaacs was a good team player. He was always totally reliable and committed, but it was eventually at a heavy cost.

At the end of the war he was a very good choice for the Central. He was still only in his early thirties but had enjoyed a very varied career. When he returned to Civvy Street, he was sufficiently highly regarded to be appointed the Mayor's chaplain in 1951, when Philip Bendel became the first Jewish mayor of Finsbury in over 50 years. He also became a member of Bnai Brith in 1953. Simeon Isaacs was conscientious and always anxious to help but he was a mild man; very approachable but never one to hog the limelight. He was recognised early on as having settled into the ceremonial role of a minister very well. For instance, he was invited to consecrate the Michael and Elizabeth Room at the Nightingale Home for Aged Jews. Founded in 1894, as a combination of three charities in Wandsworth, the Home had

150 residents and a waiting list of eighty; it needed all the support, both financial and social, it could get.

On occasions he continued in his role as a chaplain after the war. For example, in 1946 he presided at a ceremony at the East Ham cemetery to mark the death of Private Mark Feld who had been killed by an antisemitic sergeant who was also a member of his regiment. It was a case that took a long time to resolve but finally ended in a manslaughter verdict and a ten year prison sentence. It was felt that the army was not keen to admit to such criminal actions by its non-commissioned officers.

The Central lost two prominent members in 1947; Joseph Freedman died at 90. His three sons had honoured their father by having a Joseph Freedman Hall built at the Dunstan Road Synagogue and Joseph Freedman had himself been responsible for the building of a number of new Synagogues, as the United Synagogue Honorary Officer given that responsibility. He worked well with Sir Robert Waley Cohen.

Chief Rabbi Hertz also acknowledged his financial underwriting of the publication of his Chumash, which enabled it to be sold at a much more reasonable price than would otherwise have been the case. He dedicated it in memory of his wife, Rose, and he was a widower for nearly 20 years. Rabbi Dr. Schonfeld also spoke warmly of his help with his educational efforts with the Hasmonean schools.

Joseph Freedman was a patriarch in the best traditions of the community leaders. A strong supporter of the United Synagogue, he had represented the Central on their own Board for a good thirty years. One of his few failures was the repudiation by the members of the Board of Deputies of the president's letter to *The Times* in 1917, denying any desire by the community for a National Home. Joseph Freedman voted in favour of the president's action, as both were Central members anyway, but he was outvoted.

There was also the death of Myer Jack Linda, (1874-1947), a long-time parliamentary correspondent and a prolific author, notably of *The Alien Problem and its Remedy* before the First World War. He was also a past editor of the *Jewish World*. There was a well-attended memorial service at the Adolph Tuck Hall at which the Chief Rabbi spoke and many Fleet Street worthies came to pay tribute.

Emil Nemeth left the Central for the Highgate Synagogue in 1947. Highgate would make different demands on him but his contribution over many years was equally meritorious. Services continued at Woburn House as the Central struggled to recover from the effects of the war. In 1948 it was patched up, with the help of a £5,000 payment from War Damages and

£1,300 from the members. The resultant shul was consecrated by the new Chief Rabbi, Israel Brodie, in the basement of the old Synagogue and opened by Desmond Tuck. There was a full turn-out with the new Chief Rabbi, Israel Brodie, and Dayan Lazarus heading the scroll bearers. They were followed by honoured guests, Sir Robert Waley Cohen, by then the senior Honorary Officer of the United Synagogue, and the Mayor of Marylebone.

Inevitably, the result of the work was hardly impressive, but other buildings destroyed in the Blitz had to be reconstructed first. For years after the war there were shortages of any number of items and the country wasn't back to normal until the mid-1950s when the prime minister's election motto was "You've never had it so good.".

Post-war Britain didn't have anything like enough foreign currency either and bread had to be rationed, which hadn't happened even in the most difficult days of the war. Rationing didn't end completely until 1954 and repaying the last of the wartime debts to America and Canada took until 2006. The Chief Rabbi, nevertheless, struck an optimistic note:

> I feel as I survey the position of our Judaism in Anglo Jewry that there are many factors give us cause for reasonable optimism. There is an abundance of faith in our community, and there is a display of active zeal for traditional Judaism and traditional observance.
>
> I rejoice to proclaim that there are many of our youth who seek more Jewish knowledge, who evince a lively curiosity to find a spiritual as well as a historical basis for Jewish pride, and the yearning for, and tendencies towards, close and active association with our common Judaism.

It is a fact though that when conditions are particularly dangerous, the possibility of help from the Almighty makes a sound case for greater religious observance. With bombs dropping or when being about to take part in a battle, the adverse circumstances are more conducive to prayer than everyday life in peacetime. There is also an alternative argument, however, suggesting young people should reject religion, blaming the Almighty for the devastation that war brings. The advocates of traditional Judaism needed continual support and a great deal of personal commitment.

The Holocaust was an extreme example of the awful horror of the Second World War, and in addition to those slaughtered, a number of Jews turned their backs on the religion even as they survived. Bringing them back into the family of their faith was going to be a hard struggle in many cases, but this was a problem which had always faced Jews over the centuries. The Central was just the latest congregation to determinedly follow in the footsteps of their ancestors.

At the end of the war there were 500 Central members and the financial demands of their local charities led Isaac Wolfson, the warden, to regret that only £120 had been raised for the Joint Palestine Appeal. Isaac Wolfson, following his father's example, was himself very generous though. As just one small example, the Chief Rabbi came to preach as usual on the first day of Succot and it was agreed at the AGM that the best sermon of the year would be sent to the members; Isaac Wolfson, as was invariably the case, volunteered to cover the cost.

Like the Rothschilds he attributed his success in business to the beneficence of the Almighty and offered his thanks in the most practical way. He had come a long way from his birth in the Glasgow Gorbals.

In 1949 the Talmud Torah of the West End Great Synagogue decided to combine with the classes at the Central and Simeon Isaacs became the Honorary Superintendent. The classes met on Sunday, Tuesday, Wednesday and Thursday, with more Club activities on Mondays.

It was a somewhat over ambitious programme, as Simeon Isaacs reported in 1951, when he said that attendances were poor, even though there were 80 children on the roll. The children, however, would also have had their homework to do on a weekday evening and considerate parents would have to decide whether additional classes would be an educational step too far. Some children became committed, but others considered the additional religion lessons offered only unattractive boredom. Much depended on the skill of the teachers. The battle for minds was continuous as it had always been.

By 1950 the United Synagogue's 30,000 families still had a lot of ground to cover. Although there were arguments from time to time about the needs of its local communities, as against those of the central body, there was no doubt that many of the communal offices – the Chief Rabbi's office, the Beth Din, etc –could only be financed by calling on the individual communities for help. It was also desirable to recognise the contribution made by permanent staff and in 1950 Morris Roth was given a cheque to mark his 23 years as the Central's Beadle.

The additional unpaid commitment of a few individuals was remarkable. Sir Robert Waley Cohen, for instance, was still a member of the Central Board of Management in addition to his responsibilities as president of the United Synagogue. He took both roles very seriously, especially after he left Shell and Unilever's United Africa Company. He was accustomed, however, to being the undisputed authority in his business activities and when the United Synagogue appointed Israel Brodie as Chief Rabbi, he endeavoured at the outset to put more power into lay hands.

He created a body of executives who were intended to have a role in the spiritual guidance of the community but, while accepting their existence, Israel Brodie did not consult them. Robert Waley Cohen had battled for years with Chief Rabbi Hertz on a range of issues, and he was equally unsuccessful in trying to oversee Israel Brodie.

There was a great deal of help from individual lady members as well. Annie Wix died at 80 in 1951 and had financed the Julius and Annie Wix Home for Old People in London, which the Chief Rabbi opened in 1949. The Editor of the *Jewish Chronicle* wrote:

> How incongruous she found her failing strength when her spirit was ever young and virile. Others will pay tribute to her unending generosity and amazing business sense.

The recent introduction by the United Synagogue of a Religious Education Rate was another necessary move, as running the classes was expensive. It was also true that many of the poorer communities still benefited greatly from the financial support that came from the wealthier congregations, though what was actually provided was seldom recorded in the United Synagogue minutes, to avoid embarrassing those who benefited.

Aron Stoutsker was 65 in 1950 and due for retirement as the Central's chazan, but it was agreed that he should stay on for a further year. This could happen a maximum of five times before a minister had to retire. Simon Hass was inducted as his successor in April 1951. When communal activities were now starting to reach pre-war levels, the Central's Ladies Guild started their winter programme in November 1951 and £17 was raised for food for Israel. (That's over £500 today).

Many activities were elaborate. Members of the Central's new Portland Club for the 17–21-year-olds, got together to put on Noel Coward's play "I'll leave it to you" at a nearby hall, produced by the author of this book, who can't remember anything about it. The Synagogue started to show a small profit and the only change in the organisation's personnel involved the resignation of the choirmaster, A.E.Mandel, after 14 years in the post.

The Synagogue continued to recover from the effects of the Blitz on the community. By 1952 it had 600 members and the appeal for the JPA showed considerable progress when £1,140 was donated. (£32,000 in today's money.)

In November 1952 Sir Robert Waley Cohen died soon after his 75th birthday. He had been an Honorary Officer of the United Synagogue, treasurer, vice president and president for 35 years. When somebody holds a senior office for that long, he is going to acquire a host of admirers and a number of detractors. Sir Robert was like any other prominent figure. Nobody could doubt his contribution to the financial growth of the United Synagogue and, equally, his support for the maintenance of the Din was very questionable.

Simmy Isaacs became very popular with the congregation and was particularly intent on encouraging the children. Over 100 came to the classes on Sunday, though he had to struggle manfully with weekday attendances. With the older adolescents, he led the discussions at the 1952 conference of the Association of Jewish Youth. As the theme was *"Has Judaism any meaning in our times?"* he was a very good advocate. He would advise the adolescents that they were always welcome in Jewish circles and should consider making such bodies the centre of their social lives. He recognised very well the growing appeal of alternative secular attractions.

There was a lot of talent among the youngsters in the Portland Club. For instance, Jack Arbeid was a master diamond cutter from the East End and his son, Murray Arbeid, became one of the foremost fashion designers in the country, with clients like Princess Diana and Dame Shirley Bassey. Murray Arbeid always said that if there was a Nobel prize for taffeta, he would win it. He was famous for his evening wear but kept away from wedding dresses. As he cynically proclaimed:

There are enough pressures in life without having to put up with neurotic mothers of the bride, and there are no other kind.

Simeon Isaacs' warm and friendly nature was much admired. He worked hard to improve Jewish/Christian relations. In February 1954, for example, he conducted a service at a conference jointly held by the Association of Jewish Youth and the YMCA. He spoke of the significance of the service and took a lot of trouble to justify Jewish beliefs.

He had a serious problem though. Over the years, he was getting steadily more depressed as he tackled the crises of members' lives and recalled the horrors of the war years in which he had served. Eventually the stress became too great with a terrible result. In 1954 he went on holiday for a few days to Clacton and was later found drowned on the beach. He was 42. The verdict of the coroner said no more.

It had been a long war for Simmy Isaacs. Like Michael Adler in the

Great War, he would have seen horrific injuries when he visited hospitals, watched young men die in pain and had the difficult and unenviable task of writing to their families at home in the attempt to provide what little comfort he could. It would have been far more taxing than conducting services for old Central members who had died at a good age.

With some chaplains the memories might fade over the years. Some could regard comforting as simply part of the job. With others the scars remained and when they took up their peacetime ministries, they were once again called upon to help with the grief of bereaved members. Because their conversations with the mourners were in private, their efforts were not as easily recognised as was their performance in the pulpit. Every rabbinical student recognised, when he adopted the profession, what was going to be a part of his responsibilities, but the actual experiences could be devastating. The dedication of rabbis is often overlooked.

In his obituary, Isaac Wolfson recalled:

> He had played a considerable part in the resuscitation of the congregation. His inspiring sermons and leadership will always remain fresh in our memory. He possessed many sterling qualities, among them integrity, enthusiasm, and a keen sense of fair play.

The Chief Rabbi. conducted the tombstone setting in 1955. According to the Din, suicides cannot be buried in an Orthodox cemetery, but the passing of Simeon Isaacs was designated accidental death. In Judaism, with suicide, it was now invariably held that the self-inflicted death only occurred when the mind was disturbed; when therefore, the deceased was not responsible for their actions. In such circumstances the rules on suicide were held not to be applicable.

Simeon Isaacs' devoted wife, Sylvia, was a widow for over 30 years, dying in 1988. As vice-chair of the Jews' College Women's Aid Group she had the pleasure of endowing the Simeon Isaacs Memorial Students Room at the College in 1959.

The Central's relations with the nearby Western Synagogue now deteriorated. The Western was an ancient congregation (1761) and always very individualistic. They never had a distinguished building for a Synagogue, but the Western families stayed loyal to the Synagogue until so many of their children moved out of the district. They were usually on very friendly terms with the chief rabbinate; the early service they held for Hermann Adler on the morning of Edward VII's coronation was one example. but they remained independent of the United Synagogue.

In 1954 the US had decided to build a new synagogue at Marble Arch. It was questionable whether the community needed another synagogue in the West End and it was a particular aggravation to the Western Synagogue; their Synagogue was nearby and they realised the attraction of the splendid new Marble Arch building would inevitably result in them losing members. Their Synagogue had also been blitzed, like the Central, but they had turned down alternative sites in Portland Place and New Cumberland Street because they didn't want to be competition for the older shul.

They were offered sites near the New West End Synagogue and the St. Johns Wood Synagogue as well but turned these down for the same reason. They had not been consulted by the United Synagogue, however, when the site in Cumberland Place for the Marble Arch had become available and they naturally considered this discourteous. Meanwhile the Bayswater Synagogue Honorary Officers accepted that their Synagogue was not well placed for residents in the distant parts of the West End, but wanted any new Synagogue to be called the New Bayswater. This didn't happen.

The ordinary members had more important objectives. The discord between the two sets of Honorary Officers on the location of the Synagogues did not concern, for example, the helpers of the Central Friendship Club who worked well with their opposite numbers at the Western and Central Synagogues. Typically, one of their outings in July 1954 saw sixty elderly people taken to Brighton for the day, which was much appreciated.

While a successor to Simmy Isaacs was sought, the annual service of rededication of London's Jewish teachers was held at the Central. Rabbi Louis Jacobs and the new chazan, Simon Hass, conducted the service, which much impressed the leader of the London County Council who was also present.

Over 150 teachers and their friends came, and after the service the LCC leader remarked how much the Jews and the Christians had in common. The religious world had moved on. Rabbi Louis Jacobs was an inspiring speaker. He offered encouragement to the teachers who often had a somewhat thankless task. If children do not progress with their religious studies, devoted parents may well choose to blame the teachers rather than an inattentive child.

The advertisement for Simmy Isaac's replacement was terse. The successful candidate had to be under 45 years of age and would receive a salary of £1,012, rising to £1,181. (In today's money £28,000.) There was an allowance for children and a residence on the "usual United Synagogue terms". The successful candidate was expected to lein on Shabbat and supervise or take the religion classes.

Accordingly, in 1955, a successor to Simmy Isaacs was appointed; Cyril Shine (1923-2003) was born in London to Abe and Annie Shinebaum and came from the Yeshiva Etz Chaim. Although Jews' College had been Chief Rabbi Nathan Marcus Adler's creation a hundred years before, the Yeshiva Etz Chaim had been founded about 1900 in the East End and was more primarily devoted to Talmudic studies. Many future rabbonim attended both centres of learning.

Cyril Shine had been just too young to be a chaplain during the war but had served as the Peterborough minister (1944-1946), when he was only 21, at the Walthamstow and Leyton Synagogue (1946-1949) and the North Finchley & Woodside Park District Synagogue. (1949-1955). He was a precocious talent. Six hundred attended his induction by Dayan Morris Lew, who was well known for believing and teaching that a minister should lead the congregation and not vice versa. Cyril Shine took the same positive line and, in his sermon, said that it was not necessary:

> to compromise their own principles and traditions. If they maintained a practical approach to their Judaism they had nothing to fear from the non-conformist elements because they were essentially negative and secessionist in character.

Simmy Isaacs and Cyril Shine were different characters. Cyril Shine had an undergraduate sense of humour as a young man, and this was inclined to grate on Philip Taylor in the box. The Warden saw the synagogue ritual in very much the same light as the strict decorum which characterised the Freemason's Lodge meetings he taught and often conducted.

If a poor immigrant's son was trying to move up in the world, one way was to become a senior Freemason. The fraternity was open to all and the Grand Master was the Duke of Kent, so royalty was known to support it. Chief Rabbi Brodie was a clerical Grand Officer and Joseph Freedman was a Past Master of a Lodge. Philip Taylor devoted much of his spare time to Lodge meetings and became the Master of no less than four of them, (The Hercules, Samson, Silver Jubilee and Fraternal Unity), and a recognised expert on the ritual. He married Joseph Freedman's granddaughter.

A combination of an Honorary Officer at the Central and a Grand Lodge officer, promoted three times in his life, made him a most respected member of the community; a long way from the Harry Schneider 1905 choirboy. At the same time mastering the ritual in Freemasonry is no easy task. There is a great deal to learn, for everything in the Lodge is recited by heart. There are weekly meetings of Lodges of Instruction and Philip Taylor taught at these for many years.

He believed the Synagogue service was an equally disciplined occasion and strict decorum for him was a sine qua non, while the congregation members often chatted during the service. Cyril Shine was only 32 years old, though, and Philip Taylor was 60. It was one of the problems which most Synagogues had to deal with; the generation gap between a new young minister and elderly Honorary Officers.

It was agreed by the Central Honorary Officers at the outset that if the pulpit was to be awarded to Rev. Shine, he would have to earn semicha. This had never been asked of any previous minister and Cyril Shine would be the first rabbi the Central ever had with that qualification. It took him eight years' study to gain but he fulfilled his commitment.

In fact, Talmudic knowledge was now considered far more important by the community than it had been in the early days, when there were practically no ministers with semicha in the United Synagogue. By 1954 out of 21 ministers, 10 had semicha and Cyril Shine would be another. When he was awarded his rabbinical diploma in 1963 there was, of course, a reception in his honour to mark his achievement.

Michael Adler's wife, Bertha, died in 1955 and was buried at Willesden. On a happier note, in May 1955, building restrictions were abolished, ten years after the end of the war, and it was possible to plan the rebuilding of the Synagogue and to upgrade the services in the old Synagogue basement. Building a new Synagogue was a major undertaking though, and it was fortunate that the Building Committee was chaired by Leonard Wolfson, Isaac Wolfson's son, with Alfred Levy and Henry Jacobs in support. It was estimated that the building would cost over £200,000 and that figure didn't include the furnishings, and fittings.

The United Synagogue didn't, in fact, want the synagogue rebuilt. They wanted the new Synagogue at Marble Arch to replace it instead. On the other hand, the Wolfsons and many members still lived near the Central and Isaac Wolfson offered £25,000 towards the cost of the reconstruction. (£650,000 in today's money.)

As the Great Synagogue was not rebuilt after it was destroyed in the Blitz, there was substantial War Damage compensation available from that source. This could be applied to helping to finance the new building, though its new members were also very generous. With the income from War Damages, it would make the overall cost of the building quite low and the United Synagogue finally agreed to both projects. As a consequence, the Marble Arch was opened in 1957 and the new Central was consecrated in 1958.

Some would foresee that the younger generation might well move into the suburbs and reduce the pool of local West End members, but that would be in the future. Although the Din is that you may not ride on the sabbath, in the future those who did would usually not be publicly criticised from the pulpit. It would, however, become increasingly expensive to bring a car into the West End as congestion charges were introduced. This couldn't, however, be foreseen at the time.

Leonard Wolfson had seen some designs for the synagogue by the architect, Edmund Wilford, who had made his name with the construction of cinemas before the war. It was decided that the new synagogue would be of a traditional design but there would be "a touch of cinematic glamour."

It was no easy task to decide on an architectural design which would still be attractive in the generations to come. The cost of its maintenance also had to be a consideration, though the value of the building would become part of the capital assets of the United Synagogue. The raw materials for the new Synagogue were still not easy to come by, however, and the expert workers, like stonemasons, were often difficult to recruit. Some would come from as far away as Italy.

There was another problem with the number of seats planned for the new Synagogue. Originally, in July 1955, the plan had been for 597 seats for men and 425 for the ladies. By December 1956 this had been reduced by as many as 200 seats and Philip Taylor pointed to the loss of revenue, and the danger that the new synagogue would not be upgraded by the United Synagogue.

The explanation provided for the reduction was that the London County Council had raised objections to the original concept. The planning department wanted wider gangways and, on the advice they had received, the heating system would require more space than had been originally planned. The final compromise was for approximately 520 men's seats and 390 ladies.

It still meant a loss of the income from 100 seats, but this could be corrected in part by revenue from temporary additional seating for the High Holydays. Synagogues are built to accommodate all the members, but the totality of the seats are usually only occupied on Rosh Hashonah and Yom Kippur. This is why the larger Synagogues are usually only half full on shabbat, but the financial stability of the shul and the long-term finances of the United Synagogue, depended on having a full complement of members paying annual dues as often as possible, whether they attended services or not.

There was one part of the design which went against the Shulchan Aruch,, the codification of Jewish laws. This was the arrangement that members kept their prayer books in their seats. According to the Shulchan Aruch, as a righteous member of the Hull community pointed out in a letter to the *Jewish Chronicle*, prayer books have to be kept above waist level. The Chief Rabbi was asked to comment but nothing changed. The members' books are still to be found below waist level. The United Synagogue did, however, upgrade the new Central to Class 1.

The generosity of the Wolfson family and of many members, provided the necessary funds for building the Synagogue, which began in 1956. There was one small alarm when three fires broke out in June 1957, but they did little damage. It looked like arson, though, and the security at the site was strengthened. The burglary in the 1930s was the only occasion when the Synagogue security was definitely breached.

The foundation stone of the new Synagogue was laid by Isaac Wolfson in February 1956. The synagogue was finally consecrated on March 23, 1958 by the Chief Rabbi, in the presence of the new president of the United Synagogue, Hon. Ewen Montagu, the last of the Cousinhood leaders, the Israeli ambassador and the Mayor of Marylebone. Ewen Montagu recalled that his grandfather had been one of the original founders of the Synagogue and congratulated the congregation on its financial support for the new building.

The occasion was of sufficient importance for the BBC to broadcast it on TV. The commentator pointed out that it hadn't been possible to have the Synagogue face to Jerusalem in the East, as was usual, because of the other buildings in the road.

While King David had wanted the temple in Biblical times to be in Jerusalem, the equally numerous Samaritans insisted that it be in Nablus on the West Bank, as that had been designated its location in the Biblical Book of Joshua. Only the remnants of the Samaritans in Israel still pray facing Nablus, but the reference in the Book of Joshua is correct. The reporter was particularly impressed by the marble which had been brought from Israel.

The Chief Rabbi, Israel Brodie, was as inspiring as ever when he gave his address:

> After expressing his admiration for the beauty and the magnificence of the building, whose modern design was still in keeping with traditional requirements, Dr. Brodie paid tribute to the members of the congregation whose generosity and enthusiasm for the Synagogue had made the outstanding edifice possible.

NEW CENTRAL SYNAGOGUE

Foundation-Stone Laid

By a *Jewish Chronicle Reporter*

The foundation-stone of the new Central Synagogue, Great Portland Street, W.1, was laid on the site of the old one by Mr. Isaac Wolfson, Warden, on Sunday.

The Chief Rabbi conducted the service, assisted by the Rev. C. I. Shine and the Rev. Simon Hass (minister and reader, respectively, of the synagogue). The choir was under the direction of Mr. A. Hizer. Among the congregation of 400 were the President of the United Synagogue, the Hon. Ewen E.-S. Montagu, Q.C., several of the Hon. Officers of the United Synagogue, and the Secretary, Mr. Alfred Silverman; the Mayor and Mayoress of St. Marylebone (Councillor and Mrs. Robert Hampton Sharp); and Sir Wavell Wakefield, M.P., and Lady Wakefield.

It was on May 10, 1941, that the Central Synagogue was destroyed by enemy action. In 1948 a temporary synagogue was erected, which early this year was demolished to prepare the way for the new synagogue now in the course of erection at a cost, I was informed, of £200,000, with a seating capacity of about 1,200. Since the synagogue's demolition services have been held at the Adolph Tuck Hall, Woburn House.

The Chief Rabbi read the inscription on the foundation-stone, which also recalled that the synagogue was first erected in 1870. In his address, Dr. Brodie said they prayed that the building of this new

synagogue would continue without any disturbance.

They remembered that the building which was destroyed by enemy action was one of the important components of the United Synagogue. The synagogue was

Mr. Isaac Wolfson is seen laying the foundation-stone

fortunate in its ministers, in its readers, and in the lay leaders, who had devoted so much of their time, ability, and spirit of religious devotion to the welfare of the congregation. He expressed the hope that the Central Synagogue would for many years to come be a centre of spiritual light, of prayer, and of instruction.

The trowel with which he laid the foundation-stone was presented to Mr. Wolfson by Dr. Morris Schwartz and Mr. L. Ziff, members of the Board of Management.

Mr. S. M. Stoller, the Secretary of the synagogue, told me that a copy of THE JEWISH CHRONICLE dated March 12, 1869, was discovered in the old foundation-stone and that a current issue (dated October 19) was placed in the new foundation-stone.

6. Isaac Wolfson laying foundation stone

Israel Brodie always spoke ex tempore, without notes, but then he had taught public speaking at Jews' College before the war. Of greater general significance, he had an extra important quality as spiritual leader of the community at the time; he was highly regarded by the government. This was more essential than usual because when he was appointed, the situation in Palestine after 1945 had deteriorated into almost civil war and there were atrocities on both the Jewish and British sides.

The unquestioned patriotism of whoever was chosen for Chief Rabbi was, therefore, vital for the image of the British Jewish community as a whole and Israel Brodie had been a Chaplain to the Forces in both world wars; it was impossible to have a better record. Israel Brodie had, in fact, become the senior Jewish chaplain in the Second World War. Chief Rabbi Hertz had objected successfully to the suggestion that a Liberal rabbi should be appointed instead, in succession to Dayan Gallop who had fallen ill. The chief rabbi insisted that such an appointment should be his decision. The military listened, though few of the Jewish representatives supported Hertz.

Israel Brodie would be the first Chief Rabbi to be knighted and his two successors would become members of the House of Lords. The choice of Chief Rabbi always had to take into account the situation of the community and of the nation at the time when he was appointed.

He was one of only three Chief Rabbis to be born in Britain; Solomon Herschell, Israel Brodie and Jonathan Sacks were the others. He was a Newcastle man and had served as the minister in Melbourne in his time. He never wavered in his Orthodoxy. On one occasion he attended a wedding in Melbourne on the natural assumption that the menu would be kosher. When the main course was served, his waiter announced that the kitchen had run out of prawns and that they were therefore "off." "So am I," said the rabbi.

It was during the ministry of Israel Brodie that he crossed swords with Rabbi Louis Jacobs, a disagreement which caused any amount of trouble within the community. He was criticised week after week in the Jewish press, so that he came to hate Fridays, but like his predecessors, he stuck to his guns.

Rabbi Jacobs was the author of *We Have Reason to Believe*, a book which queried some of the normally accepted facts in the Bible. The Bible is, of course, a work of history and ancient historians did, on occasions, distort the historical stories. The new book was naturally contentious, but Louis Jacobs was a fine Talmudic brain and had been expected to become the new principal of Jews' College, when the incumbent, Isidore Epstein, retired. His views were rejected by the Chief Rabbi though, who denied him the appointment and refused to reappoint him to his former New West End Synagogue pulpit.

Louis Jacobs was, however, very popular with the New West End members. They supported him and set up a new congregation in the old St. Johns Wood Synagogue, which eventually became the Masorti. In the lifetime of Louis Jacobs, the new community didn't stray from the Orthodox norms but, as time went by, some of its practices became more akin to the Reform and would no longer be acceptable to the congregations of the United Synagogue. It is now a separate community.

In addition to the consecration of the new Synagogue, 1958 saw the 10th anniversary of the State of Israel and a religious service was held at the Central in the presence of the Chief Rabbi, the Haham, Solomon Gaon, and the Israeli ambassador.

With the new Synagogue now available, its communal and social activities were extended. It was unusual for a Synagogue like the Central to have such extensive assembly facilities and the members benefited:

> This will incorporate a raised stage with dressing room accommodation, as well as a lecture or committee room. The kitchen will also be included adjacent to the Hall for the preparation of light refreshments. A School section will be included in the building but planned so as to comprise a complete entity, having its own entrance. This will include four classrooms, and assembly and recreation rooms with ample natural lighting throughout.

There are always critics though, even if, for most members, the design of the synagogue was very difficult to fault. The favourite adverse comment was on the design over the Ark which Sir Ben Barnett, for one, said looked like a cross. It is still in place. The touch of cinematic glamour had its critics too, but the finished building was worthy of its predecessor.

The decoration of the new synagogue was enhanced over the years by the installation of many stained-glass windows, designed by Rabbi David Hillman. (1893-1974). Apart from the original ones, many members gave windows in the future in memory of their parents. So generous was Isaac Wolfson that the contemporary joke was that the Synagogue should be renamed St. Isaacs.

The one discordant feature of the windows was the metal grille protecting each of them from vandals on the street side of the Synagogue. The Church in Britain had, however, suffered far more in its time. Many thousands of stained-glass windows were smashed during the dissolution of the monasteries by Henry VIII in the 16th century; the custom of producing stained glass windows for religious buildings disappeared in Britain thereafter until the early 19th century.

There was the disastrous ruin of whole buildings, like Fountains Abbey, Rievaulx Abbey and Glastonbury Abbey, which are only three of the 800 monasteries destroyed on Henry VIII's orders. Much of the damage is still unrepaired. A stained-glass window at Canterbury Cathedral has recently been restored and probably dates from before the 13th century.

There is a tendency today perhaps to take stained glass windows for granted as just another form of artistry, but they have a very long history and involve a great deal of technical knowledge. They are called stained glass because in the 14th century silver nitrate was applied to the surface of glass and produced a range of colours from orange-red to yellow. The original production of coloured glass, however, goes back at least to the Egyptians and has been part of the buildings of many cultures subsequently.

David Hillman came from a family of rabbis. He was born in Latvia and brought up in Glasgow, where his father, Rabbi Samuel Hillman, was the minister. One of David Hillman's childhood friends was Isaac Wolfson, so their cooperation and friendship was of long standing. Rabbi Samuel Hillman went on to be the head of the Beth Din in London and was not keen on his son's passion for painting. Nevertheless, he allowed him at the age of fifteen to become a student at the Charles Rennie Macintosh School of Art in Glasgow, which was very avant-garde.

When the family moved to London, David Hillman studied with Haham Moses Gaster who awarded him his semicha, but he also became a member of the Society of Master-Glass Painters and was a founder member of the Jewish Association of Arts and Sciences. During his lifetime, David Hillman designed some 300 stained glass windows for Synagogues both in Britain and Israel. His sister married Isaac Herzog, the first Ashkenazi Chief Rabbi of Israel.

David Hillman's original teacher was Solomon J. Solomon, R.A., the wartime army officer who had become a friend of Michael Adler when he was designing the decoration of tanks in the Great War. Solomon was a portrait painter in civilian life, but he had also studied with Rabbi Simeon Singer, and his sister had married into the Joseph family of architects who had created the first Central synagogue. It was a small world.

In designing stained glass windows for synagogues, David Hillman had to take into account the Jewish prohibition on portraying human beings, as these were considered graven images. Late in life he occasionally broke the rule, but the windows at the Central are strictly according to the Din. There are 26 windows in all and they reflect Biblical subjects, the festivals and Jewish months.

One, for example, shows a flock of sheep, and expresses the thought that just as sheep are in the hands of their shepherd, so we are in the hands of the Almighty. There are three on the Sabbath and one on the end of shabbat; Havdalah. One is on Rosh Hashonah, and one on creation. Yom Kippur is illustrated with one window on the Kol Nidrei evening service, another on the day itself and a third on Neilah, the concluding service.

There is also one for Succot and another for Hoshana Rabbah, the seventh day of the Festival. Another window is for the prayer for rain, and there is one for Chanukah, and a second for the eight days of the festival. There is one for Purim which translates as Lots. This reflects the decision of Haman to draw lots when choosing which Jews to massacre on Adar 13. He was foiled by Queen Esther. Purim and Chanukah are minor festivals but still recall important events in Jewish history and the favour of the Almighty thousands of years ago.

Passover is represented, and two further windows cover the prayer for dew. There is one for Shavuot and one for Moses receiving the Ten Commandments on Mount Sinai. Another window reminds us that the mother bird has to be sent away before taking her eggs, which is designated necessary to be granted a long life.

There is one covering the commandment to honour your father and your mother, and one for Rosh Chodesh, the blessing for the new month. Part of the biblical harvest had to be given to the Temple, which is represented by another window and one for the end of days. The last one covers the future of Passover, when the lion will lay down with the lamb.

The windows are 4 metres by 2 metres and it took 15 years to create them all. They were very much a labour of love, because David Hillman didn't charge anything like the amount he should have done. Three windows at the Central cost less than £500 in all.

David Hillman had a wide knowledge of the source material, which often made his work superior to the other windows which existed at the time. When Synagogues closed as their congregations left the district, his windows were redistributed to other communities. They are still to be found decorating their new Synagogue homes, except for one which finished up in the Ely Cathedral Stained Glass Museum. Nobody quite knows how or why.

The Museum has 1,000 panels and the work of David Hillman can be seen alongside works from mediaeval times and from the Royal Collection and the Victoria and Albert Museum. It was opened in 1979 and its patron is King Charles III, so the Synagogue panel is in very good company.

The construction of stained-glass windows involves the necessity of creating a whole range of colours, and each requires a different technique.

7. Rabbi David Hillman – Renowned Designer of Stained Glass-Windows

They have developed over the centuries. In mediaeval times, for instance, blue glass was made by adding cobalt blue, and it is now recognised that sulphur added to boron-rich borosilicate glass also imparts a blue colour. If you use copper oxide it produces a turquoise colour and nickel produces blue, violet or black glass.

Ruby gold glass is usually made of lead glass with tin added, and selenium is important in making pink and red glass. Added to cadmium sulphide, it produces a brilliant red colour known as Selenium Ruby. Add manganese and you get an amethyst colour, and purple manganese glass has been used for at least 5,000 years since early Egyptian history. All of this, and a great deal more, had to be mastered by David Hillman, who would work on the design of the windows in his attic, deciding what would be in each window and then painstakingly write the design in words as a plan.

One other famous artist in stained glass was Roman Halter, (1927-2012) a Pole who had survived the Holocaust. He provided a window showing an idealised Jerusalem for the stairwell mezzanine and in 1978 a window depicting Jacob wrestling with the angel.

The stained-glass windows were an important part of the Synagogue's decor, but there needed to be a committed congregation in the future to appreciate them. There were other good causes to support as well and there were often grand occasions to raise funds with very substantial donations from the guests. A typical dinner was one to raise money for a children's Synagogue in 1958, held at the prestigious Grosvenor House Hotel by the West Central Parents Association, and there would be many more.

When it was completed, the new Synagogue was a very imposing building. It covered a block between Great Portland Street and Hallam Street, and in addition to a Synagogue which could seat nearly 1,000 worshippers, there would be offices, classrooms and a major hall for receptions. The outside of the building would hardly change over the years, but modern architecture would go through a number of phases comparatively quickly. Whether, like Tudor or Regency, the 1950s style of architecture would stand the test of time, as has a Synagogue like Bevis Marks, only the passing of the years will tell.

The interior, however, would be improved in the future and the generosity of the members would enhance what was already a beautiful Synagogue. It was not surprising that over the years Central became a major tourist attraction in the West End.

8. Stained-glass windows

10

A Brand New Building

The new Central synagogue ritual didn't depart from tradition in any way, but the shul was designed to be contemporary in its architectural details. Gold carpeting was one of the features and this had been donated to the Synagogue by a Christian well-wisher. A commemorative brochure was produced for its consecration and described the building:

> The frontage on Great Portland Street, constructed of well-tested weatherproof materials, is of impressive appearance and consistent with the dignity required in a House of Worship. The main walls are constructed of natural Portland stone, and columns supporting the stone arched window heads are of imperial red Swedish granite, and rest upon a plinth of the same material. Below this plinth the wall between the windows to the lower rooms is faced with ebony black granite.
>
> The main entrance doors, set in a recess, are of polished hardwood heavily moulded. The surrounds of these recessed doors reach to a height of 36 feet [11 metres] and are faced with Venetian glass mosaics, enriched with symbolic designs. There is an additional entrance from Hallam Street to the main foyer and this is treated externally with selected facing bricks and Portland-stone dressings. Immediately within this entrance is a Bride's Room which is exquisitely decorated in a scheme including a fibrous plaster ceiling and damask-covered walls. The synagogue has a minimum seating capacity of 484 on ground-floor level and 386 in the Ladies Gallery.
>
> From the foregoing it will be seen that the new Synagogue aims at achieving a manifold purpose by extending upon its primary religious foundation, facilities for social and recreational activities, both for its adult membership and the younger generation.

The charges for membership had been increased, much to the annoyance of Ewen Montagu, the president of the United Synagogue. As he said at the Council meeting:

It is a dreadful thing that a Synagogue the size of this should have to set a schedule as high as this in order to be able to pay its way, despite the fact that through the generosity of Mr. Isaac Wolfson and his family, the Synagogue will start almost uniquely with no capital charges whatsoever.

As the contribution to the United Synagogue funds from any surplus profit would assist poorer communities, Ewen Montagu's thinking was questionable. He did like the design, though:

A most interesting approach to the theme of Synagogue architecture which hitherto in our experience has tended to be somewhat hackneyed.

The enthusiasm aroused by having a brand-new synagogue gave a fillip to all kinds of new ideas for the members. A parent's association was formed for the children at the Hebrew Classes and from this came the Portland Jewish Youth Club. This was aimed at the adolescents and met twice a week; later there was to be a club for the 10–13-year-olds.

The appeal of the Synagogue was most difficult to advance for these age groups. The very young children had the attraction of going with their parents to an event designed for grown-ups. The newly married wanted to give their children a proper spiritual upbringing. It was part of their lives for the older people, and the very old took comfort from the religion being there at the end of their days.

The rabbis have a saying, however, which is "Forget not the Lord in the days of thy youth" and the alternative attractions of pop concerts, raves, sports matches and non-denominational social gatherings are powerful alternatives for young people.

The members realised that just ordering their children to obey the Din was not enough, and the Synagogue became a lot more of a social centre as the years went by. The older members were not neglected though; The Diplomats, for the over 35s was established and met regularly in the synagogue hall, while the Friendship Club was designed to attract the pensioners. Mrs. Max Williams and Mrs. Arnold Klausner, as they were then called, became joint chairs of the Ladies Guild.

Cyril Shine's relations with the non-Jewish world were always warm and friendly. He had started greeting parties of non-Jews visiting the Synagogue as early as 1958 and he was always concerned to counteract the distorted views they might gather from some of the media. He would visit the Middle East all his life to see for himself what was happening in the Arab countries as well as the Holy Land; for example, 1982 would find him in the Lebanon when he was nearly 60 years old. He was also well known though for sitting next to a BBC disc jockey at Arsenal midweek matches.

In 1958 he could be found talking on the BBC's Woman's Hour programme on the Jewish view on divorce. He pointed out the importance of the family in Judaism but its denunciation of adultery. If an adulterous relationship was proven, then a divorce was mandatory and it was against the Din for the adulterous couple to marry each other.

Israel celebrated its 10th anniversary in 1958 and there was a service of thanksgiving at the Synagogue. It was sponsored by the United, the Sephardim, the Federation, the Zionist Federation and the Mizrachi-Hapoel Hamizrachi Federation; closed circuit television was necessary in the adjoining hall to carry the service to those who couldn't squeeze into the Synagogue. Among the congregation were representatives of the Israeli army, navy and air force in uniform and the Chief Rabbi gave his usual inspiring address.

The new Synagogue continued to attract considerable groups of non-Jews, from 20 – 200 in number, who came to see the synagogue or attend a service. Cyril Shine always tried to make himself available. Careful attention also continued to be paid over the years to the daily morning services. Those who came were recognised in the shul magazine and there was no shortage of participants.

Of course, the children's services weren't neglected; Sidney Diamond, who would become a warden in the shul for 18 years, had been instrumental in amalgamating the Hebrew classes of the Dean Street Talmud Torah with the Central. He now formed a parents association with Rosie Randall to build a small Synagogue for the children. A succession of worthwhile dinner dances and other functions provided the necessary finance.

Rosie Randall led the Ladies Guild and was not to be trifled with. Along with the consecration of the new Synagogue came its dedication. Sidney Diamond and Rosie Randall were given the honour of opening it. on April 3 1960. It was the only children's synagogue in the Metropolis.

The Synagogue was built on a scale suitable for the youngsters. It had a miniature Ark, Reading Desk and Scrolls and permanent seating for 70 children. It was refurbished and rededicated through the generosity of the Alan and Sheila Diamond Charitable Trust in 2011.

With refurbishments, the children's synagogue for some years was amalgamated in the other buildings, but the inaugural plaques are still in a place of honour. In its time the Synagogue was used for many purposes; one family was blessed with a daughter in the 1970s but there was, of course, no event on the scale of a briss to mark her arrival. Cyril Shine offered to name her in the children's synagogue with just the family there. It was a typical gesture of the rabbi. Naturally, it is never easy to judge just how successful the appeal to children will be.

The Hamas massacre of Israelis on October 7, 2023, brought the members even more closely together. Much sympathy was evinced by local organisations, though the initial refusal of the nearby BBC to call Hamas terrorists was a matter of great concern.

There was little the members could do except voice their support and solidarity for Israel, but the positive statements of all the political parties in the House of Commons were very much appreciated. Pro-Palestinian demonstrations reflected the views of only a very small percentage of the population and condemnation of Hamas was almost universal.

In times of trouble the synagogue becomes a gathering place where members can unite and attendances at services increased. Central received many letters of sympathy from their neighbours and the local police were very supportive as well.

At such times of crisis it is reassuring to know that all the organisations which matter in this country are united in condemning antisemitism. If you have the government and the Crown on your side there is really not too much to worry about.

Many organisations continued to use the building, but these were strictly peripheral to its main raison d'être which was, of course, to provide a place of worship. Over the years there was now a solid base of attending members and the morning and evening services continued to be conducted in the traditional way.

There is a limit, however, to the influence a Synagogue body can have on its members. Faith has to come from an individual's personal beliefs and is often a very private aspect of someone's thinking. It can also change over the years and wax and wane. The Synagogue is a potentially powerful way to help a member through life.

Morris Roth, the Beadle, died in 1958. He came from a family of Beadles, where his father, Tobias Roth and his brother, Raphael, had both served as Beadles for London Synagogues for many years; Raphael at the New West End. Philip Taylor wrote in the *Jewish Chronicle*:

> He earned the respect and esteem of the members as well as many visitors to the Synagogue by his unswerving zeal and devotion to his duties.

It was unlikely that anyone would have noticed that the Minister who had served for eight years had the obituary provided by Sir Isaac, but not the Beadle who had served 31 years. The Roth family would have been proud to have a tribute from an illustrious leader like Sir Isaac, but it was still a society where class mattered.

Certainly, Morris Roth had worked hard for various volunteer organisations. He was a long-time member of the St. Johns Ambulance Brigade and for many years the Scoutmaster of the 24th St. Marylebone Troop. The new Beadle had to be under 45 and the salary was £500 a year, which was the starting wage of a university graduate at the time. He also had to assist the Secretary.

A memorial service was held in July 1958 for another distinguished member, Sir Louis Sterling. (1879-1958). He had started life as a newspaper boy in New York, but came to Britain and became the doyen of the gramophone industry. Few businessmen were as well liked as Sir Louis and the Synagogue had a full complement of recording artists in a service conducted by Rabbi Louis Jacobs.

The charitable benevolence of Sir Isaac Wolfson led to the creation of the Wolfson Foundation which had assets of at least £6 million, mostly in Great Universal Store shares. Among the trustees, beside members of the Wolfson family, were Lords Nathan, Burkett and Evans and the Director and Secretary was Lieutenant General Sir Harold Redman. An immense number of major charitable donations would be forthcoming in future years. In 1958 alone, the Westminster Hospital School of Nursing, London University and the British Empire Cancer Campaign each received £150,000 and among other gifts were £120,000 to the National Playing Fields Association. (£150,000 in 1958 is £3,500,000 today.)

In 1959 a student room at Jews' College was dedicated to Simeon Isaacs, who had studied there for five years. Simon Hass conducted the service and the Chief Rabbi said:

> He had been one who had understood and appreciated the difficulties as well as the aspirations of students, particularly those

who proposed to dedicate their lives, ambitions and energies to the service of the Almighty and of the Jewish people.

There was a lot to celebrate in 1960. In July the Golden Jubilee of the Girl Guides was marked by a service in the shul attended by 500 girl guides from all over the country. There were many from overseas, including the commissioners for the West Indies, Northern Rhodesia and Ireland and girl scouts from Israel. The chief rabbi conducted the service in the presence of the chief guide, Lady Olave Baden-Powell.

In November Cyril Shine received a signal honour when Sir Bernard Waley-Cohen became Lord Mayor of London, representing, appropriately, the Worshipful Company of Clothworkers. He appointed the rabbi as his Domestic Chaplain. This was the first time a Jewish Chaplain had been selected for the role although there had been several Jewish Lord Mayors before Waley-Cohen. Four of the seven had been members of the Central.

It was an additional distinction when the Lord Mayor in full ceremonial dress, came to the shul on the first shabbat after his inauguration; another first, with the Chief Rabbi giving the address and a congregation of 800. He came again with the Sheriffs and officers of the City of London for a civic service in the synagogue in December; the Chief Rabbi recalled the occasions in the 19th century when the Lord Mayor held meetings at the Mansion House to protest at the persecution of the Jews in Russia. It was typical of the status of Britain and its empire in those days that a London politician could make an international statement of this kind.

Sir Bernard was the son of Sir Robert Waley Cohen. One of his predecessors as Lord Mayor had been Sir Henry Isaacs, who had held the office in 1889. Sir Henry was very concerned about riding in the Lord Mayor's coach in the inaugural procession on the Sabbath, but the City fathers would not compromise and Sir Henry went ahead. Sir Bernard did likewise. The Central members supported all the political parties; in 1961 Charles Gilbert became chair of the new South Paddington Liberal Association and welcomed Lord Samuel, who at 91 was still able to address the audience for half an hour.

A further notable service in December 1960 would be the centenary of the London Board of Jewish Religious Education, at which the Chief Rabbi spoke again. The Central was, of course, packed as the congregation awaited the VIPs. When everybody was settled, the doors were opened and a long line of distinguished clerics marched through the synagogue in a stately fashion to the area of the Ark. Now Jewish ceremonies are not noted for the perfection of their organisation, there are more than a fair share of individualists. This procession, however, looked more like the Trooping of the Colour than the children milling about for sweets on Simchas Torah.

Fortunately, the Jewish traditions were in safe hands because when the procession reached the Ark, nobody had the faintest idea where they were supposed to sit. The column broke up into small revolving circles, while an official came out of the congregation, armed with a notebook, and tried to make sense of the arrangements. At least one member of the congregation, the present writer, breathed a sigh of relief as the procession tried to sort itself out; our great traditions were maintained. Membership increased by 100 in the next year.

The relations between the Church and the Synagogue were always very friendly. At one official dinner, the Archbishop of York, Dr. Donald Coggan, addressed the Lord Mayor in Hebrew and asked Rabbi Shine for his opinion of its quality. Cyril Shine assured him that the Hebrew was excellent but that it was delivered with a Manchester accent! Dr. Coggan had taught semitics at Manchester University. Cyril Shine's undergraduate sense of humour still came to the fore on occasions.

The quality of Simon Hass' singing was becoming well known. In December 1961 he was invited to an evening organised by the Friends of the Zionist Federation Educational Trust, the Educational Branch of the Jewish Agency and the Israeli Students Association. The lecture that evening was on the Maccabees and given by the famous Anglo-Jewish historian, Cecil Roth. Afterwards Simon Hass performed in Hebrew and Yiddish, and there was a contribution by the Central childrens' choir who sang Chanukah songs. Simon Hass helped raise money as well for a Hospital compound in Herzliya when he sang at the beginning of the Jewish Music Month in December 1962.

In September 1962, Cyril Shine and Simon Hass had gone to the Combined Charities Committee home for the Aged and Infirm in Grayshott in Surrey to consecrate the Hyam and Jessie Hyams wing. In his address Cyril Shine said that the home must be a source of envy to social workers throughout the country but not all hard work for charity is successful. The location in Grayshott was, in fact, too far to be easily accessible for relatives and the home closed in 1975.

In 1963 too Simon Hass started a Selichoth midnight service on the eve of the festival of Rosh Hashonah. The crowds who came had to be marshalled by the police. Over the years the services were widely reported and became known as the Jewish Midnight Mass. This was popularly changed to Midnight Hass. His very intelligent and charming wife was Elaine, but she died of cancer at 62 in 1995. She had been an enormous help

9. Reverend Simon Hass – A great Cantor

to her husband who she had married when she was eighteen and was a pillar of strength to the synagogue's Ladies Guild.

Educated at South Hampstead High School, Elaine Hass was clever, vivacious and committed to good causes. She was a member of the 35s, trying to get permission for Russian Jews to emigrate, helped sufferers from Alzheimers and was part of the Synagogue's Chevra Kadisha, looking after the bodies of the deceased. She was also a good poet and worked with her husband for 42 years. It was unusual for the wives of chazans to be so prominent and there was some envy, but she carried on with her work unperturbed. In her memory Simon Hass created the Elaine Hass Memorial Trust which has since made substantial donations to good causes.

Another innovation in 1963 saw London Synagogues combining to offer a Combined Adult School for Jewish Studies. Cyril Shine was the lecturer on Basic Judaism on Wednesdays. Providing friendship and company for the members always depended on a few people doing a lot of work. The Central Friendship Club, started in 1958 fulfilled that role and an anniversary lunch was held at the Synagogue in December 1965. There was a relaunch in 2014 when Ze'ev Galibov offered his home for similar gatherings.

One event which was well supported was a concert by Simon Hass in aid of the Hebron Jewish Youth Club in November 1963 with the London Jewish Male Choir. His devotion to the Central was well illustrated at the time of the Holydays in 1964. He had fallen and been taken to hospital to deal with an injured leg. He insisted, however, on being released to conduct the service on Yom Kippur and went back to hospital the day after. He had done a concert tour of Israel in the summer and faced criticism at home that chazzanut was becoming more like concerts. He replied:

> People tend not to apportion the importance of beauty in our services but we have hundreds of laws concerning the importance of beauty. There is a Talmudic saying "where there is song there is prayer." There is no doubt that the souls of young people are today hungry and searching for something beyond the materialism of their everyday lives. They can be brought to religion through music. They often tend to feel that Judaism is morbid and depressing, and we must prove to them that this is not true.

A notable service was held at the Synagogue in December 1964 to mark the 65th anniversary of the No: 30 (East London) Division of the St. Johns Ambulance Brigade, at which the Drummers of the Infantry Battalion of the Honourable Artillery Company played the Last Post and Reveille.

In 1965 the Greater London Council were intent on building a new ring road which became the Westway, and to do this they needed to buy and demolish the Bayswater Synagogue. There were considerable protests but the needs of the West End Jewish community were well covered by the Central, the Western, the New West End and the new Marble Arch synagogue. The Marble Arch contained a fine banqueting suite and, like the Central, was wholly owned by the United Synagogue.

The loss of the Bayswater was particularly hard on the rabbi, Raymond Apple, and in his valedictory sermon, he voiced his regret in a way which would not have been necessary at the Central. He said of the task of the rabbi:

> He must try to take no notice of those who speak contemptuously of him and deliberately misinterpret his work - and I cannot pretend that there are none such at Bayswater....The historic concept is that of a Bet Am, a house of the people, which brings together people of all kinds, of different backgrounds, of diverse intents, all initiated by their common Judaism, to have Jewish experiences and be inspired intellectually and emotionally, to carry the values and teachings of Judaism into daily life.

This was well understood at the Central and it would now be up to them to carry on the traditions, while Raymond Apple would do the same back in his native Australia, where he became the rabbi of the Great Synagogue in Sydney and the Av Beth Din for many years. Synagogue politics are often not helpful.

The Bayswater Synagogue had nearly been destroyed in an arson attack in 1965. It was one of several crimes of arson against Synagogues from November 1964 to October 1966. It stopped when ten members of Colin Jordan's National Front fascist organisation were charged at the Old Bailey. The offences included daubing swastikas on the doors of the Central and the Old Bailey building. Found guilty, the men were sentenced to between three and five years' imprisonment. Every British government was determined to protect the many religious congregations in the country.

The demolition of the Bayswater left the Central as the oldest major synagogue in the West End, apart from the Western which joined the Marble Arch in the years to come. The Central had the more imposing building and it, therefore, became the centre for many tourists anxious to worship in a fine Synagogue which had stood the test of time. It was also a target for antisemites and during the trial of offenders at the Old Bailey more swastikas were daubed on the Synagogue doors.

Where the Russian Jews could not emigrate, the BBC Russian Service tried to reassure them that they were not forgotten. Simon Hass recorded the Central Kol Nidre service in 1966, with Dayan Maurice Swift giving a sermon which was translated into Russian for the broadcast. Simon Hass had given three concerts in Israel that August and had to deny that he was thinking of accepting one of several offers he had received from the United States. He said:

> I have been deeply disturbed by the recent split in the Orthodox community

but he continued to conduct the full Selichot service in September, which still started at midnight. The Jacobs affair had been very disruptive, but Simon Hass was too attached to the synagogue to really think of moving. Events in Israel were now of major concern to the congregation and in 1967, when another war broke out, a day of Prayer and Intercession was held. The synagogue was thronged with worshippers who left work to attend continuous services.

During the Six Day War crowded meetings were held at which the support of the community was paramount. When the war was won, a Thanksgiving Service was naturally held, and it was also a recognition that after thousands of years Jerusalem was once again united under Jewish government. A year later the Central Synagogue Joint Palestine Appeal was formed by Alec Coleman and Cyril Shine and was soon very active. Cyril Shine joined a delegation of rabbis who visited Israel in 1967 and gave a first-hand report of his findings to the Central Cultural Society, in association with the Zionist religious Mizrachi Federation.

In 1967 the Central had filled another gap for the community. Hillel House, a major social centre for Jewish students was to be knocked down so that a better one could be put up in its place. That would halt the provision of kosher meals for a time and so, during the rebuilding, the Central undertook to provide them out of Hallam Street. A report of the financial position of the Kosher School Meals Service made the point that only 24 Central members had donated to its funds, which were considerably in deficit, but the cost of the student meals and the Synagogue's generosity in providing them, was unfairly not mentioned.

Israel Brodie had retired in 1965 and Immanuel Jakobovits was appointed to succeed him in 1967. He had been the Chief Rabbi in Ireland for 10 years and was currently the rabbi of the prestigious Fifth Avenue Synagogue in New York. He was well settled there and didn't want to take on the onerous position of Chief Rabbi in Britain. There had been an alternative choice, but unfortunately he fell ill and there had to be a replacement.

Isaac Wolfson went to New York to try to persuade him and managed to do so, with the aid of Immanuel Jakobovits' wife Amelie, whose father, the Chief Rabbi of France, told him that it was his duty. Jakobovits was installed in 1967 and worked well with Isaac Wolfson.

The new Chief Rabbi was an expert on Jewish medical ethics and a first-class diplomat. Like his predecessors, he was to be found at the Central on the first day of Succot and worked hard with Solomon Schonfeld to produce more Jewish schools.

It was, however, in keeping to Jewish traditions that he gained the favour of Margaret Thatcher, the prime minister. The Archbishop of Canterbury had produced a paper complaining that the government wasn't doing enough for poor people. He wanted the maximum support and asked the chief rabbi to sign the document. Immanuel Jakobovits kept to Jewish traditions and had to regretfully decline. He pointed out that the principle of government helping poor people was not the Jewish way. It was the Jewish practice to provide the poor with a sum of money at no interest, in order that they could start a business and work their way out of poverty.

Margaret Thatcher was delighted because it was her thinking as well. Immanuel Jakobovits found himself in the House of Lords, the first chief rabbi ever to gain the honour. He was robed in the Moses Room at the Lords and when he made his first address pointed out that he was following in the footsteps of the prophet.

Leonard Wolfson took over from his father from 1963 to 1970 and the generosity of the Wolfsons continued to benefit non-Jewish causes as well as those of the community. In 1966 Wolfson College, Oxford was opened, and the Queen did the honours when Wolfson College, Cambridge was opened in 1977. The only other name to be found attached to university colleges at both Oxford and Cambridge was Jesus.

Leonard Wolfson did not want to have coteries of Honorary Officers sitting for indefinite periods as Synagogue wardens. He was on a United Synagogue committee in 1968 which recommended that Honorary Officers should only serve for seven years and he, therefore, stood down in 1970. He was elected again, however, when he had become Lord Wolfson in 1972, and some Honorary Officers in the future did serve more than seven years.

Jack Steinberg served as a warden from 1963-1966. He was, by marriage, part of the Wolfson family and a very generous supporter of the Synagogue. In business he was for some years the Vice Chairman of the Clothing Export Council and a member of the Clothing Economic Development Committee. He served alongside Alfred Levy with the distinguished lawyer, Lionel Swift as Financial Representative. Lionel Swift was the son of Rev. Harris Swift, who was the minister at St. Johns Wood for many years.

Aron Stoutsker died in July 1968 when he was 86 years old. His wife had died in the January. The regard in which he was held was well illustrated by the nine ministers who took part in his memorial service. Aron Stoutsker had been the cantor in Synagogues in Regensberg, Paris, the Great in Amsterdam and the Central. He was so well liked that Leopold Grabowski came from the Krystalgade Synagogue in Copenhagen to participate in the memorial service. It was difficult to accept that he would no longer be part of the cantorial world.

Obituaries recall the highlights of a life and those for Aron Stoutsker followed a common pattern. He had been born in Poland and appointed to the Great Synagogue in Amsterdam in 1913. His voice was so good that the congregation overflowed into the street for the Friday night service. In 1924 Queen Wilhelmina came to the shul and Rev. Stoutsker was presented to her. In 1925 he became the chazan at the Central and stayed in post for 25 years. He entertained a good deal and celebrities like Sophie Tucker, the Broadway star, was just one who enjoyed his hospitality. The Stoutskers had been pillars of the synagogue all that time, but the obituarist recognised their difficulties when he said of Dora Stoutsker:

> Dependent on the rather meagre salary of a minister, she contrived nevertheless not only to educate her children at the best schools but also to ensure for them a musical education.

There was, of course, a well-attended memorial service for Aron Stoutsker but the "meagre salary" attached to the office hardly reflected the value of his long-term contribution.

In 1968 Emil Nemeth also died; he was only 57. He had served the Central from 1940-1947. Emil Nemeth had been born in Hungary but left for England in 1921. He went to the yeshiva Etz Haim and obtained his BA. In 1963 at Jews College he was given semicha. After his stint at the Central he spent 21 years at the Highgate Synagogue where he was remembered for never saying an unkind word. He was also noted for having a tremendous strength of character and he rebuilt the membership of the small Synagogue so that it now remains in existence under Rabbi Nicky Liss, the grandson of Hyman Liss, the Financial Representative of the Willesden Synagogue for many years.

Among the distinguished speakers in the Synagogue in 1968 was Rabbi Simcha Teitelbaum, the principal of the Yeshiva High School in Queens, New York. Simon Hass was prepared to travel as well and in February went to Sussex University at the invitation of the Jewish Society, to give a concert of liturgical music, which was very well received.

The Synagogue continued to have one great advantage for Jews everywhere. It had full services morning and evening every day of the week. Many synagogues couldn't muster ten men for evening services but there was always the necessary minyan (ten men) at the Central.

Today one of the devotees is Michael Bayer who arrives about seven in the morning and produces plates of bagels, bridge rolls and other delicacies for the regulars. Prayers are followed by breakfast, generally sponsored to commemorate happy events, like birthdays, wedding anniversaries and other family occasions. To enable everybody to get to their offices, the congregants can always get away by 8.30. A pool of more than 100 congregants support the morning services.

One of those who took advantage of the daily services was Michael Howard. He became the leader of the Conservative party in opposition in 2003 and the question it raised was whether a Jew could become prime minister. In the event, the Conservatives lost the election and Michael Howard resigned. He was born Michael Hecht in Swansea of a Romanian immigrant father, was brought up Orthodox, but married out of the faith. He would go to the Central, though, when he had yahrzeit, (the anniversary of his father's death), and take the service in the manner born.

Throughout the years in which the Synagogue had existed, the appearance of the Ministers and Honorary Officers had only enhanced the image. The appropriate dress for a synagogue minister and Honorary Officer is not to be found in Jewish law though. The vicar's "dog" collar was invented by a Church of Scotland minister, Donald McLeod, in 1865.

In the time of Hermann Adler as chief rabbi, the influx of Jews from Eastern Europe made it desirable to emphasise the English nature of Jewish ministers. So, the Chief Rabbi decided that they should be referred to as Reverends and many wore dog collars. Indeed, there is a picture of Chief Rabbi Hertz at a meeting with his ministers in the 1920s, and while few of them were wearing yarmulkes, almost all of them were wearing dog collars.

As the Victorian dress of the male upper classes included a top hat, the Central Synagogue Honorary Officers always wore them until long after the new synagogue had been consecrated. The Beadle wore a top hat as well, together with a long black coat, and this mode of dress is illustrated in the picture of the first wedding in 1872.

Aaron Levy Green only wore a minister's large yarmulke, but Samuel Lyons, the second reader, wore a top hat.

One of the contentious issues which all the synagogues faced was the introductions of the Israeli Hebrew pronunciation. Chief Rabbi Brodie had ruled against it, but in 1968 Chief Rabbi Jakobovits had said that synagogues could choose which form of pronunciation they preferred. There had been a lot of support for the Israeli pronunciation, but after three years the *Jewish Chronicle* reported that few Synagogues had actually taken up the option. Cyril Shine had to admit that while it was taught in the Hebrew classes, that was as far as it had gone in most cases.

Cyril Shine was becoming a public figure. In January 1969 the Iraq government publicly hanged fourteen alleged Israel spies in Baghdad to the horror of the Western world. A major demonstration at the Iraq embassy followed, where over a thousand Jews and non-Jews gathered to protest. It ended at midnight when Cyril Shine said kaddish to the assembled throng.

By 1969 Cyril Shine had been appointed chair of the council of United Synagogue ministers. The cause of Jewish education was dear to his heart. He joined the committee of the London Board of Jewish Religious Education in 1970 and immediately suggested that all United Synagogue ministers be invited to such meetings as they had a major part to play in the education of the children. In some ways the ministers were still treated like second class citizens. He also thought that parents should pay for the education. He was reported as castigating the state of barmitzvahs too.:

> For the majority of Anglo-Jewry the Barmitzvah today is a farce, a fetish, nothing more than the medium for a party in the West End.

What Rabbi Shine wanted was for every Barmitzvah boy to have to pass an examination before being allowed to be barmitzvah. The situation at the time was that this applied only if the boy wanted to say the Haftorah. The Rabbi was helped in both his objectives by Reginald Phillips who gave a £500 prize to the best pupil in the classes and £50,000 to help deaf and blind children. In all Reginald Phillips, a property developer, gave over a million pounds to charity.

It was also in 1969 that the Joint Treasurer of the Israeli Philharmonic Orchestra, Manya Brodetsky, died in London. Her colleague, Victor Mishcon, wrote with affection about her as the wife of Selig Brodetsky, (1888-1954) the second president of the Hebrew University. Selig Brodetsky was another immigrant from Eastern Europe who broke many barriers.

The son of a Russian synagogue beadle he won a scholarship to Trinity College, Cambridge and then became the Senior Wrangler. Boys from poor families were not expected to win such high honours and Selig Brodetsky went on to a distinguished career as a mathematics academic. It wasn't his only ability though. During the First World War he had much to do with the development of submarines periscopes.

The daughter of an Antwerp diamond merchant, Manya Brodetsky's memorial service at the Central brought Israel Brodie to the pulpit and many distinguished members of the community to pay her tribute. She was so highly regarded that the memorial service was held in association with the Board of Deputies, the British Council of the Shaare Zedek Hospital, the Federation of Women Zionists, the Friends of the Israel Philharmonic Orchestra and the Zionist Federation. The Brodetskys were a great example of what could be achieved from humble beginnings.

Another member of the synagogue was knighted in the 1969 New Year's Honours list. Sir John Cohen, the founder of Tesco, commemorated his wife's parents by funding a room at Jews' College and the Chief Rabbi consecrated it with Cyril Shine in attendance. The emeritus chief rabbi, Israel Brodie gave the second Sir Winston Churchill Memorial lecture to the Central's Cultural Society on Jewish Scholarship in Mediaeval England. A year later there was another memorial service for Charles Wolfson who had done a great deal for the synagogue; the Chief Rabbi conducted the memorial service. In his lifetime Charles Wolfson had done immense good and the Charles Wolfson Charitable Trust is still a major supporter of many organisations.

Another problem for the United Synagogue was demographic. The Jewish population continued to leave some districts and set up home in others. As a result there was no Synagogue for 260 families in Chigwell, or for 300 families in Belmont. The solution considered by the US in 1975 was to sell some synagogues in areas where there were more Synagogues than were needed. In the West End this was the case, but suggestions that the Central give up its independence by joining with another West End synagogue were firmly resisted by the members. In a time of rampant inflation the Central was still well able to keep its financial head above water.

One of the longest traditions of the Jews is providing help to their communities in trouble anywhere in the world. Appeals for assistance in rebuilding desecrated synagogues, supporting communities expelled from their native lands, ransoming those captured by mediaeval pirates and looking after displaced emigrants, were standard practice ever since the Romans expelled the Jews from the Holy Land. It was natural, therefore, that donations came for Israel from the Central members, and that days of prayer were held in the Synagogue when the wars broke out in the Middle East in 1967 and 1973.

Israel's main need was still to grow its population and the British Aliyah Movement was started in 1969 and moved its headquarters to the Central. The tragedy of the Holocaust remained difficult to bear over the years. It was not unhappily the first massacre of Jewish communities, though by far the worst. One traditional way in which the memories of the congregations are kept alive has always been by saving their sifrei torahs.

There is, for example, a very small community in Dubrovnik in Croatia where the synagogue is just a room in a house in a side street. In the place of honour, however, is a Sefer Torah which dates from the 13th century and its wording is as clear today as it was when it was written.

In 1967 the Central had received a Sefer torah which was among over 1,500 hidden away during the war by communities in Bohemia, Moravia and Silesia. It is no: 866 and was written in the 19th century in Lipnik in Czechoslovakia. The Baltic communities who had perished in the Holocaust were certainly not forgotten. A commemorative service was held at the Synagogue by the Association of Baltic Communities and Israel Brodie gave the address.

In the creation of a Jewish community, the possession of a Sefer torah is more important than anything else. Services can be held in any room or in the open air, and marriages should be conducted outside. During the festival of Succot, members should eat and pray outside as well. The Sefer torah in the Synagogue though is traditionally to be found securely housed in the Ark.

Jewish Ministers are teachers and not intermediaries with the Almighty. The Sefer Torah, however, is a fundamental. The continuity stretches back to Biblical times and their importance cannot be overestimated. All Sifrei Torah are handwritten and there can be no corrections; they have to be perfect and the scribe is particularly highly regarded for his skill.

In November 1968 Charles Wolfson had presented a new Sefer Torah to the Synagogue at a special service. It was the first celebration of its kind for 50 years and the honour of writing the last letters was given to the family and senior members of the congregation. The original Central Sefer Torah was, of course, brought from the Great Synagogue for the Branch.

Over the years other sifrei torah were presented to the Synagogue for safe keeping; 23 were accumulated by 1973. When two more were brought to the Synagogue from Gruzia in Russia by Eric Miller, it was pointed out that at least three congregations in Australia were short of sifrei torah and the Central didn't need so many. This was corrected. The other viewpoint was identified by Simon Hass who said:

> I spent the war years in a Russian camp in Siberia and being able to feel the scrolls that came of so much suffering affects me very greatly. We are going to give them a good home.

The essential need was to keep the sifrei torah intact, and many had moved for centuries from community to community and would continue to do so.

In 1970 the Synagogue celebrated its centenary and the Emeritus Chief Rabbi, Israel Brodie, came to conduct the service. Reginald Maudling, the Home Secretary, was the principal guest and Alfred Levy, the warden, paid tribute to the minister's predecessors who:

> have earned our heartfelt thanks for their steadfast protection of our religious and other freedoms....That we should, any of us, be privileged to celebrate this Centenary is due in no small measure to the admirable, even enviable, tolerance of the country in which we live, and we should not forget that many of our brethren elsewhere are less fortunate.

This was particularly true behind the Iron Curtain. The struggle to get permission for the Russian Jews to emigrate to Israel was ongoing and the Rumanian Jews had to be ransomed at vast expense to get visas from their country's dictator. The total of the bribes ran into millions of pounds which were donated by Jews all over the world.

In 1970 Cyril Shine wrote a history of the Synagogue. The honorary officers, Alfred Levy, Eric Miller and Lionel Swift commented in it:

> The tolerance of others, whilst a most favourable background, would not of itself have sufficed to create and nurture our unique Synagogue. We needed three more elements: a unique tradition, a unique congregation and a unique Ministry. We hope we will be forgiven for our proud assertion that we have through the years been blessed with all three.

The Synagogue was certainly a credit to the community though "unique" applied primarily to its longevity. Like so many fine old traditions, its eminence could arouse envy. Chaim Bermant was the foremost Jewish newspaper columnist and in 1971 he wrote of the Central that it "was a unique example of gown merchant baroque". He added that "the interior of the Central is so gaudy that one would be advised to approach it with a pair of sunglasses."

But then, as Aeschylus, the ancient Greek playwright said, "It is in the character of very few men to honour without envy a friend who has prospered". Chaim was a fine writer, but he was devoted to the Shtiebel in Hampstead Garden Suburb, reminiscent of his family's original East European shul. Any suggestion of the superiority of a so-called Cathedral Synagogue was likely to arouse his journalistic ire.

Talmudic study, involving members of the community, was not neglected by Cyril Shine. For eight and a half years he had been leading a group of members analysing Tractate Berakhot. This is the first tractate of the Mishnah and the Talmud and covers the rules of daily prayer and the blessings, including the shema.

It was an important enough exercise for the Chief Rabbi to come to the Synagogue to mark the ending of the study. It was typical of very Orthodox congregations. One synagogue in Sunderland studied a page of the Babylonian Talmud every day, which took them 25 years and was completed four times in their existence. Many Sunderland professionals – lawyers, doctors, accountants –would regularly attend. Studies of this nature have been a feature of Synagogue practice for centuries.

In December 1971 the Central was chosen for a service to mark the 50th anniversary of the Royal British Legion. There are 2,500 branches of the British Legion and one of them is the Monash Branch, named after the Jewish General who commanded the Australian forces during the Great War. When he died in 1931, he was given a state funeral in Australia and 300,000 were estimated to have taken part. John Monash is considered by many experts to have been the most effective allied general in the Great War, though the comment at the time was that the allied armies consisted of lions led by donkeys.

Field Marshall Haig was said to have postulated that as the allies had a quarter of a million more soldiers than the axis, if the casualties were equal, the allies would win on numbers alone. The casualties were certainly horrific and included the Centrals' losses.

The Monash branch was formed in Winnipeg in 1934 for Jews who had served in the Canadian forces and were anxious to counteract the growth of antisemitism by the Nazis at the time. Members of the British Monash branch now paraded their standards in the Synagogue and the Emeritus Chief Rabbi Brodie gave the address.

After Israel became a reality in 1948 it was agreed to have an appeal on

Yom Kippur and this produced substantial funds for Israeli charities. The argument over the coming years would be whether Israeli charities needed the money more than local charitable organisations. Initially, when Israel was in poor straits, it was not so contentious, but as the state became wealthier, the arguments became more heated.

How the money was distributed was not often disclosed. In 1972, however, the Joint Palestine Appeal did give a comprehensive breakdown of what happened to the £410,000 raised at Yom Kippur that year. It noted, however, that only one synagogue kept some of the money for local charities and that was the Central. Leonard Wolfson was in the Box at the time with Lionel Swift, and their concern for local charities was well known. Lionel Swift had been the Financial Representative and knew how much support many home charities needed. It was not very welcome publicity but there was a principle at stake.

It wasn't that the Synagogue lacked enthusiasm for the State of Israel. An Aliyah exhibition was set up in the hall to provide advice and publicity for those thinking of emigrating. Apart from an information desk, there were such diverse attractions as children's paintings on the subject of "How I see myself in Israel", a multi-coloured illuminated map portraying Israel's absorption facility, and other illustrations of life in the Holy Land. The exhibit went all round the country during the summer. There was also an Aliyah Club which had been established in December 1969 and proved so popular that 200-300 attended regularly and it had to be moved to the Central as it outgrew the original meeting room.

11

The difficult years

With inflation skyrocketing in the 1970s there was a need for more finance for the Synagogue's charities and the question arose again of how the results of the Joint Palestine Appeal should be used in future years. All the British synagogues continued to devote their whole collection to Israel, but once again the Central decided to only give 50% of the money raised to the JPA.

The thorny question of race relations was achieving more prominence now and in May 1971 there was a Race Relations shabbat service which Sir Samuel Fisher, the chair of the Working Party on the subject attended, together with Lady Fisher. It was a busy weekend. On the Sunday Eric Miller laid the foundation stone of a new club house at the East of London Jewish Youth Club, of which Viscount Bearsted and Louis Mintz, were presidents.

The Synagogue's central position in the West End of London was naturally a favourite for tourists. One who came for the High Holydays one year was a famous American opera singer who was also an outstanding cantor. He recounted that he had been asked to take the service at the Synagogue in Independence, Missouri, to which town the former president, Harry Truman had retired.

Truman invited him to lunch, but he arrived an hour late because the service in the Synagogue had been a long one and he was davening. He said he apologised profusely for keeping Truman waiting and the former president said "You had to choose between G-d and the President of the United States. You made the right decision."

Naturally, the community and the Israelis wanted to increase understanding of the new state and one result was the Bridge in Britain Association. What was the country really like? A part of the public relations campaign was when twenty-three, mostly non-Jews, including participants from Eton, Gordonstoun and other public schools, came to the Synagogue for a get-together before going to Israel for six months, prior to university. They found it a very worthwhile experience.

At the Munich Olympics in 1972 there had been a horrific massacre of Israeli athletes. It was a terrible outrage and Albert Rothschild decided to give an ambulance to Magen David Adom as a memorial to the tragedy to mark his 83rd birthday. Its consecration was at the Central. Over the years the Israelis killed the assassins.

The long process of creating the Synagogue stained-glass windows was finally completed in 1973 and Rabbi Shine consecrated them at the end of Passover that year. During the Yom Kippur war he also presided over a Service of Intercession for Israel on Shemini Atzeret. He had actually heard of the start of the Yom Kippur War on the day and announced it to the congregation from the pulpit. The previous week the congregation chose to leave by the back door of the Synagogue. About six people had come to picket the Synagogue with placards reading "Remember the Israeli-Jewish domination of the Palestinian-Arab people".

They themselves didn't remember that the Arab League said in 1948 that the aim of its five armies invading the country, was to massacre all the Jews in Palestine. Fortunately, their rhetoric was more than their fighting ability. In the years to come the ambition of many Arab governments in the Middle East was to destroy Israel, but their public emphasis was always on the Arab refugees who had left the country during the War of Independence. They had fled when the Mufti of Jerusalem told them that if the Jews won, their lives were in danger. Although this proved untrue, those who left the country were lodged in refugee camps in Arab countries rather than being absorbed into the general population.

The congregation's view was, nevertheless, that discretion was the better part of valour and the demonstration was allowed to continue.

In the 1974 war the Arabs attacked on Yom Kippur. The Israelis suffered substantial casualties and both Jewish and non-Jewish volunteers responded to the appeal for blood for the Israeli wounded. The need was urgent, and the Chief Rabbi agreed that Synagogues could be used on Succot for blood transfusion volunteers. The Synagogues chosen in London were Marble Arch and St. Johns Wood. It was a question of attending Succot services or being a blood donor, and many Central members chose to give blood.

They had been angered by another anti-Israel demonstration outside the Central on Rosh Hashonah. On a happier note Simon Hass had conducted a full Selichot service between Rosh Hashonah and Yom Kippur.

There were rabbis who did not feel that giving blood should take precedence over observing Succot, but Chief Rabbi Jakobovits held strong opinions and was a firm leader. In 1972 he had aroused criticism when he refused to allow the chief rabbi of Denmark, Rabbi Bent Melchior, to preach at the Kenton Synagogue. The reason he gave was that Rabbi Melchior was a Vice President of the World Council of Synagogues which had been founded by the American Jewish Conservatives who were not Orthodox and advocated their own form of Jewish practice.

Cyril Shine, still occupying the Chair of the Chief Rabbi's Council of Ministers, criticised the decision from the pulpit as unnecessarily discriminatory. He was not alone, and he felt that there could be more tolerance. He reminded the congregation that a well-known rabbi had refused to preach at the Central because it now had a mixed choir. He believed that the "narrowness and insularity" of some of the younger ministers could be harmful. The Chief Rabbi stood his ground.

In the spring Cyril Shine conducted Thanksgiving Services for the Israeli victory in the War. The other side of the coin had been a lecture in February by Salmond Levin, a senior member of the community, with the ominous title "For Whom the Bell Tolls".

In 1974 Sir Desmond Tuck died. He had not only served the synagogue with devotion, but his country as well. He was one of the first pilots when the Royal Flying Corps was founded during the First World War and spent many years in the Territorial Army. Another member of the Royal Flying Corps and the Central was Alfred Harrison, who was an air gunner and spent a year in a prisoner-of-war camp after being shot down. He would die in 1977. The Tucks, for nearly a century, were pillars of the Central community and their contribution deserves to be an important part of the Synagogue's history.

Philip Taylor also died in 1974. In a long association with the Synagogue, he had been in the choir in 1905, was the Financial Representative in 1947 and served as warden from 1948–1963. He was devoted to the Synagogue, but his later years were difficult, and he is only remembered by a plaque in the Synagogue hall marking its unveiling at the opening of the new synagogue. The stress of wartime when he served as an air raid warden, often looking in the dark for unexploded bombs, had resulted in his suffering a burst gastric ulcer. Philip Taylor took it in his stride and was in the Box the next Shabbat. The Synagogue had no more devoted servant for the next 20 years.

Cyril Shine was involved in many events in 1975. One was the memorial service for Rose Leigh, who died at 90. Many readers offer their condolences with entries in the *Jewish Chronicle*, but there were as many as 35 for Rose Leigh which was exceptional.

Another memorial service was held that year for Esther Immanuel whose employment company had found jobs for 200,000 people in its 100 branches. Among her benefactions was the Balfour Chair in the Economics of Government at Heriot Watt university in Edinburgh. The Rabbi also opened a block of flats for the elderly which had been financed by Sir John Cohen. It was the 33rd block built by the Jewish Welfare Board since its inception.

The year saw the 27th anniversary of the State of Israel and to mark it Cyril Shine again addressed the congregation at a joint service with five other communities, accompanied by both the Chief Rabbi and the Emeritus Chief Rabbi. Sir Ernest Chain's 70th birthday was celebrated at the Synagogue in June 1976 and to add additional distinction to the occasion, his son, Benjamin, leined.

The increasing average age of the members of the Synagogues in the West End led the United Synagogue to again consider reducing their number and this would also be a subject of discussion at many future meetings. In 1976 the synagogue lost its choirmaster when Pinchas Baumberg passed away. A noted scholar of Hebrew Literature, Pinchas Baumberg had worked well with Simon Hass and they had formed a very good team. The choir were still in good voice when a communal thanksgiving service was held on Sunday, 12 June 1977 to mark the Queen's Silver Jubilee; the Chief Rabbi gave the sermon to a congregation of 900.

The Chief Rabbi, Immanuel Jakobovits, was born in Germany and came to Britain as a refugee. Now, 40 years later, he was able to point out that Prince Philip was more often to be seen in a yarmulke than most Jews, and to congratulate the Queen for ensuring that Britain was:

> still the most civilised country, where decency, toleration, refinement, fair play and the simple courtesy of conduct - the concept of gentlemanliness - continue to prevail against the erosion of vulgarity, discrimination and the assertion of self, rampant in so many other parts of the world.

The annual Selichot service conducted by Simon Hass had its attraction reinforced in 1977. In September both the chief rabbi, Immanuel Jakobovits and the emeritus chief rabbi, Israel Brodie, joined the members of five other London synagogues at midnight. Timekeeping is not always a consideration with a Jewish service.

Simon Hass took the opportunity on several occasions to dedicate the service to such good causes as Soviet Jewry. He had celebrated his own silver jubilee as chazan in 1976 and had taken the opportunity to remark that he never quarreled with the rabbi "only about football teams". His eminence in the community was further illustrated by being asked to say kaddish at a meeting of the Polish Jewish Ex-Servicemen's Association.

Another Central tradition which marked its silver jubilee that year, was the Central Friendship Club, which provided an acceptable amelioration of the loneliness which many elderly members suffered otherwise.

It was natural that, on retirement, many members chose to leave London and the congregation may not have been aware that the long-time and popular Financial Representative, Jack Harris, had moved to Brighton and lost his wife, Ada, in 1973. In her memory he gave a handsome Megilla to the Brighton and Hove congregation. It was appropriate that there was a memorial service at the Synagogue addressed by the Chief Rabbi. Jack Harris had been the Financial Representative at the Central for sixteen years and on the Board of Management for 40 years. He, himself, died in 1975. He was a gregarious and popular character and kept the finances of the Synagogue in very good order at all times.

One of the most flamboyant wardens in the early 1970's was Sir Eric Miller who served from 1970-1974. From a humble background, Eric Miller became chair of the largest property company in the country and a friend of prime minister, Harold Wilson. There were, however, accusations of fraud and a great deal of adverse media coverage. Eric Miller took to carrying a gun and, in 1977, when he was 50 years old, he died from two gunshots at his home on Yom Kippur. The inquest returned a verdict of suicide but friends, like RAF hero, Douglas Bader, said that it couldn't be the case with the gun in question. The question was how and why would someone who committed suicide shoot himself twice?

The England football captain, Bobby Moore, came to the funeral at Willesden and a stand at Fulham Football ground was named after Sir Eric, who had been a director for many years. During his lifetime he had also been an important ally of the Israelis. He had even chartered a plane to take family and friends to Israel for his son's Barmitzvah. At the same time, he had removed him from Harrow after the boy complained of antisemitic bullying. Many grieved, as Eric Miller had done much good in his lifetime.

Over the years the Synagogue had lost a number of wardens and financial officers prematurely. Even so, the private lives of honorary officers seldom affected the performance of their Synagogue duties. There was much difference, however, between a mortal illness and a suicide. Eric Miller's relationship with the prime minister made it inevitable that his death would become major news and suspicion of malpractice reflected badly on the community. As friends questioned his death, the story would continue to be news for a long time.

There were always members of the medical profession in the Synagogue. In November a distinguished American member retired as the children's psychiatrist at the Leytonstone House Hospital. William Livingstone fought with the 8th army during the war and was so highly regarded by the hospital that he was both presented with a portrait when he finally left office and had a ward named after him. His interests included serving on the JNF Executive Golfers' Committee and he was very popular, together with his wife, Anne.

Leonard Wolfson took over the chair of Great Universal Stores when his father retired. His cousin, David, also a member, became Margaret Thatcher's Chief of Staff when she rose to be prime minister and was awarded a peerage in 1991. The records of David Wolfson's work for Margaret Thatcher show an important role in advising her on the full range of government actions. In 1977 Sir Isaac Wolfson turned 80 and the Chief Rabbi in the pulpit at the Synagogue praised his commitment to the community and said he could be considered as notable as the Rothschilds and Sir Moses Montefiore, which was praise indeed.

Sir Isaac had been a member of the Central for 54 years and president of the United Synagogue for eleven. He had also given £500,000 to build the Great Synagogue in Jerusalem and at this point the Wolfson Trust had donated £400 million to charity.

There was yet another peer in the Central congregation; Lord Victor Mishcon. Like the Wolfson family, the Mishcon ancestors were from Poland and his father, Rabbi Arnold Mishcon, was the minister to the Derby and Brixton communities. Arnold Mishcon was also one of the translators of the Babylonian Talmud into English but, unhappily, died at only 55.

His son set out to study law and started his own firm when he was only 18 years old. Throughout his life he was a regular attender at the Central and his practice became one of the most notable in the country. This was particularly the case when he represented Princess Diana in her divorce proceedings. He was an unsuccessful parliamentary candidate, but served as Chair of the London County Council when he was only 39 years old.

He was appointed to the Wolfenden Committee on Homosexualism, and the Mishcon Lectures were established in 1990 by University College London in his honour. After the passing of Sonny Freedman, he took on the responsibility of reading the book of Jonah on Yom Kippur afternoon, but he did so in English.

One of the members and a great name in retail clothing was Cecil Gee, who was the first to display clothes on rails rather than shelves. He was the epitomisation of the Swinging Sixties and Kings Road, Chelsea, producing everything from Demob Suits to James Bond outfits. Behind the scenes, however, he was born in Lithuania as Sasha Goldstein, a descendent of the Vilna Gaon. He was brought to Britain when he was seven and died in 1980 aged 77. The descendants of poverty-stricken immigrants were still making the grade.

Cyril Shine spoke his mind but was naturally on the Chief Rabbi's side on most occasions. He went to his defence when he was attacked by right wing members of the community for maintaining the traditional Anglo-Jewish approach. It was Cyril Shine who was reported as calling for more commitment, more loyalty and more tolerance.

He was also among the leaders in a 24-hour vigil outside the Soviet embassy, organised by 25 Pinner members of BBYO, the young people's social organisation, in December 1978. The Jews in Russia were still not allowed to emigrate and a group of Jewish women, known as the 35s, were also demonstrating, particularly on behalf of three Russian Jews – Josef Mendelovich, Josif Begun and Dr. Abram Kagan. During the day £1,000 was raised to finance their activities. The ranks of the 35s included Central members.

In January 1979 Cyril Shine was to be found presiding at the Synagogue at the 80th anniversary service of the East London branch of the St. Johns Ambulance Brigade. It was a busy life, representing the Synagogue on many different occasions. His wife, Sylvia Isaacs, was also a very hard worker for the Synagogue. In June 1977 when the Central Friendship Club celebrated its Silver Jubilee, this was only one of the charities which she had embraced.

The rabbi and Simon Hass were now called upon for the funerals of many leaders of the community. Lord Fisher had been the first Jewish mayor of Camden and there was a large gathering at Willesden for his interment in 1979, conducted by the two ministers. They worked independently as well. At the memorial service for Lord Fisher at the House of Commons, it was Simon Hass who was invited to say Kaddish. In April 1979 he participated in the World Symposium of Humanity Conference at Wembley, holding aloft the Star of David alongside the Moslem representative carrying the Red Crescent.

Leonard Wolfson presided at the Annual General Meeting and was able to announce that there was now a 300 waiting list for seats at the Synagogue. New faces were forthcoming to run the Synagogue administration, although those who had played their part in the past were only to be found in the minute books. In 1969, for example, Josey Freedman, the warden from 1940-1947, died at the grand old age of 94. He had contracted cancer in his seventies, but his nephew, who was a blood specialist, forecast correctly that as he was very slim, the cancer had little chance of killing him.

The Synagogue was a haven of calm in a country ravaged by terrible industrial relations. The average annual number of days lost to strikes in the 1970s was 12.9 million. In the winter of 1978-1979, that number increased to 29.5 million. This has to be compared with the figure for 2018 of 273,000, the lowest for 120 years. The result of the Yom Kippur war in 1973 was inflation which reached 24% in 1974. The price of a litre of oil was 16p in 1975 and £1.40 today.

The Synagogue was affected, like everybody else, by power cuts and dustmen on strike, but the combination of Cyril Shine, Simon Hass and Honorary Officers like Sidney Diamond and Leonard Wolfson kept it in good order. Sylvia Shine, Cyril Shine's wife, also played her part in recommending a degree of austerity when it came to weddings:

> It doesn't seem right to dress up too much when the whole world is in such turmoil. Nice to go for the simpler things. Anyway the sweetest dresses today are quite simple, high-necked long-sleeved styles, perhaps with a small unelaborated hat, like a turban.

When eventually the public had the opportunity to vote in a general election, they elected Margaret Thatcher, the first British woman prime minister, and the community provided her with a substantial number of Cabinet members.

As the members of Central had come from the East End, so the support for the Labour party, so strong in the 20th century, had moved towards Margaret Thatcher and the Conservatives, as the community became more middle class.

At the end of the decade, the congregation also lost one of its stalwarts in the death of Sir Ben Barnett at 85. Sir Ben (1894-1979) had been the Deputy Director General of the post office and much involved in the start of commercial television in 1954. He had been born in the East End and won the MC in the First World War, also being mentioned twice in dispatches. A jovial character, he well deserved to be in the National Portrait Gallery.

There was also a memorial service for Sir Ernest Chain, (1906-1979) who had been responsible for the development of penicillin and was awarded the Nobel prize for doing so. Ernest Chain was an emigrant from Germany before the war and Imperial College created a centre for him after the conflict to encourage him to stay in Britain. The death of such an eminent scientist made the choice of the Central for the memorial service and the presence of the Chief Rabbi an illustration of the Synagogue's importance for such Ashkenazi community occasions.

The service was held in conjunction with the Board of Deputies, the Anglo-Jewish Association, the Anglo-Israel Chamber of Commerce, B'nai Brith, the Friends of Bar Ilan and the Hebrew University, the Weizmann Institute and the World Jewish Congress. The world recognised that it owed a great deal to Ernest Chain.

In their own quiet way many members continued to do a great deal of good. A major supporter of the Yesodey Hatorah schools, Leslie Paisner, died at 70 in 1979. The Chief Rabbi said:

> As a Jew, a lawyer and simply as a beautiful human being, Leslie Paisner had few peers. He was possessed of an extraordinary capacity to radiate friendship and kindness, lavishing his own wisdom and help on numerous communal causes and countless individuals whose lives he enriched.

The Synagogue was also fortunate at that time to have Jack Linden as headmaster of the religion classes for a few years. He had been a teacher for the London Board of Jewish Religious Education since 1946 and was both highly experienced and very knowledgeable.

In 1980 Cyril Shine celebrated his own silver jubilee as the Central's minister and a weekend of celebrations saw the Chief Rabbi attending the shabbat service to pay honour to his efforts. There was a reception on the Sunday when further tributes were made and the rabbi was given a silver salver and a cheque which, if not speaking louder than words, was a fitting gift.

Cyril Shine's standing in the community was emphasised when he was asked with Simon Hass to conduct the commemoration service at Willesden for Chief Rabbi Israel Brodie who had died in 1979. He was also to be found at Hillel House with Rabbi Cyril Harris talking to the Yavneh students. He ministered to the congregation until 2002 and there was a memorial service after his passing at the age of 80 in 2003, which the Deputy Lord Mayor attended.

Leonard Wolfson was now a peer and gave an address. It reflected the state of play during the years Cyril Shine and Simon Hass worked together. He referred to Cyril Shine's "wise and witty sermons" and to "our superb Cantor".

That was the key point. Where the ministers at the Synagogue had always been senior to the chazanim, Simon Hass was the exception. He raised Jewish chazanut to a higher level. He gained the qualification of LLCM, which is a Licentiate of the London College of Music, and the equivalent of a third-year undergraduate degree.

He also recorded seven records with London Records and Decca. These were four versions of *Great Hebrew Prayers*, a record of *Cantorial and Jewish Folksongs* and *The Lord is my Strength*. When the Warsaw Ghetto annual memorial meetings were held, it was Simon Hass who was asked to say *El Mole Rachamim*, the memorial prayer.

It wasn't surprising that he was still regularly offered important and well rewarded pulpits in America, and it was appropriate that this was dealt with by members of the synagogue, like Jack Steinberg, supplementing his more inadequate United Synagogue salary. Not much had changed since the experiences of Aron Stoutsker. Simon Hass was always prepared to work for good causes. In 1981 to mark his 30 years as the chazan at the Central he gave a concert at the Royal College of Music, sponsored by the B'nai Brith and the Council of Christians and Jews.

It was always likely that Simon Hass' experiences in Siberia would affect his health in the long term and in 1988 he needed a heart bypass. He was lucky in one way that medicine had moved on to a point where the operation was possible. The first had only been in 1960. Philip Taylor would have survived if that had been generally possible in his time. The operation was now so successful, thank G-d, that the Chazan is still with us 30 years later, but died recently.

Cyril Shine, for his part, worked tirelessly to raise funds for the Jewish National Fund and did a great deal of charity work. The Hass family remembers that the two worked well together, which says a lot for both men. The Rabbi was always helpful. A man called Roderick Young, brought up as a Christian, discovered he was Jewish and called at the Synagogue one Saturday. He was about to be turned away when Rabbi Shine invited him in and talked to him at length.

The rabbi told him to find the necessary ketubim. (marriage certificates). Roderick Young became a Reform rabbi and served the Finchley Reform Synagogue for some years. Cyril Shine didn't turn people away, from wherever they came.

A lot of members did a great deal of good in their lifetimes but are long forgotten except by their families. In 1981, for instance, the distinguished barrister Lionel Roffe died at only 49. He was also a concert pianist and gave many recitals for charity. He supported the Red Cross, Talking Books for the Blind and in helping Israel's crippled children. As Shakespeare said "The evil that men do lives on; the good is oft interred in their bones." It was a difficult problem and to recognise extensive contributions when members ceased to be wardens, they were on occasions appointed Elders of the congregation. In 1982 Sidney Diamond and J. Castle were given that honour.

The Chief Rabbi as an expert on medical science, as it affected Judaism, gave an important address at the Central in 1983 to clarify the Din where new medication had been created. He made it clear, for instance, that fertility drugs were approved in the Talmud, which, as with many other laws, once again was way ahead of its time. He did not approve on the other hand of plastic surgery for sufferers from Downs Syndrome simply because the parents wanted their child to change its appearance. The only acceptable criterion he insisted upon was whether it would benefit the child.

The United Synagogue Community service chose the Central for a series of other lectures. They ranged from the Chief Rabbi giving another talk on the Jewish response to the latest advances in medical science to Rabbi Rosen considering whether Anglo-Judaism could survive. It was often postulated that Jews could survive persecution more easily than they could toleration.

Memorial services were held at the Central for non-members of the Synagogue but distinguished members of the community. One such was for Dr. Israel Feldman who died at 92 after a lifetime of support for a considerable number of the community's charities, particularly Children and Youth Aliyah. Dr. Feldman had been a warden at the Great Synagogue and had tried unsuccessfully to have it rebuilt after the war. He was a senior lecturer in Physiology at the London Hospital and for 27 years the president of the Royal British Legion (Hampstead branch). He came from a very Orthodox family, as his father was a founder of the Machzikei Hadath Synagogue. At the memorial service the Chief Rabbi spoke very warmly of all his efforts.

In 1983, in the Church of St. Georges in the East in the City, an Auschwitz exhibition attracted many thousands of children. The Bishop of Stepney pointed out the support the exhibition had had from all the nation's political leaders and took the opportunity of castigating the attacks on East End Moslems which were taking place at the time. More than 150 British Jews had died in Auschwitz. The exhibition had cost £30,000 to stage and the Bishop emphasised the importance of teaching children about the horrors of the Holocaust. At the opening. Simon Hass came to say Kaddish and sing a song which had been written by a victim.

One of the Synagogue's most distinguished members, Ellis Stanning, died in 1984. He had founded Lloyds Pharmaceuticals as a young man and had a very full life. For 30 years he had worked for the Jewish Lads and Girls Brigade, as chair of the council. He had also been on the Council of the Royal Albert Hall and had been made an Honorary Fellow of the Royal College of General Practitioners. The Ellis and Edna Stanning Jewish charity helped many worthy organisations and there was keen competition within the Jewish Lads Brigade for the Ellis Stanning Rose Bowl.

Whether there were too many Synagogues in the West End was a subject raised again at this time. The popularity of the Central was not matched by the numbers joining the Marble Arch synagogue and preliminary discussions were conducted in 1985 to consider the merging of the two synagogues. A committee of enquiry had suggested that if there wasn't a merger, both synagogues would decline over the years, but at an extraordinary general meeting at the Central only four of the 300 attendees voted in favour of the idea. For that many members to attend the meeting, the subject was obviously of major importance to them.

The members might be quite satisfied to leave the running of the Synagogue in the hands of the Honorary Officers as a general rule. If, however, the sheer existence of the Synagogue was ever threatened they could be guaranteed to turn out in large numbers to protect it. There was even support from New York where a former American London University student, Harold Aspis, remembered when the wardens had given him a free seat for the Yomim Nora'im. and always welcomed him warmly when he came on Shabbat.

The Central was over 100 years old, financially sound and had a 900-year lease. The Central Financial Representative, Peter Goldbart, assured the Jewish media that it would take at least ten years to come to any conclusion on amalgamation and no more was heard of it. In fact, it was the Marble Arch and the Western which eventually merged.

Peter Goldbart also represented the synagogue on the Board of Deputies and in 1986 was instrumental in solving one of their problems It was on the vexed question of how to stop deputies talking too long. Peter Goldbart and his wife built an electric light control system which flashed green, amber and red to warn the speaker how time was passing.

The US Council meeting at the time showed up some serious discord among the delegates, led by Cyril Shine. He was fighting for the middle ground again. He took the opportunity to criticise the "intransigence and extremism" of several United Synagogue ministers who he said were increasing the polarisation within the community. He still remembered the rabbi who objected to the Central's mixed choir, and he said he spoke for a number of ministers.

He also questioned the United Synagogue appointments committee, whose notable members consisted of the Chief Rabbi, the principal of Jews' College, (Jonathan Sacks at the time), a rabbi and a United Synagogue council member. He pointed out one minister who had abandoned bat chayil ceremonies, and refused to permit a wedding reception if there was mixed dancing. The very popular Rabbi Eddie Jackson, the Kenton minister, deplored the raising of the subject at the US Council meeting, preferring to let sleeping dogs lie, but the publicity was considerable. The traditions of Anglo-Jewry had no more devoted defender than Cyril Shine.

The children's classes at the Synagogue were now quite small and the London Board of Religious Education wanted the younger pupils to go to St. Johns Wood and the older to Hampstead. The parents' association at the Synagogue and the Board of Management rejected the idea and split from the London Board after two years of fruitless discussions. It was an expensive move, as the Synagogue still gave the Board £13,000 a year as their contribution to its activities.

The Board's case was that with such small numbers, the curriculum couldn't be sufficiently wide, and that in any event the families didn't live near the Synagogue. The parents though wanted the children to learn at the Synagogue and hence the split. It was an embarrassment for the London Board, but it kept the members with young children close to the Synagogue.

There were many forms of education. One lady member was author Rosemary Friedman, who in 1982 published *Proofs of Affection* which chronicled the life of a Jewish family throughout a year. As she said:

> I wanted to be informative about Jewish life without having to provide a glossary.

She has now published 21 novels and three non-fiction works,

On Sunday, June 23, 1985, the Association of Jewish ex-Servicemen and Women held a service at the Central to commemorate the 40th anniversary of VE Day. The Chief Rabbi officiated with Rev. Isaac (Harry) Levy, who was a chaplain to the forces in the war. It was Harry Levy who was sent to Bergen-Belsen when the concentration camp was liberated and did much good work for the survivors with the cooperation of the British armed forces. By coincidence, the events of June 23rd 1985 would remind everyone that terrorism had not been ended by the culmination of the war; an Air

India plane was sabotaged on that day with the loss of over 300 passengers, most of them Canadians.

One of the foremost Jewish charities is the Jewish Blind Society and Cyril Shine and Simon Hass conducted a memorial service in 1986 for their respected Chief Medical Office, Dr. Jakob Rabinowitz.

One Jewish branch was known for its very positive opposition to anything non-religious and that was the Lubavitch. In 1986 a dozen of the senior rabbinical students at their Friends of the Lubavitch Yeshiva in London, signed up to spend two years going round the country lecturing and teaching anybody interested in Judaism on a one-to-one basis.

A large advertisement in 1988 thanked them on behalf of the community and the Central was happy to join with the other synagogues in endorsing the acclamation. The educational activities of the Lubavitch were very varied. They would include going to Cambridge with bottles of whisky and inviting the students to a party. The Lubavitch were strongly Orthodox but very much of this world.

A series of lectures on politics and religion in 1986 saw Cyril Shine presiding when the Chief Rabbi addressed the subject of the modern Aids disease. Rabbi Jakobovits said, as memorably as ever:

> Issues that affect the stability of our society mean that we as Jews ought to be seen as pioneers. We were not told to return to Zion merely to export oranges, but to export Torah values.

A long-time member, Alec Colman, (1916-2004), the Life President of the British Friends of Bar Ilan University, was 70 in 1986 and to mark the occasion, Rabbi Professor Emanuel Rackman, the Chancellor of the University, spoke at the Synagogue. Alec Colman was a highly successful property developer and founded the E. Alec Colman Charitable Fund to relieve poverty. He lived to be 88 and his fund continues to do much good work.

The Central was now the last of the original United Synagogues and it was a focal point for Israeli visitors. As many as 350 might come to Shabbot services and tour operators were taking to providing packed kosher lunches for them in the Wix Hall.

The world wars were long over, but in 1987 there was a reunion at the Synagogue of the Second World War Jewish Brigade after over 40 years. Some of the Judeans from the First World War came as well. The Jewish forces were part of the Royal Regiment of Fusiliers and were known informally in the First World War as the 'Royal Jewsiliers'. A bronze plaque had commemorated them at the Central, but it had disappeared and had only recently been rediscovered. It was now presented to the Fusiliers.

Simon Hass' chazzanut was still in great demand throughout the community. To such an extent that he had been asked in January 1986 to conduct the memorial service at the New West End Synagogue for their minister, Raphael Levy.

To mark its 120th anniversary, in 1989 the financial position of the United Synagogue was clarified in a major article in the *Jewish Chronicle*. The organisation at that point was running an annual deficit of £500,000 but owned 66 synagogues and had assets estimated at £120 million. A quarter of its budget was spent on education and the Chief Rabbi's office cost over £200,000 a year. The value of the Central was estimated to be £12 million. The salary of the rabbi at a synagogue like the Central was now £29,000, which in today's money is about £74,000. He was also entitled to a Ford Sierra and an entertainment allowance.

Being a warden was not just an honour. There could be disputes. In 1988 Rabbi Dr. David Miller's contract as Student Chaplain was not extended by the United Synagogue and he refused to leave his flat which was over the Central. The court confirmed the action of the United Synagogue and for a time it was likely that Rabbi Miller would sue the wardens, Sam Peltz and Herbert Samek, for defamation. The case was abandoned, but the rabbi had to pay £1,700 costs. As he had nine children, it was a situation which everybody would have liked to have been avoided.

The New Year's Honours list saw another of the members knighted. Sir Anthony Jacobs was the chair of the British School of Motoring and the former treasurer of the Liberal Party, working closely with David Steel. He was also a governor of Haifa University.

In 1990 Eric Charles started a 20-year stint as Financial Representative. He was also the Treasurer of the Ben Gurion University in Israel and, on a lighthearted note, could be found singing at the Synagogue's Purim party in the style of Frank Sinatra and acting as chef.

When Margaret Thatcher resigned in 1991, one of the Central's members became a peer in her resignation honours list. This was Jeffrey Sterling, who was chair of the shipping line, P.&O, from 1983-2005. Jeffrey Sterling was born in Stepney and was another example of a member of an East End family who had succeeded in life. He was also made chair of the Golden Jubilee Weekend Trust, arranging the celebrations for the Queen's fifty years on the throne in 2002. As recognition of all his hard work he was made a Grand Knight Commander of the Royal Victorian Order.

In 1988 Cyril Shine officially retired after more than 30 years in office but the Board of Management asked him to stay in post until a successor could be found, which they didn't consider an easy task. The rabbi wanted to spend more time with his children in Israel but was still called upon when, for example, an obituary was needed for Evelyn Bloom, the matriarch of the family of restaurateurs, which had been a favoured institution in the East End since 1920. Blooms was a favourite eating and meeting place where the tables were shared and complete strangers would often find they had relatives and friends in common.

Central was involved in every kind of good work. Typically, on Boxing Day a few years before, members of the Borehamwood and Elstree Synagogue held a Quiz evening at the Central in aid of the Kisharon School for children with special needs. Members also took political office; Marion Harrison became the first woman chair of the Hampstead and Highgate Conservative Association in 100 years.

Cyril Shine was succeeded by Rabbi Vivian Silverman. The new minister was traditionally educated at the Etz Chaim yeshiva, Jews' College and London University and had created the Clayhill Synagogue before going on to Cape Town and Chigwell and Hainault. It was in Rabbi Silverman's time that the minister was finally invited to meetings of the Board of Management. It was in 1988 as well that Coral Jewel arrived as the new administrator and held the post for the next 14 years.

An excellent communicator, Coral Jewel worked well within and without the synagogue. For example, one of the beauties of Westminster is the vast number of trees. There are something like 15,000 of them and there is a Westminster Tree Trust and protection orders in profusion. The synagogue decided to present a tree and plant it in Portland Place, which Coral Jewel organised.

In September 1991 Ellott Bernard and Sir Anthony and Lady Jacobs presented the Synagogue with a new Sefer Torah. The honour of writing the last letters in the scroll is highly prized and a hundred men queued up in the Synagogue to play their part.

It would also be Coral Jewel who advertised for an administrator in 2002 when she retired. The qualifications required for the successful candidate were extensive:

> highly computer literate, fully conversant with M Microsoft Office programmes, able to work on his own initiative, strong interpersonal skills and a good telephone manner.

Craig Levison ticked all the boxes and had served the Synagogue for nineteen years in 2021.

Coral Jewel remembers Rabbi Silverman as a lovely man but not considered sufficiently dynamic for the Synagogue. Born in Liverpool, he is the brother-in-law of Chief Rabbi Ephraim Mirvis. He also had an impressive CV and he has had a distinguished career after the Central.

Rabbi Silverman left the Synagogue after five years when the Honorary Officers decided not to renew his contract. The Rabbi appealed unsuccessfully for the decision to be altered, denouncing it as:

> sacrificing sincerity and dedication for charisma and image.

He had no difficulty in finding another pulpit when he became the rabbi of the Hove community from 1995-2016. As such in 2014 he showed his independence by denouncing from the pulpit a decision by the Orthodox Jewish community in Brighton not to allow a Reform rabbi to enter the cemetery prayer hall to join a service on Holocaust Memorial Day.

Three noted members were remembered with services in the shul in the autumn of 1991. Jack Steinberg, a member of the Wolfson family was remembered in September, Alec Colman's memorial service was held in the same month and the memorial service for Sir Isaac Wolfson was held in November. Sir Isaac had died at 93 in Israel, having built the largest mail-order company in Britain, with 2,200 stores. He was most noted for his generosity, ranging from new Oxbridge colleges to a vast sum to buy a Goya painting back for the nation from America.

On his 80th birthday he had summed up:

> Running through the whole of my life is the fact that I was born a Jew. I attend Synagogue services regularly and I never fail to be present at a Shabbot service. I have always associated myself in Jewish affairs and would like to be known not as a businessman but as a man who built 50 Synagogues in Israel.

The community always needed volunteers to help people with day-to-day problems. In December 1991, for instance, a hundred supporters of the Visitation Committee of the United Synagogue, met at the Central, and one of the pressing challenges was the necessity to support patients who could not go home from hospital because there was nobody to look after them, as would be the more satisfactory case in a convalescent home. Some of the people involved had been on the list of the Visitation Committee for many years. The good work of the Committee, of course, went all the way back to Aaron Levy Green.

In December 1991 there also occurred the 70th anniversary service of rededication of the members of the Association of Jewish Ex-Servicemen at the Synagogue. They had started to get together annually in 1921 and although most of the original members were no longer alive, their successors made a brave show with standards and decorations.

One unusual event which took place at the Synagogue in 1993 was a copy of the popular TV programme "Any Questions". This is one of the best methods of communicating between the public and senior members of the community. The panel for the Central evening was Lady Jakobovits, Ned Temko, the Editor of the Jewish Chronicle, Deena Coleman, the Head of the Hasmonean Girls School and Tony Lerman, Director of the Institute for Jewish Affairs.

10. Rabbi Cyril Shine z'l

12

The Barry Marcus years

When Simon Hass retired in 1993 after forty years' service to the community, Shlomo Kreimann took his place for a short time, but decided to pursue a legal career instead of being a chazan. He was succeeded by Rev. Moshe Dubiner, who was a Jews' College and Etz Chaim graduate and had been the cantor at Bayswater after he qualified in 1964 and served in other synagogues. He was very much a stop-gap, however, and the Jerusalem born Yaacov Reichmann took his place in 1994. At the end of his two-year contract, however, he also did not seek an extension.

A lack of dynamism couldn't be said of Rabbi Silverman's successor in 1995. Rabbi Barry Marcus was a modern rabbi, creating a different image from the traditional. He was, for example, not to be found regularly in formal clerical garb. He was just as likely to be in a T shirt emblazoned with the message "God is busy. Can I help you?"

He also had an exceptional quality; he had been trained to be a Sofer, a scribe. There is hardly any Jewish official more important than the Sofer. All legal documents have to be absolutely perfectly written and the Sofer is given the responsibility. He does not just write the Sefer Torah. He writes legal documents like wedding certificates, and no error of any kind is permitted. So important is his work considered that while a member of the Beth Din does not have to be a rabbi, the Sofer does.

In 1995 it had been decided that the synagogue would be known as Central rather than 'The' Central. One memory of the past was the rediscovery of the memorial candelabrum to those who had fallen in the First World War, which had been lost when the synagogue was blitzed. Happily, it was found in a storeroom by Rabbi Marcus and warden Leonard Fertleman, broken in pieces, and it was completely restored by Leonard Fertleman in 2004.

It was one of the few things which has survived the destruction of the Synagogue in the bombing. It now has a permanent place in the Synagogue and the eighteen memorial candles are lit every year before Kol Nidre on Yom Kippur. On a lighter note, Josie Murray started the Central Bridge Club in 1997 and it can still be found attracting enthusiasts on

Wednesday afternoons, after the costs of the congestion charge have been absorbed.

Rev. Reichmann's successor in 1997 was Jonathan Murgraff who had dual interests; he was both a fine voice and a dentist. He stayed until 2002 but then left to concentrate on root canal treatment, which might well have been more financially rewarding. At the same time he didn't want to neglect liturgical music and the result was his association with the Cantorial Singers, who still give concerts all over the country and sing with Jewish cantors from all over the world. Founded by Ian Lyons in 1995, the Cantorial Singers both raise money for charity and perpetuate cantorial music, both Synagogue based and perpetuating Israeli and Yiddish melodies.

Barry Marcus was always in touch with his native South Africans. One charity founded by a few of them was the One-to-One Children Fund, which originally set out to help Russian Jews who had gone to Israel. With sponsored walks organised every year in Israel, and in many other countries like Peru and China, a lot of money was raised for good causes.

Barry Marcus soon came up with several initiatives of considerable value. In December his inauguration was marked with supervising the coordination of 200 people who had been encouraged to trek to Israel and Jordan to raise funds for the One-to-One charity. £250,000 was raised in all, 500 families benefited, and the participants climbed Mount Sinai and Mount Nebo in Jordan. As the oldest was 79 years old, it showed considerable determination in a good cause. One of the participants recalled the influence of the Rabbi:

> He instructed us to lie on the ground, place our hands flat on the earth and close our eyes....Amid a silence which seems to reverberate all the way to the heavens, it was a moment of palpable peace and extraordinary beauty.

Of equal but different impact, in 1998 Barry Marcus pioneered the concept of one-day educational visits to the former concentration camp of Auschwitz-Birkenau in Poland. Among those who joined him was Andrew Dismore MP, who afterwards initiated the establishment of Holocaust Memorial Day in Britain.

Groups visiting Auschwitz were not confined to Jews. For instance, the rabbi led 150 Chelsea supporters and club employees to the former concentration camp one year. It ended with a memorial ceremony next to the gas chambers and illustrated the concern of the football club to continue its campaign to 'Say No To Antisemitism'.

As one of the Chelsea participants wrote:

> It afforded the chance for those present to see with their own eyes locations where human history reached its lowest point and the trail of destruction of life left behind....This week's visit by Chelsea conceded with a powerful memorial ceremony adjacent to the remains of those same gas chambers.

Barry Marcus didn't stop there. In 2000 he had gone to Belarus and stayed in Minsk, home since 1815 of the Mir Yeshivah. He visited the Rabbi and was told that the Synagogue Sefer Torah had been lost. Rabbi Marcus' father had been a student in the Yeshiva and the rabbi contacted the community in his native Cape Town to see what could be done.

As a result, Cape Town donated two Sifrei Torah to Minsk and Rabbi Marcus persuaded the Central to twin with the area and to help the community on an ongoing basis. All the original members of the Cape Town community had come from Europe and the family feeling still persisted.

Minsk is part of Belarus now, and a memorial to the Jews massacred in the war was unveiled in the presence of the country's head of state. There were arguments about whether the unmarked grave should have a memorial at all but it was a popular decision with the townsfolk. Central has been of considerable assistance over the years to Minsk and it was necessary because, as the Minsk rabbi told Barry Marcus:

> Whenever there are large projects organised by one section of the community, it is opposed by others.

Minsk was not alone in having such problems. As every effort was made over the centuries to convert the Jews, it was essential that they remained individualists and resisted pressures when necessary. It can still be seen to be a feature of Jewish communities.

Minsk is within Belarus and Barry Marcus found there the only Jewish orphanage in the country. It was founded by Rabbi Moshe Fhima and it now looks after 150 boys and girls from deprived homes, or who are orphaned or abandoned. Rabbi Fhima aroused similar enthusiasm for the project with Barry Marcus, who in his turn got Sir Richard Desmond's financial support and that of the Gerald and Gail Ronson Family Foundation.

The Beis Aharon orphanage was also twinned with Central and now has a Synagogue, Yeshivah, mikveh and soup kitchen. The Ukraine had a large Jewish population before the war, but the vast majority were lost. Now rabbis come from abroad to teach the children, who know Russian, Hebrew, English and Belarussian when they leave the school, many for universities in America and Israel.

It is another example of the dogged determination shown by so many to ensure that the faith survived the war. There are estimated to still be about 100,000 Jews in the Ukraine and the prime minister from 2016-2019 was the Jewish Volodymyr Groysman. The President today is the Jewish Volodymyr Zelensky, who made his living before his election as a comedian.

The international nature of the attraction of Central continued unabated. In 2000 there was a memorial gathering of former pupils of Rev. Yonah Balkind, who had headed a cheder in Cheetham Hill, Manchester for over 70 years. People came from as far away as Israel and the United States to create a fund to now encourage youngsters to go to Israel for their further education. It was due to Jonah Balkind's persuasion that Rabbi Louis Jacobs decided to make his career in the rabbinate.

Barry Marcus has also taken over 20,000 school children to Auschwitz over the years. By 2008 the Holocaust Education Trust, with government support, arranged 17 visits a year for schoolchildren. At the 2012 Holocaust Education Trust Appeal Dinner the hard work was enthusiastically recognised. As far as the Holocaust was concerned, it wasn't just Barry Marcus leading groups to visit Auschwitz, though he was said to have counselled another 17,000 people on the Holocaust.

Barry Marcus was asked to be a Trustee of the government appointed Holocaust Memorial Day Trust, as well as serving as a Trustee of Yad Vashem UK. This organisation supports the international school for Holocaust Studies which holds seminars in Jerusalem, and which gathers in 300,000 visitors a year. He also spoke at the anniversary of the Rwandan Genocide at City Hall and was asked by the Survivors' Organisation to visit Rwanda in 2007 to offer support and guidance.

In 2000 it was also finally agreed that women could be elected Vice Chairs of United Synagogues. This decision was improved upon and the first woman to be elected chair of a United Synagogue was Karen Appleby, who took the seat at the St. Albans Synagogue in 2013 after the United Synagogue Council approved such appointments in 2012. The Central decided to have a vice chair as well as a chair in 2000 and Sam Peltz and Terry Same were the first incumbents.

Dr. Sam Peltz was on the Board in the 1980s and served as a warden and then Chair from 2000, with Eric Charles as Financial Representative, for fifteen years until 2011. Sam Peltz was known as Mr. Central. He came from a poor Soho family and was still a graduate of Trinity College, Dublin where he had won a gold medal for diagnostics.

He went on to be a much-loved doctor in Soho but was best known for inventing Executive Medicine in the 1970s. This was a service for the senior executives of companies, whose importance made it sensible to monitor their health carefully. The idea was later taken on by BUPA and PPP. It was another example of Jews finding the hole in the market. Sam Peltz was also the first to recognize the connection between cholesterol and obesity.

Although he was a member of the Central, Sam Peltz was also a warm supporter of the Lubavitch. His wife, Lois, was a Westminster Councillor and he was once asked if the two offices clashed. He replied "Oh no. Lois worries about the world. I only worry about the Jews." When he finally stood down in 2011, he was made Honorary Life President of the synagogue and died in 2014 when he was 82.

Lois Peltz decided to stand for election as a Westminster Councillor because both she and Sam Peltz were upset at the standard of some of the housing in Westminster. She sat as an Independent for twelve years and managed a deal of improvement. She was also a first-class ceramic designer and served on the Board of Management for many years. As ladies could now be elected to the chair of a synagogue, Nicola Burns, her daughter, took on the responsibility. She had been an honorary officer since 2008 and Melvin Lawson became her vice chair and Harold Schogger a warden.

In 2001 Paul Samek died at the age of 82. He had served twelve years in the Box at the Central and was a very colourful character. One of the Austrian refugee's children rescued by Rabbi Solomon Schonfeld before the war, he was categorised as an enemy alien but still managed to join the army in 1943. His mother and sister died in the Holocaust. He rose to the rank of major, which was astonishing for an alien, as he didn't become a British citizen until 1947. He became a member of the Chief Rabbi's standing committee and was on the council of the Board of Deputies. He was also treasurer of Ajex.

Seventy years may have passed, but in commemorating the Holocaust, it isn't anything like enough. It has only just been tacitly agreed to condemn the Spanish Inquisition to history after hundreds of years, and the Spanish are still embarrassed by their historic persecution of the Jews. Fanatics still exist though. In recent years there was still a Spanish NCO guard outside the new Madrid Synagogue carrying a machine gun.

Spain is, however, making a determined effort to apologise for the past. It was recently decreed that if a Jew could trace his ancestry back to Spain in 1492, he could claim Spanish citizenship again. There are still connections. When a new Synagogue was finally built in Madrid, Rabbi Abraham Levy from the Sephardim in London, was invited to the opening and addressed the audience in Ladino, the ancient Sephardi language, just as Yiddish is the traditional Ashkenazi tongue. Ladino is Classical Spanish, which the Spaniards can no longer speak, and they were delighted with Rabbi Levy's contribution.

The problem of congestion in central London was ameliorated when Mayor Ken Livingstone introduced a congestion charge of £5 in 2002, but it was a disastrous innovation for the Central and Barry Marcus led strong but unsuccessful protests against it. It wasn't so much a problem on the Sabbath when walking to shul was the norm, but weekday activities were made far more costly. It wasn't that far to walk from Regents Park outside the congestion zone, but with elderly people and inclement weather it was highly inconvenient. Within 20 years the cost would rise to £15 a day.

In 2003 there had been an important innovation in the creation of Tribe, a division of the United Synagogue aimed specifically at the young people in the community. Allied to Tribe, by the summer of 1911 Central was appealing for funds to enable youngsters from poorer families to go to Israel during the summer. It was called the US Chesed Bursary Fund and it was well supported. As the synagogue magazine explained:

> It is about attracting Jewish youth from all across the spectrum of observance, and showing them, bringing them, into the richness of Jewish life and culture, building their pride in their people and cementing them into the Anglo-Jewish community.

It wasn't the only charity trying to give poor children a visit to Israel and much was achieved. Tribe also created events which the children would enjoy in London. "Chanukah on Ice" saw 200 members at the Tower of London ice rink, lighting a giant Chanukah menorah and singing *Ma'OzTzur*, while devouring numerous traditional doughnuts.

There is, perhaps, not enough clarity about the distribution of money raised by some charities, but Tribe's Bursary Fund is crystal clear:

> The money we raise is ring fenced and goes directly to enable a young person to visit Israel, which is central to their personal Jewish identify and education.

Cyril Shine died in October 2003 at the age of 80. He had been the Synagogue rabbi for 35 years. He was buried in Bnei Brak in Israel and the

Chief Rabbi officiated at the memorial service at Central. Over the years Cyril Shine had become an inspiring speaker and devoted to many causes. He was the founder and chair of the Synagogue's JIA committee for many years and was well known for collecting the blue boxes in which charitable offerings were kept in many homes.

Cyril Shine had served in the army during the war and his experience of going into the Belsen concentration camp in 1945 had a lasting effect; he said the mourner's kaddish at every service in the Synagogue. He lived to celebrate his Golden Wedding to his wife, Sylvia; his son, Jeremy, chose to teach Jewish history in America which must have given him particular pleasure.

In 2003 also, Jonathan Murgaff was succeeded by South African Cantor, Steven Leas. The tradition of British and Commonwealth ministers occupying pulpits across the world was still in place. Chief Rabbi Israel Brodie had served in Melbourne and Rabbi Raymond Apple had served the Hampstead synagogue before returning to his native Australia. Chief Rabbi Mirvis, who succeeded Chief Rabbi Lord Sacks is a South African and from the St. Johns Wood synagogue came Rabbi Cyril Harris, who became the Chief Rabbi in South Africa and played a notable role with Nelson Mandela in the development of the country after the end of apartheid.

Steven Leas is in the tradition of Simon Hass, though he is also a trained accountant. He is not only a first class chazan but notable in the wider world of music. He appeared in two BBC television programmes commemorating the 60 years since the liberation of Auschwitz, which received an International Emmy award as well as a BAFTA.

He started singing when he was 10 and became the chazan of a leading synagogue in Johannesburg when he was only 23. As such he appeared on several occasions on South African television and pioneered the "Three chazans and a cousin" concert format which was copied in many countries.

He became the Trustee of the Jewish Music Institute and he has set up the Jewish Music Central which is a cooperation between the Central and the JMI. He also formed a new choir who sing modern liturgical settings of traditional chazzanut. They joined him in 2005 at the Holocaust Memorial Service, when he sang the memorial prayer at Westminster in the presence of the Queen, the prime minister and the chief rabbi.

In addition, along with the London Symphony Orchestra at the studios in Abbey Road, he recorded music for the 60th anniversary of the Commonwealth in 2009. When the Queen heard the record, she was sufficiently impressed to invite the group to Buckingham Palace to play the compositions again.

He has now appeared all over the world and is the resident chazan of the London Jewish Male Voice Choir. The choir has toured internationally and he has sung in operas as well. If all that wasn't enough, he appeared at the reopening of London's Roundhouse with Michael Ball, Brian Conley, Maria Friedman, Michael Legrand and Don Black in a tribute to 350 years of Jewish Music. Like Simon Hass he has also produced records and a CD - *Central in Song* - on the shul's website.

Stephen Leas is a first-class communicator, and he gave the congregation an example to follow when his son, Jonathan, was to be barmitzvah. He taught him to lein and Rabbi Marcus was pleased to call on him to do so monthly afterwards.

The chazan also tackles one of the most difficult of the problems of many of the members. He recognizes that as Hebrew is not their first language, they may have difficulty in understanding the significance of many of the prayers. In a contribution to the Synagogue magazine in 2018, he explained what was behind the voice of the Chazan:

> If I had to have a "Top of the Pops"….at the top of the list would be Shema Koleinu "Hear our Voices", which is the first of a group of Biblical verses beseeching G-d to answer our prayers favourably. Picture the scene. The Ark opens, people stop talking and words of heartfelt petition set to the most haunting tune fill the Synagogue. The Chazan leads the congregation as he pleads before G-d. It is at this stage of the service where I feel my biggest obligation in leading the congregants. We pray to G-d that He should have compassion, accept our prayers, keep us connected to Him and not cast us away.

The plea for compassion was not confined to the members. There was an occasion in 2005 when Rabbi Marcus invited the German Ambassador, Thomas Matussek, to come to the synagogue for a shabbat service. That day the ambassador spoke to the congregation of the dignity of the service, and if nothing could excuse the murder of the Jews who suffered in the Holocaust, the ambassador did his best to make the right gesture. It was a good idea to invite him and Barry Marcus called the concept Building Bridges. The Polish Ambassador and other notables followed on.

In 2006 Elie Wiesel was knighted for his literary achievements and service to humanity. He marked the occasion by coming to Central on shabbat. During the war he had been imprisoned in Auschwitz and Buchenwald and his book of memories brought the full horror of his experiences to the attention of the world. He wrote more than 50 books and was awarded the Nobel Prize. In the same year Jeremy Hunt, the Foreign Secretary, went to Auschwitz with Barry Marcus and found the rabbi inspiring.

In 2007 John Bull, a notable politician who had been Lord Mayor of Westminster as far back as 1983, passed away. He was born in a poor home in Cable Street in the East End, but founded a notable antiques shop in the West End whilst pursuing his political career. It was at Central that he talked of the Jewish links with Westminster which certainly went back to Norman times.

The members worked hard at the full range of business activities. Amir Chen, for example, founded the Apostrophe Coffee company and sold it to the Tower of London's caterers after some years for upwards of ten million pounds. Coffee shops were coming back into fashion again and Amir Chen was the only one who saw the opportunity.

The challenges Barry Marcus faced were very diverse. For instance, a Nigerian had decided to become Jewish and was readily accepted when he came to Central for services. Barry Marcus guided him on the necessary process, much to his appreciation.

In 2008 Rabbi Barry Marcus conducted a service in the shul to mark the 50th anniversary of the reconsecration of the new synagogue. He had already served the community for thirteen years and, as he said in his address:

> I am both humbled and honoured to serve this remarkable community that continues to be blessed with such fine, active and extraordinary members. Today we pay tribute to the vision and efforts of those who faithfully occupied themselves with the rebuilding of our Synagogue as an act of faith in the future….What is so particularly heartwarming is that so many of those families are still involved and take an active part in the life of our community and in many cases, occupying the seats of parent and grandparents. It is equally fitting to acknowledge the selfless contributions of my predecessors, Rabbis, Cantors and lay leaders who served with distinction.

The Chief Rabbi, Jonathan Sacks, said that,

> the list of its members, past and present, reads like a roll-call of the great and good of Anglo-Jewry, and between them they have been responsible for many of the proudest achievements and most important institutions.

Among a distinguished gathering were Elihu Elath, the president of the United Synagogue, Ewen Montagu, a past president, and the local MP, Sir William Wakefield. The opportunity was taken to dedicate the new Communal Hall, which had been given by the tobacco magnate, Abe Wix, in memory of his parents. The Children's Synagogue was rededicated as well.

Barry Marcus was always there to give guidance. For example, he was asked about Rosh Hashonah by the *Jewish Chronicle* in 2008. He pointed to the hard work it involved with 1,000 worshippers coming to the Synagogue, but revelled in the compassion and humanity which epitomised the festival. He did advise his readers that it was not the custom to make New Years resolutions in case there was a failure to abide by them.

Considering the many thousands of members over more than a century, there were bound to be some historical occasions which those involved in them would rather forget; the Central was not designed to be filled with monks, but the good deeds of the members far exceeded the lapses.

The sentiments of Lord Sacks would have pleased Chief Rabbi Israel Brodie, who in a sermon one Succot had wondered how many of the families in the congregation he was addressing would still be represented by their descendants in the future. Jewish communities have faced that problem for centuries, but there have always been sufficient among them to ensure that they carried on the faith.

July 2008 saw the organisation by the Jewish Music Institute of the Third Cantors Convention at the Synagogue. Participants came from Britain, Canada, Czechoslovakia, Denmark, Germany, Israel and the USA. Three days were spent discussing chazzanut and there were even lectures by three medics on how to protect the voice during protracted services like Yom Kippur.

In November 2008 Barry Marcus' initiative in arranging visits to Auschwitz culminated in a delegation of religious British leaders joining together to make the journey. Led by the Chief Rabbi and the Archbishop of Canterbury, representatives of the Hindus, Moslems, Sikhs, Janes, Buddhists, Bahai and Zoroastrians were joined by Lord Michael Howard and Sheikh Ibrahim Mogra, chair of the Moslem Interfaith Committee. It was a very welcome illustration of the multi-faith cooperation of religious leaders in Britain.

One organisation which increased in importance was the Spirituality for Kids society which lectured to children in schools. They were known as part of Kabbalah and had the support of celebrities like the singer, Madonna. Because Kabbalah was associated with Jewish mysticism, the critics of the organisation were concerned at its alleged connection with the Orthodox faith, and the Chief Rabbi and the Beth Din instructed their ministers to state from the pulpit that the organisation had no connection with them. Barry Marcus was one of those who was very much against the SFK influence.

In spite of overwhelming evidence of the atrocities of the Holocaust, a number of Holocaust Deniers came to the fore as the 20th century ended, and Central played its part in countering this falsification of history. For example, in 2010 the Deputy Prosecutor at the Eichmann trial, Gabriel Bach, gave a well-attended lecture on the subject at the Synagogue.

In 2010 Leonard Wolfson died at 83. Though never in his father's shadow, he followed in his footsteps and gave enormous sums to charity. Even as a young man he worked hard for any number of good causes. In 1953, for example, he raised £20,000 with a dinner for the Board of Guardians, which is over £500,000 today. He well deserved his peerage.

A number of women members now decided to study Judaism on a regular basis. Liat Mayerfield played a major part in the programme and although lady lecturers have not always been welcomed by the rabbis, Barry Marcus gave the initiative his warm support. Jacqueline Charles made the case for attending:

> About every four weeks, Jewish holidays permitting, the Central Synagogue holds a Shiur in the Beth Hamidrash. It starts at 11am (Jewish time) on a Wednesday and at around ten past eleven, several ladies gather together and Liat Mayerfield, our educator (we don't consider her as a lecturer) rushes in having finally found a parking spot. If there is an imminent festival, we tune into that or if not, we discuss some interesting event or philosophical point from the Torah. Happily, it is a free-for-all in points of view, mostly with a very modern take on any subject….by 12.30 we really feel we have been enthused with new ideas of interpretation….the shiur is open to all ladies, whether members or friends of the Synagogue and we welcome new faces.

A special Bat Mitzvah course was started as well and:

> aimed to provide a practical grounding in all aspects for what it means to be a Jew in modern times.

In an increasingly secular world, there continued to always be a danger of youngsters drifting away from the Synagogue. Not following in a parents' footsteps can be a part of growing up. Many were coming to Synagogue primarily on Rosh Hashonah and Yom Kippur.

The relations between the Orthodox and the Progressives had been a source of contention since 1840. They would continue to disagree to the present day, but the tendency to refer to past events to justify the Progressive's present status was unfair to the position of the Orthodox. For example, Chief Rabbi Hertz had visited a Reform social centre in the 1930s where this was unlikely to happen today, but he was trying at the time to get the entire community to unite against Nazi Germany and he did not attend a Reform religious service. Except for such exceptional occasions Progressive and Orthodox ministers did not pray together after the 1930s.

Due to his eminence as a leader and a scholar, Chief Rabbi Hertz has been claimed to be more Progressive in his outlook than was ever the case. He was the first graduate of the Jewish Theological College in New York, which is now the centre for American Conservatives, but when he studied there it was strictly Orthodox, which Masorti promotional material fails to point out.

It was, of course true that a United Synagogue minister had preached at a Reform Synagogue in Victorian times, but there was precious little difference between the Orthodox and Reform until the 1930s. In the early part of the century the Reform, for example, rejected the suggestion that men and women in Synagogue would sit together. By contrast the ambition of the American Conservatives is now to undermine the Orthodox, as their comments on Orthodoxy made quite clear. One New York Conservative rabbi toed the party line when he told his congregation that the Orthodox had the Din, but the Conservatives had love.

So, as in the case of Rabbi Melchior, the Chief Rabbi and his ministers were supporting Orthodox beliefs against the views of the Progressive movement. He did not believe that there were a number of types of authentic Judaism, any more than the Progressives did, and he was not going to approve of rabbis who took that view. However, he also spoke out against the way the Israelis treated their Arab citizens, which aroused a lot of opposition in the Holy Land. The Central gave Cyril Shine complete freedom to express his own opinions. The arguments continue.

The community's attitude to Jewish schools started to change because of two factors; the inflation of the 1970s, which made the cost of public-school education prohibitive for many, and the efforts of Rabbi Dr. Solomon Schonfeld whose Hasmonean schools achieved first class results in Barnet. The Hasmonean schools were the first Jewish schools to educate their pupils for university, but their success in this endeavour was soon copied, even though Hasmonean didn't have entrance exams and were financed by the local Council. Chief Rabbi Jonathan Sacks was happy to report in the synagogue magazine that:

> There have been more new Jewish day schools opened in the last two decades than in any comparable period in the 356-year history of Anglo-Jewry. The percentage of Jewish children at Jewish day schools has moved from some 25% to almost 70%.

It was a first-class educational effort, although Rabbi Dr. Schonfeld made life very difficult for the Barnet educational committee by ignoring many of the conditions they laid down. For example, he spent a good deal on a science block but, for years, the school had no fire escape.

Part of Hyde Park had been dedicated to the Holocaust and on Yom Hashoah in April there is now always a memorial service. More than 500 people attended in 2012 and Steven Leas and Central Synagogue choir took various parts of the service. In 2013 there was a Jan Karski Holocaust Memorial evening to mark the centenary of the birth of a courier for the Polish underground during the war. Jan Karski was one of the first to warn the American government of the Holocaust.

In 2011 there were Young Professional Sephardi Friday Night Dinners in January and May. In 2012 there were five Jewish Society Friday Night dinners and a Purim party with the Marble Arch synagogue.

When children marry, they often leave the district and the continuity of the Synagogue depends to a considerable extent on those who become old-timers. In 2013, for example, Laurie and Adrienne Phillips celebrated their golden wedding at the shul. Laurie Phillips had served on the Board of Management for 26 years at the time. He had been the synagogue's chair, the security officer for seven years, sat on the United Synagogue council for fourteen and the Board of Deputies for two. Adrienne Phillips was the Ladies' Guild chair. With a soft furnishing business and acting as a magistrate for twenty years, Laurie and Adrienne Phillips didn't seek a quiet life and the synagogue benefited from their devotion to it.

Another exercise in Jewish learning was Limmud, a major annual gathering, across the community to examine a wide range of topics. It was not originally welcomed by Barry Marcus when it invited speakers from organisations like the Kabbalah Centre in 2013. He denounced the invitation as a grave mistake, welcoming a different cult to Orthodox Judaism. In later years Limmud became increasingly popular, but its participants continued to have very different views.

A substantive report that year covered Synagogue membership in Britain. It identified that the community split into 53% Orthodox, 19% Reform, 13% Charedi, 8% Liberal, 3% Masorti and 3% Sephardi. Over the years there had been a substantial drop in the Orthodox numbers, but an over 100% increase in the Charedi community.

Barry Marcus found time in 2013 to work for non-Jewish organisations as well as Jewish. Among other events, he talked to King Charles at a meeting of the Campaign for Youth Social Action and spoke of Judaism to the St. James Senior Girls School. The impression he left in the minds of his audiences could only be beneficial.

The United Synagogue women began 2013 by electing a new executive and campaigned successfully to change a bylaw so that women could become chairs of synagogues. Nine women were elected chair that May, including Nicola Burns at Central. After 143 years women were recognised as on a par with the men. Nicola Burns stepped down as editor of the Synagogue magazine after six years and handed over to Raquel Amit, the Community Development Officer and Daphne Schogger.

What was noticeable about the year was the determined effort to provide more reasons for coming together at the Synagogue. The new chief rabbi, Ephraim Mirvis, made the point in the Synagogue magazine. That as the Beit Tefillah it was where members came to worship; as the Beis Knesset, it was where members met together, and Shul is taken from the German word for school.

Mandatory education was introduced in Britain in 1870, but the first Sephardi school in Britain, the Gates of Hope School, was opened in 1664. It was also exceptional that provision was made to educate girls, which put the Sephardim centuries ahead of the general population and it was, therefore, not surprising that Jewish schools were often housed in the Synagogue building.

Keeping up with the times, the Synagogue created its own website, with a lot of help from Michael Fishberg. Rabbi Marcus played his part with press articles, radio and TV appearances and public speaking to many differing audiences. Using a more old-fashioned means of communication, over 200 members of the Wolfson family got together for a reunion in the shul in 2012 as well.

It should not be forgotten how much support for the community came from non-Jewish sources as well. For example, a questionable cartoon in one of Rupert Murdoch's newspapers led to his writing a personal letter of apology to the president of the Board of Deputies.

In 2012 Lionel Swift died. He had been a warden at the synagogue for seven years and financial representative for another five. A highly distinguished barrister, he was best known as a peacemaker and was nicknamed the 'Corridor Kissinger' in legal circles. He was a thoroughly nice individual but unhappily he suffered a stroke during an operation and the last four years of his life were very difficult. He was fortunate to have a devoted wife in Elizabeth Swift.

The Olympics were held in London in 2012 and the Synagogue made special efforts to welcome Jewish visitors. Daily kosher refreshments, television relays of the top sporting events and a celebratory dinner were all on offer. The Synagogue also had a system of volunteers who offered to be on "Greeting Duty" to welcome strangers.

The ladies were particularly busy at this time. One of the most active was still Coral Jewell. She also served as the Treasurer and Secretary of the Ladies Guild. In what was described as "a groundswell of female agitation" it was now decided to have a ladies shiur. Jewish women have been prominent in education from Biblical times onwards, and in England the education of girls was encouraged by the Sephardim in the days of the Stuarts. Judaism may be an ancient religion, but its laws are extraordinarily modern and many were far ahead of their time. Mrs. Pankhurst would have been pleased.

The team needed to run the synagogue had grown over the years, and by 2012 it would have an Honorary Life President in Dr. Sam Peltz; a chair; a vice chair; wardens; a financial representative; eighteen members of the Board of Management, including eight women; a security officer; a welfare officer; a Ladies Guild chair; four United Synagogue representatives; two looking after the children's services; two members of the Board of Deputies; an Administrator; a Community Development Officer and four members of the Building Management team.

The building had to be looked after, of course, and Douglas O'Halloran served as the able caretaker for many years. It was appropriate that the Administrator, Craig Levison, has won a United Synagogue award for his excellent efforts, and behind the scenes, the Administrator holds a great deal of the work together. There were also a number of members who volunteered to be on "Greetings Duty" on Shabbat to welcome visitors to the Synagogue. The founders of the Branch Synagogue would have been very proud of the progress which had been made.

One member of the Board of Management, Michael Fishberg, maintained the finest Jewish traditions when he found himself stranded by an air strike in New Delhi just before Passover in 2012. Many more were

11. Rabbi Barry Marcus MBE

similarly inconvenienced and Michael Fishberg, in cooperation with the local synagogue, took it upon himself to bring from London all that was necessary for a seder for 100 people.

He flew it all in by cargo aircraft which weren't affected by the strike. The congregation were from all over the world and it was agreed that it was heartwarming to gather them together for the ancient festival. Michael Fishberg died in 2020 and was remembered as larger than life, writing in green ink and fond of flamboyant bow ties. In an emergency, however, there was no better man to have on your side.

In 2012, 400 guests and dignitaries attended the Holocaust Educational Trust's Appeal Dinner at the Savoy to honour those who had dedicated their lives to Holocaust Education and Rabbi Marcus was deservedly given an award. The Rabbi was now well known as a spokesman for the Jewish people and was even interviewed by Sky to discuss how the situation in Gaza affected the Jewish community in Britain. Another of the distinguished members was Lord David Young, who had served in Margaret Thatcher's cabinet and watched with satisfaction the newly acceptable understanding of Jewish festivals. He was particularly pleased with the singing of *Moatz Tsur* at Chanukah which seemed to now ring through both No 10 and No 11 Downing Street.

13

Recent Days

In 2013 the focus was on the completion of the original Hallam Street wing which housed the small Synagogue, the children's Synagogue, as well as the administrative offices.

One of the ancient traditions in the Bible was that of Temple elders and the Sephardim had continued to have such officials. Now the Ashkenazi Synagogues appointed elders as well and in 2013 Laurie Philips and Nigel Gee were given the honour. Nigel Gee is the son of Cecil Gee and served as a warden for nine years, besides holding the office of vice chairman of the charity, British Ort.

In 2013 Harold Schogger became a warden and served for six years. He is very well known in the bridge world and his tips on playing the game feature in the Synagogues' annual publication. He had been teaching bridge for over 40 years and organised an annual trip to Israel for bridge lovers. Jews have always taken to bridge and are keenly competitive. At the top-level, arguments often rage across national boundaries but Harold Schogger sees to it that little disturbs the calm of the Synagogue Bridge Club.

One outstanding musical event for Central was hosting the Eighth European Cantors convention in 2013. This international organisation works to maintain the quality of cantorial music and the convention was very well supported. Sol Zim, who is a legend among cantors, came from New York, and Yechezkel Klang from Israel. At the convention concert there were six cantors, five adult choirs and a 35 voice children's choir. As Stephen Leas recorded:

> The week-long excitement ended with a magnificent Shabbat where we were treated to a great exhibition of different musical styles. We had a lovely dinner on Friday night where all the cantors sang and spoke until late into the night. Shabbat morning was a treat with five cantors singing at the Ark together with the choir and all joining the choir on the Bimah to lead the Musaph service.

Of particular pleasure for the chazan was a duet between Sol Zim and his son, Jonathan Leas, singing *Avinu Shebashamayim*.

In 2013 Stephen Leas set out to widen the appeal of the synagogue by asking members what else they would like it to provide. From the meeting came events as diffuse as a Bridge lessons and varied concerts. The attraction of the Friday evening service was enhanced by a sushi and schnapps event, and there was an old Central favourite, Challah baking.

To bring them more into the community, Young US was created in 2014, led by a group of young adults in their mid-twenties who set out to build a more vibrant young community that spoke to them specifically. Some of the London Synagogues joined together the next year to create a Jewish learning initiative called Connect. It drew substantial audiences, but it was noticeable that the report on its activities in the annual magazine said:

> People from both sides of the divide packed into the this sold out venue. If only we had the same problem in Shul.

If the weekly congregation didn't fill the Synagogue, the problem remained the sheer size of the building. It could seat about 900 and it was too large for the average shabbat. It didn't help that members looked back to a mythical age when attendances were thought to have been far greater. The likelihood was that they weren't.

In 2014 a series of monthly themed Children's services were introduced and were very successful, thanks to the hard work of Yoav and Raquel Amit, Nicky Burns and Harold Schogger.

The importance of new ideas to attract members to use the Synagogue more was now emphasised by the creation in 2014 of a new Events Committee, led by Guy Ornadel. He was the son of Cyril Ornadel, the orchestra leader at the popular Sunday Night at the London Palladium TV show. Guy Ornadel introduced Bowling competitions, among other events, which were very popular.

The attempts to make the Synagogue a more attractive location for the members had led to a wide range of social activities as well, but although these were welcome, many of them had little to do with the religion. Movie nights, concerts, tours, functions and kiddushim were not a substitute for prayer, but they were in English and the services, for many, were in a language they didn't comprehend in toto. There was, however, always a hard core of members who supported the services over the years.

When a good cause needed publicity, the Central was often the setting for its promotion. In 2014, for example, an evening devoted to the singing of three Chazan tenors, Rabbi Danny Bergson (Pinner), Jonny Turgel, (Stanmore) and Stephen Leas was the setting to introduce the audience to the concept of hospital clowns. This was an innovation to help sick youngsters and was first tried at the Hadassah hospital in Israel in 2002. Teams of clowns gain the children's confidence, and then it is easier for the medical staff to do the same. Clowns have now helped victims of trauma in Nepal, Haiti and Ethiopia. The world would be a more peaceful place if the standard of cooperation in the medical world was mirrored in political circles.

The needs of old people were still very much in the minds of the Board of Management. Carole Murray took on the task of making regular phone calls to elderly and possibly isolated members, to see if there was anything they needed and keeping them in touch with the shul.

Among its long-term Central members, in 2014 Ben Rudolf made it to 100 years old. He had been a member of the Synagogue for 70 years and his marriage lasted 72 years. He died a year later. On the first day of Rosh Hashonah, the new Israeli ambassador, Daniel Taub, came to shul. His family had been members of Norrice Lea in North London, so the United Synagogue was well known to him from an early age.

It was in these years that a number of publications were contributed by the clergy and members of the congregation. The Ladies Guild also produced a cookery book "Jam-packed with recipes to cater for all the Festivals and Shabbat". *The splendours of the Central Synagogue* was written by Leonard Fertleman and the Lawson, Lewis and Townsley families would make it possible for the 150th anniversary to be celebrated with an elegant history of the shul by Leonard Fertleman and Mervyn Druian. An annual magazine was also produced and Talia Goldman, the editor, made a substantial contribution to communal life.

When Nicola Burns stood down, Barry Townsley CBE., became chair and Melvin Lawson remained vice chair. The team would remain in office until the present day and, in addition to their Synagogue work, were to be found on many charity committees. Barry Townsley was an early Hasmonean boy and well-schooled in Yiddishkeit. He is married to Laura Wolfson, Leonard Wolfson's daughter. They have four children.

It was not surprising that he was awarded the CBE for his charity work as he sits on boards as varied as the Child Bereavement Trust, the Weizmann Institute Foundation, the Royal National Institute for the Blind and the National Gallery East Wing Development Project. He sold his stockbroking firm and founded Hobart Capital Markets, but still finds time for Central. He has in common with Rabbi Lerer that they are both former

Hasmonean boys. He is deeply involved in education, health and fine art charities for which he received his decoration.

The groups Barry Marcus took to Auschwitz were warmly welcomed by the Polish government. In 2014 he was awarded the Polish Knights Cross of the Order of Merit for Holocaust Education and for fostering dialogue and building bridges with Poland. He also went to Bergen Belsen for the 70th anniversary of its liberation, taking part in a service at the Jewish memorial.

In 2015 he was awarded the MBE for service to Holocaust Education. He had received an award for his dedication to the cause in 2013 and the government minister, Eric Pickles, said of him:

> There is no better way to remember than education. Rabbi Barry Marcus has done so much, coming into contact with over 17,000 students and teachers. He has made us all proud of the work he has done.

There were antisemitic terrorist attacks in 2015 on the Continent and Nigel Gee, as the Synagogue Security Officer, was responsible for the safety of the members. A high-powered panel discussed the problem at a meeting attended by 300 in February, but 33,000 saw it on You Tube as well. It was pointed out that although French Jews were only 1% of the population, 50% of the violent hate crimes in France were committed against Jews.

This was, of course, not true of Britain, where a large majority of the antisemitic incidents were graffiti and verbal abuse, and a violent the crime was exceptional. The existence of antisemitism in the Labour party would, however, become the subject of endless debate in the coming years.

The international image of the Poles certainly needed refurbishing. They had a terrible record of antisemitism over the centuries and, of course, a large proportion of the Holocaust victims were Poles. Visiting Poland after the war Solomon Schonfeld eased the suffering of many of those who had survived. He still needed armed guards to avoid assassination in the face of Polish pogroms. It appeared that these attacks would now be a thing of the past when dealing with Rabbi Marcus, but they could still be found below the surface.

In 2020 there would be a very close presidential election between the incumbent, Andrzej Duda, and the Mayor of Warsaw, Rafal Trzaskowsky. To attract antisemite votes Andrzej Duda accused the Mayor of being prepared to pay restitution to Jews who had lost property during the Second World War.

Whether the Mayor's view was popular in the country or not, Andrzej Duda won a close contest. The battle of the Polish hustings contrasted with Central holding a joint Klezmer concert with the Polish Embassy in 2013. Yet the practices of Judaism were under attack in Poland again a few years after.

This time there was a movement to stop the export of meat killed by shechita. A bill was passed in the Polish parliament to that effect and only after a major effort, was it agreed to delay any such legislation until 2025. The bill was justified on the grounds of animal welfare, although there is no scientific evidence that shechita is anything but the most humane way of killing animals.

Polish wild boar shooting apparently remains very popular throughout the country, though the animals can suffer severely. Apparently, wild boars are not covered by animal welfare advocates. In direct contrast, shooting for sport is, of course, against the Din, but hunting has a lot of followers around the world.

The Ladies' Guild were still hard at work and organised the Supper Quiz which raised more money in 2015 than ever before. A whole range of educational areas were now available to members as well. The aim of the events was also to learn more of lesser-known intellectual subjects, for those who wanted to combine entertainment with deeper study. The lectures would be introduced by highly qualified writers, film makers and academics, who could discuss their creations in a personal way. From 2016 there was also a Sephardi minyan service once a month on shabbat and there were Ivrit (Modern Hebrew) classes in conjunction with Spiro Ark.

A further initiative which Central supported was Mitzvah Day when people from all over the world and from every faith, set aside a day to offer their time to help others. In 2016, for instance, the synagogue asked the public to buy extra items from supermarkets to give to charities such as St. Mungos, the Separated Child Foundation and the Refugee Council. People responded very generously and as an example of inter-faith cooperation, Mitzvah Day gives out all the right messages.

In the heart of London, there had been a small synagogue in Dean Street in Soho from 1880. Its members had been small shopkeepers and newly arrived immigrants; fertile ground for Labour Party recruitment. There was a lot of deprivation among its original congregation but the differences in income between the members of the two synagogues had diminished over the years and society was no longer so class conscious. In 2016 the Dean Street community moved to Central where its members were made very welcome.

Every kind of meeting had been held at the Synagogue over the years. A strong case could be made that the saddest took place in September 2016 when the Lost Shtebl Complex was launched in Britain at the shul. It commemorated one of the strongest Jewish communities in Europe over the centuries, which had been based in Lithuania; among its most notable members was the famous Talmudist, the Vilna Gaon, Rabbi Elijah ben Solomon Zalman.

During the 19th century large numbers of Lithuanian Jews had emigrated to countries like South Africa but there was still a large community in its home base. It suffered grievously, however, in the Holocaust and the Lithuanians were complicit in the massacres. At last, 70 years after. the war ended, it was decided to bring the horrific events back into the light and try to apologise.

As a consequence, the Berlin Holocaust Memorial Information Centre arranged with the Lithuanian government to take some positive action. It repaired the old Sedova cemetery and built three memorials at the sites of horrific massacres. A museum would be founded as well. Publicity for the Lost Shtebl Complex was organised internationally and the meeting at the Central was the first in London, and attended by Mrs. Asta Skaisgiryte, the Lithuanian ambassador. Like so many other Jewish communities, the Lithuanians had suffered terrible oppression but, like the Central, Judaism survived.

The lower ground floor at Central was now turned into the Alan and Caroline Cultural Centre. It incorporated totally refurbished function rooms, meeting rooms and a state-of-the-art kitchen. There was also the beautiful Children's synagogue and a stunning glass-roofed atrium. One of the latest innovations was a Hebrew Reading Crash course and an Understanding Shabbat course, from which almost everybody would benefit.

It was perhaps overdue, but the alternative attraction of Yiddish had waned and this helped, with Hebrew as the language in Israel, to make the idea more popular. It was astonishing that Hebrew had survived over the centuries when so many ancient languages hadn't. Among those who deserved credit for this are the Samaritans who retained Hebrew for their services throughout all those years.

To strengthen the academic standards on offer to members, Rabbi Dr. Rafi Sarum was appointed the Scholar in Residence in 2017. One event he conducted which was much enjoyed was a visit to the British Museum before Pesach to learn about the Jews in Egypt.

Looking back, the Central membership had inevitably changed over the years as the original community had absorbed its East End immigrants. The son of Aaron Stoutsker, Stephen Stout-Kerr, knew the old synagogue and was not happy with the new one. He gave his own impression in 2017:

Light years away from the grandeur of the original Synagogue with its marble splendour, its magnificent marble Bima and its giant chandeliers. Its sweeping and grand red carpeted white marble stairway leading to three arks, the massive central one flanked on each side of it. The Roman pavement at the foot of the stairs. The two imperial royal crowns on top of the large marble tablets on either side of the Prayer for the Royal Family. The grand stairways facing each other in sweeping, majestic, even palatial steps in the great hall leading to the two galleries above. This was no cinema and the architects employed had never built one. The tinsel look of the new Synagogue is in stark contrast to the Versailles quality of the materials and its construction. This was a Synagogue befitting its aristocratic Eton/Harrow membership.

The original members may have wanted their children educated at Eton and Harrow but for those who still did, it would often be social climbing. The eminent Rabbi Kopul Rosen, as long ago as 1960, had said of the children sent to Eton that they were:

Offered up as sacrifices on the altar of parental vanity.

The new Synagogue continued to safeguard the culture of. a monotheistic religion where, by contrast, Eton and Harrow offered an excellent education, but one which had no relevance to the survival of Judaism. There was also a lot of antisemitism in many public schools and, as Christian foundations, they had no responsibility for the religious education of their Jewish pupils and had to adjust, as they saw fit, to the new multi-cultural British society.

Furthermore, in an increasingly secular world there continued to always be a danger of youngsters drifting away from the Synagogue. Many were coming to Synagogue primarily on Rosh Hashonah and Yom Kippur, but then Michael Adler had made the same complaint after the First World War and Simeon Isaacs after the Second.

Another problem area was efficiently addressed. It is inevitable that some members will run into difficulties in their lives and would appreciate help in overcoming them. In 2017 a new Chesed (kindness) group was formed with new volunteers like Susan Lesner and Rosalie Stevens. For members who are elderly and on their own such a body does a great deal of good. Susan Grant would also create the Central Community Cares in 2019 to offer assistance in such cases, and more volunteers were not hard to find.

The needs of the poorer members of society as a whole though were not neglected. In 2017 Central combined with Holland Park, the New West End, Western Marble Arch and the Westminster Young Professionals to collect gifts for Mitzvah Day and were rewarded with large scale donations.

The local authorities had always been extremely cooperative with the needs of the Synagogue. There was a hiccup, however, in 2018 when the North London coroner announced that no death would be prioritised in any way over any other because of the religion of the deceased or family, either by the coroner's office or by coroners. Both Judaism and Islam rule that the dead must be buried within 24 hours, but this, it was now declared, would be honoured no longer. It was no surprise though when the coroner was overruled by the High Court which arbitrated and quashed the ruling. They said:

> To treat everyone in the same way is not necessarily to treat them equally. Uniformity is not the same thing as equality.

They decreed that Jewish and Moslem deaths, referred by the coroner, would, as before, be given priority to enable the burials to take place within the usual time span. It was a typically British judicial decision, protecting the culture of minorities. The Din has a strong case for being centuries ahead of other civilisations; this time in the rules on bereavement. The loss of a loved one is hard to bear, but the mourners are comforted by the shiva process, lasting seven days, with visitors coming every day to offer their support during that time. The rule that the burial should take place within 24 hours avoids prolonging grief at the outset of internment.

Central had many attractions for visitors which made it almost unique. As Rabbi Marcus said:

> although one of the downsides to an inner-city synagogue is that access to families is limited by virtue of property prices and location, there is an annual regeneration of students because of all the universities in the area. There is another sadder source of people, because the synagogue is surrounded by hospitals. Almost every week there are people who come to services at the Central because a family member is in hospital.

When it came to students, Central didn't just offer Synagogue services. It also helped the University Jewish Chaplains. The London Region Chaplain is Rabbi Gavin Broder, a former Chief Rabbi of Ireland, and Central provides him with a lounge at the Synagogue where students could meet, enjoy lunch and socialise during the week. This was very necessary after the Hillel House centre in Euston Road was closed.

Friday Night Dinners were also provided and Jo Hochauser raised the money to pay for them. On average, more than 50 students come every week. If it can't be just like home, it's a very acceptable substitute. Rabbi Broder also has an office in the Synagogue.

Students are often to be found at demonstrations and there were a number of vigils in 2014 and 2015 in which Rabbi Broder participated. They were for the victims of terrorist attacks in Paris, Holocaust Memorial Day at Kings College and the March of the Living in Poland. There are estimated to be about 2,500 Jewish students in London, so the rabbi has a very full-time job. He doesn't differentiate between the sects; as he points out, chaplaincy is non-judgmental and provides for students from across the religious spectrum.

As the country became less class conscious, so some of the formality which was so noticeable in the early days began to disappear. There was no longer any question of ministers wearing vicars' dog collars. The community was now more comfortable in setting its own standards rather than copying a national clerical approach.

This individual approach reflected the difference brought about by multi-culturalism. Widespread antisemitism is only a bad memory now, but it had existed for most of the 20th century. It had never been characterised by official discrimination in Britain but the stereotype image of Jews as unpleasant people, just because they were Jews, had been portrayed in popular books, plays and media.

Where in Victorian times the members of the Central wanted to be seen as gentlemen, a favourable image in much of society was seen as an unattainable ambition. The shock of the Holocaust taught the dreadful results of such attitudes and laid the foundation for the growth of multi-culturalism.

In spite of the massive publicity antisemitism gets, the total number of reported incidents in Britain are very small, though they still need to be reduced

The customs of Central were still sometimes unusual in that married ladies still did not have to wear hats in Synagogue. It was ironic that one of the foremost Central members was David Shilling, who was one of the most famous milliners in the country. His mother, Gertrude Shilling, had been a national figure, noted for her extravagant hats for many years. There was a Jewish tradition here. For many years in Victorian times hats with ostrich feathers had been very fashionable and many Jews had reared ostriches in South Africa. The fashion passed during the Great War except with ladies like Gertrude Shilling.

It was very much a minor issue though. As Stephen Leas said:

> It is comforting to be able to come to Synagogue and join together in harmony, while time is suspended. A time to pray and take stock of our lives, while participating in the traditional and modern settings of our beautiful prayers.

Many of the notable days in the Jewish calendar are now marked with communal events at the Synagogue. There has been a large barbecue on Lag B'Omer, the only day between Passover and Shavuot when parties are allowed. There have been events at Succot, Chanukah and Purim. The concept of the neighbourhood, with everybody knowing everybody else, is difficult in the West End, particularly as pubs lack attraction for most of the community. The role of the synagogue, therefore, in filling the gap is very welcome.

Jonathan Metliss took on a new role of Events and Marketing Manager to give the Synagogue a still higher profile with its members. He already represented the Synagogue on the Board of Deputies. As chair of a major law firm, he has every excuse to say he is too busy to find the time for these roles, but his commitment is typical of so many of the members,

It was still contentious that the proceeds of the Kol Nidre Appeal were allocated "primarily to the needs of our growing community." The same explanation had been given a century ago, but the financial situation of another beneficiary, Israel, had changed for the better.

Since independence in 1948, through hard work, Israel had become one of the richest fifty countries in the world. For a tiny country like Israel to reach such a level meant it needed new industries. It was significant, for example, that over the years 40% of the multi-national companies around the world had based their research departments in Israel. The deciding factor was that there was a highly educated work force available to staff them. The needs of Central charities might very well be greater now than the nation state.

In 2018 the United Synagogue created a Woman's Officer and Roz Loren accepted that role. The position of women in the community had improved a great deal since the early days of the Branch Synagogue, but there were still limits. An academic, Dr. Lindsay Taylor-Gurhartz, had served as a Research Fellow with distinction at the London School of Jewish Studies, formerly Jews' College, for many years. She had, however, studied to be awarded semicha in America and would be initially dismissed in 2021 because women rabbis did not have the approval of the Orthodox authorities. It was only when it was decided that a Research Fellow was not a religious position, that she was reinstated.

In 2018 there was a complete rebuild of the lower ground floor of the Synagogue, so that a newly refurbished communal hall for up to 300 was created. There was also a fully fitted kosher kitchen now, new toilets and cloakrooms, new large meeting rooms, and a storage area. The atrium was enclosed and the extra £3 million needed came from the members. The chair of Central Ladies, Sara Cohen, was also able to report that no less than 12 charities had been supported during the year, including the Jewish Blind and Disabled, the Jewish Deaf Association, and Hatzola, which is a free ambulance service.

As Michael Goldstein, president of the United Synagogue, said on the 150th anniversary:

> You can boast regular services every day of the week, a revamped children's programme to ensure your future is strong, regular Lunch and Learns, and dedicated opportunities for women's learning. You run high quality events throughout the year to attract a broad range of your members; at the Central, there really is something for everyone.

The status of Central had grown to a point where distinguished members of the Jewish public considered it something of an honour to be invited to address the members. A new initiative was called Connect and offered Jewish learning from the views of experts. Among the speakers were Professor David Hochauser who talked about Diabetes, Richard Desmond on self-made businessmen, and Malcolm Rifkind, the former Conservative Foreign Minister, on Russia.

Michael Sherwood came from Goldman Sachs to talk about bankers and Dr. Eli Lewis from Ben Gurion University. It meant that the Synagogue addressed both religious and secular learning. There were also distinguished speakers after the service on some shabbat. These included the distinguished journalist Melanie Phillips, for the pulpit was now available to both women and men after the service.

The tradition of Jews recognizing a hole in the market and consequently becoming very successful businessmen, continued in very modern times. One of the most successful Central members was Harvey Goldsmith who had been studying pharmacy in Brighton as a youngster and had the initiative to start a live music venue for the students.

From this beginning he became one of the most prominent concert promoters in the world. In 1985 he put on the famous Live Aid concert with Sir Bob Geldof and he is generally credited with making rock history. His artists ranged from Elton John and the Rolling Stones to Luciano Pavarotti, but he served on the Central's Board of Management for several years and his wife, Diana, still does so.

The United Synagogue now has 62 congregations, 40,000 members. and it is the largest Synagogue body in Europe. It has been described as:

> the religious parent organisation for the largest section of Anglo-Jewry with a dominant role in its national institutions.

It has been a steady growth. From the original half a dozen communities, it had grown to 21 in 1914 and 19 more congregations joined between 1931 and 1938. There were 52 in 1939, and 60 by 2008.

Another lady member who made an impact outside the Synagogue was Inez Benjamin, who in 2018 became the first woman to be installed as president of the City's Bishopsgate Ward Club in its 230-year history. As a Freeman of the City of London and president of the club, she could now herd her sheep across London Bridge, walk around with her sword drawn, be drunk and disorderly in the City without the fear of being arrested and turn the traffic lights red on Tower Bridge during the rush hour. Such nachas.

In 2018 many members of the Synagogue joined the demonstration in Parliament Square of Jews protesting against antisemitism in the Labour party. The demonstration was about 2,000 strong and participants had come at 24 hours' notice from all over the country. They included 30 MPs and the message was "Enough is Enough". Although the recording machinery failed to work, the fact that the demonstration took place at all was widely reported.

On a lighter note, Shabbat UK in 2018 saw the ladies gathering for a Challah bake, instructed by Rebbetzin Ilana Epstein. The making of Challah is not only complicated, but the plaiting of the loaves has religious significance. It is a memorial to the Manna sent to the Israelites in the Wilderness.

It was in the same year that the second official visit of a foreign country's representatives came to the shul, the first having been the Emperor of Brazil 100 years before. In May the Nicaraguan Minister of International Relations and Policy, Siddhartha Marin and the Nicaraguan Ambassador, Guisell Morales-Echaverry, came to the morning service. The minister addressed the gathering during the breakfast after a tour of the synagogue.

Barry Marcus lost his mother, Esther, at the age of 95 in South Africa in 2017. She had brought him up to follow in the footsteps of his family, whose rabbinic predecessors in Eastern Europe had been widely admired. In 1939 the family had left Poland for South Africa in time to avoid the Holocaust. Barry Marcus retired himself in 2018 after 23 years as Central's rabbi and nearing seventy years old. He had made many political friends. Michael Gove, the Environment Secretary, called him a truly wonderful man at a reception at the House of Commons.

Rabbi Barry Lerer was appointed to succeed Barry Marcus in 2019. After seeing Rabbi Lerer, the Central honorary officers said they were struck by:

> a dynamic, passionate, innovative, caring, inspirational and friendly rabbinic couple.

Born in America, Rabbi Lerer served the Barnet community for many years and taught at Hasmonean High School for seventeen. He now discusses the weekly parsha on Zoom every Tuesday at eight o'clock in the evening, making the best of the problems caused by the pandemic closing the shul not long after he was appointed, but this should be a temporary setback. The difference between Barry Lerer and Aaron Levy Green is that between the modern British rabbi and the Victorian. Barry Lerer does have Semicha from Jews College but he also went to the Hokotel Yeshivah in Jerusalem.

He has a BSc in Psychology, a qualification far beyond his predecessors. Blessed with four sons and a daughter, and experience as the minister in Watford as well as Barnet, with his wife Naomi, the spiritual side of the Synagogue is in safe hands. Indeed, the one shortcoming in Barry Marcus' ministry was that there was no Rebbitzin.

It is true that only members of the Sanhedrin in Biblical times had to be married and have children, but a congregation normally benefits a great deal from having a Rebbitzin. The Rebbitzin set to work to get the younger women members to participate to a greater extent in the organisation of the Synagogue. In order to establish the new equality of the lady members even more, the office took over the organisation of the kiddushim.

Sara Cohen was the last chair of the Ladies Guild and took the opportunity to recall and recognise some of those who had done so much in the years gone by. She specified the Life President, Sylvia Shine, the Hon. President Lady Brodie, Elaine Hass, Edith Wolfson, Jeannie Williams, Ruth Klausner, Sally Lee, Denise Cohen, Lily Cappin, Cecilia Colman, Lois Peltz, Adrienne Phillips, Jacqueline Charles, Terry Samek, Anita Winkler, Esna Galibov, Coral Jewel, Daphne Schogger, Isabel Ritblat, Susan Goldbart, Margaret Grant, Carole Murray, Raquel Amit, Roz Laren, Clarice Shamash, and Jose Murray. There were, of course, many others as well, but 150 years is a long time.

There are some things which don't change. A synagogue thrives or declines according to the ability of the minister. Some synagogues in London have been revived by charismatic ministers and some have lost their congregations in a wave of indifference. The minister is that important as a public figure, but he also has the additional task of being at the side of the bereaved and being available to be consulted on family matters if they become difficult. In a society which is increasingly secular he also, of course, must defend Jewish traditions.

Fortunately, the British Jewish community have had many good spiritual leaders over the centuries. Today's United Synagogue ministers will have been inspired in their younger days by the example of Chief Rabbi Lord Sacks, who achieved the extraordinary status of being "a moral light unto the nation."

For example, when the riots in London in 2011 subsided, *The Times* commissioned an article on what might be learned from the disturbances. The logical author would have been the Archbishop of Canterbury, but Jonathan Sacks was chosen. It showed what was possible for a minister to achieve, even if he was not part of the dominant faith in the country.

Unhappily, Jonathan Sacks died in 2020 but his many speeches to distinguished gatherings have been collected on You Tube and his words of wisdom are still available in that form.

Barry Lerer introduced his own Torah teaching with a session he called the Power Half Hour. The title may have been modernised, but the old tradition of offering Talmudic education continued.

Another innovation was a number of lunchtime shiurim, notably by Rabbi Nicky Liss from the Highgate Synagogue. Rabbi Nicky Liss is a Gateshead man but is very much a modern rabbi; one of his lectures was on *The Oldest Building Regulations in the World* and many members from the City were happy to learn. Rabbi Liss' recent experiences in rebuilding the Highgate shul made the comparisons with ancient Talmudic rulings particularly pertinent.

It is true that the present synagogue does not look like the Victorian structure it replaced, but synagogues have adopted different styles of architecture over the years and the tastes of the members change. The ark is the key element in the synagogue and the sifrei torah haven't altered.

After 150 years of continuous services to its members, the coronavirus pandemic in 2020 proved an obstacle even Central couldn't overcome. To avoid the disease spreading it was necessary for several months to shut the Synagogue and although the administration continued as effectively as ever, it was not possible for minyans to gather under the circumstances. Where some Synagogues ignored the dangers, the Jewish community as a whole didn't always comply and consequently suffered more deaths than their percentage of the general public warranted. The effect of gathering to read the Megillah at Purim in 2020 was particularly damaging.

The situation could have been ameliorated if the community had obeyed the rules for dealing with pandemics laid down in the Torah. Isolating the infected and washing hands are only two of the 6th century regulations which had to be reinvented by modern scientists after 1,500 years.

Other diseases covered in the Talmud range from leprosy and apoplexy to gonorrhoea, dysentery and emerods. From this approach comes the Jewish contribution to medicine over the centuries, which include no less than 60 Nobel prizes in that category.

The pandemic created challenges which had never had to be faced in such volume by the community since the Spanish Flu epidemic in 1919. The Central Community Care committee needed additional support and Rabbi Lerer, pointed to:

> the amazing group of volunteers who inundated us with offers to help those who were isolated or vulnerable.

The Welfare team distributed parcels to many households and a Weekly Challah Run saw to it that as many as seventy challas were obtained for those who couldn't leave their homes. The Rebbetzin hosted Wednesday Women's Hour for the ladies. In the 2020 synagogue magazine there was also a new innovation, a Rosh Hashonah message from Naomi Lerer. Her Talmudic expertise was obvious. There was also a weekly Zoomed Mincha and Maariv, as well as Havdalah services.

The scholastic ability of the women in the congregation was now equally as recognised as the men. After the Saturday service, for example,

12. Naomi Lerer – Where would the Synagogue be without the ladies

Roz Laren addressed the congregation on the Fourth Annual Mental Health Shabbat. Much had improved since the days of the Branch synagogue, though the pandemic meant that the 150th anniversary celebrations had to be delayed. So many of the activities of the Ladies Guild were now being carried out by separate committees that the Guild was dissolved in 2019.

Rabbi Ari Cohen joined the synagogue as Assistant Minister when the aging community of the Dean Street Synagogue finally closed its doors. He also continued to be the official Jewish chaplain at the Imperial College Healthcare Trust. Ari Cohen had been the minister at the West End Great for nearly a quarter of a century and was very highly regarded. During the pandemic he conducted Friday night services on Zoom. He had also studied a great deal and was awarded semicha in 2018.

Central continues to be a West End Jewish presence after 150 years. The new Chief Rabbi, Ephraim Mirvis, decided he would like an office in the West End, as well as at the headquarters of the United Synagogue in North London, and Central was delighted to accommodate him in 2018. Members help Israeli institutions as well; Mervyn Druian, for instance, is the UK governor of Tel Aviv University.

Stanley Salter served as the Financial Representative from 2011-2021. As a notable accountant he has also given a lot of time to the Variety Club Children's charity. After ten years in the role, the Central's finances are in good order. Eric Charles, though, who had set a United Synagogue record for serving as Financial Representative for 21 years, died in December 2020 at the age of 89. It was a good innings, but he will be sadly missed in the Synagogue.

So, in 2020 Central was 150 years old. The current 700 members would have found little difference between the rituals of 1870 and the present service, but the British Jewish community has changed a great deal.

There were the traditional members of the community and there were the 19th century immigrants from Eastern Europe who were usually more observant. The refugees at the end of the century had formed the Federation of Synagogues, on the initiative of Samuel Montagu, later Lord Swaythling, and although they had the Din in common with the original community, a larger percentage of their members paid more attention to it.

In the latter part of the 19th century another element started, which was to grow into the Yeshiva community at Gateshead in North East England. Where Jews' College and the Etz Haim Yeshiva had produced most of the native-born ministers, there would now be graduates from Gateshead whose standards of observance as ministers was very high. In addition, the dispute over Rabbi Louis Jacobs led to the creation of the Masorti movement in Britain.

As the whole country became more secular, the religious faiths declined in the number of members. It affected the Church of England congregations as well as the Jewish. The British Jewish community sank from its largest number of about 400,000 in 1945, to 260,000 by 2020. It is still the fifth largest Jewish community in the world and about half the members of Synagogues belong to congregations like Central. The United Synagogue now has 62 communities, the Federation 24, the Reform 40 and the Liberals 40. Nineteen per cent of British Jews are Reform, 8% Liberals and 3%

Masorti. The Masorti allow women to have a greater say in the services but remain primarily Orthodox.

The very Orthodox British Jews are the Charedi communities who comprise about 4% of the community, but whose numbers are increasing fastest. They divide into the Lithuanian, whose concentration is on study, and the Hasidim who add the importance of joyful spirituality. The evangelical Lubavitch are another segment. The Charedim have large families, partially as a result of a determination to replace the Jews murdered in the Holocaust. The more Orthodox the community, the greater the authority of the rabbi.

Of course, a major change over the years has been the establishment of the State of Israel. The United Synagogue is now proud to be a Zionist organisation, though this was not the case until the Second World War. Zionism still splits the community because the Charedim hold that the Jews should not be in control in Israel until the coming of the Messiah.

Whenever there is conflict between the Jews and the Arabs, there is a marked increase in antisemitic incidents in Britain, although the British community has no say in the conduct of Israeli government policy. The Israelis have now appointed a cabinet minister for the Diaspora but the British Jews are loyal to Britain and the Diaspora minister is an anachronism.

Many Jews all over the world, disapprove of aspects of Israeli government policy, but at the end of the day, it is the only Jewish country, fighting for its life and the Jews have a millennia old tradition of sticking together and helping each other. It has enabled them to survive against all the odds. In the Middle Ages when the Moslems ruled in North Africa and much of Spain, they treated their Jewish communities very well, and the period is often known as the Golden Age. Today the Board of Deputies still make strenuous efforts to improve relations with the Moslem community, who have their own problems with racialists.

There are about 3 million Moslems in Britain and a recent study established that 94% believe that they can practice their religion safely in this country. This is about the same percentage as the Jewish community.

A secular society does not regard inter-marriage as objectionable. Where it was considered a disaster for Jewish families in the 19th and 20th centuries, as many as 50% of Jewish youngsters marry out today in Britain. The Reform Synagogues make consequent conversion less difficult than the Orthodox, where the Beth Din demand a higher standard of observance in the convert than most native-born members ever achieve. It also takes up to two years to be converted by the Beth Din.

Central, going forward, have to tackle all these developments. To appreciate a faith it is necessary to know about it. Education is, therefore, a top priority and the number of Jewish schools has grown in recent years, so that 35,000 Jewish children attend Jewish schools today. Their results are normally excellent, but the Charedi schools often teach in Yiddish and argue with the government on whether schools should teach sex education and how much of the curriculum needs to be secular.

Central pay even more attention to the children than used to be the case. A number of social events are mixed in with children's religious services and they are involved in running their own shul and enjoying many forms of outings. There are not, however, sufficient children of members now to justify religious classes and these have been discontinued. It does mean that the children whose families are members, often cannot say the

13. Barry Townsley CBE

prayers in Synagogue when they come with their parents, and Rabbi Lerer is anxious to repair this deficiency.

There is also a policy now to teach youngsters about other religions while they are at school, and that often involves visiting a Synagogue to learn at first-hand what, in this case, Judaism is all about. A natural setting for these visits is Central, which is an impressive building, and its ministers are well able to communicate the faith. These Synagogue tours had to be suspended during the pandemic, but they will no doubt continue to be a fixture when the situation returns to normal.

14

Epilogue

A hundred and fifty years is a long time. When the Branch Synagogue was consecrated there were no more than 35,000 Jews in the country. The community included the Sephardim, the Orthodox, the Secessionists and, within 30 years, the Liberals.

There were then added to the traditional members of the community, the immigrants coming from Eastern Europe. They formed the Federation of Synagogues, on the initiative of Samuel Montagu, later Lord Swaythling. In the latter part of the 19th century another element began life, which was to grow into the Yeshiva community at Gateshead in North East England.

As the whole country became more secular as the 20th century wore on, the British Jewish community sank from its largest number of about 400,000 in 1945, to 260,000 by 2020. It is still the fifth largest Jewish community in the world, and about half the members of Synagogues belong to congregations like. Central. Nineteen per cent of British Jews are Reform, 8% Liberal and 3% Masorti.

What concerns a substantial proportion of the community today is the perceived increase in antisemitism. The number of incidents involving graffiti and internet hatred is around 1,500 a year. What is forgotten is the acceptance of antisemitism by society until after the Second World War. Take an instance as innocuous as a favourite detective character, Lord Peter Wimsey, created by author Dorothy L. Sayers. The characterisation of Jewish characters in her books are very stereotypically antisemitic. The same applies to a number of other popular authors, like T.S.Eliot, Hilaire Belloc, Graham Greene and Evelyn Waugh. The situation has markedly improved in recent years.

To the horror of very many Moslem leaders in the country, there is an element in their community who commit terrorist acts and this is a millstone round their necks in trying to present their true image as equally good citizens. By contrast, as Woody Allen, the American Jewish comedian said, you don't cross the road when you see a Jewish accountant.

Central's readiness to cooperate with communities from overseas resulted in their linking with the Jewish Learning Exchange. This led to gatherings like two Friday night dinners for a French speaking community; more than fifty young professionals came to Central to enjoy the evening. The political situation in France has led to a considerable number of French Jews coming to live in Britain.

There are many young Jews who have grown up feeling that there is a gap in their knowledge of their religion. Being family minded, Central reminds them of their forebears when they visit and this is an important part of its attraction.

Life goes on for the members. For example, in 2021 the Moss family celebrated a century's connection with the Synagogue. It began with the marriage of Louis and Beatrice Moss in 1921. Louis was the house doctor for all the West End theatres and took a keen interest in acupuncture, journeying to China to learn more about it. During the Blitz he saw the Synagogue on fire and hurried to rescue the sifrei torah before they were consumed. The family have now celebrated five weddings in the Synagogue.

To mark the 150th anniversary, Leonard Fertleman and Mervyn Druian produced an excellent book about the Synagogue's history.

The Rabbi and Naomi, his wife, contributed to the occasion. The Rabbi said:

> It is a true honour and a privilege to be the Rabbi of the Central Synagogue. A world renowned Synagogue, steeped in the annals of Anglo-Jewish history and a jewel in the crown of the United Synagogue. How much more so it is an honour to be writing this message as this wonderful Synagogue celebrates its 150th Anniversary.

It is worth noting that in Hebrew we call a synagogue a Beit Knesset, a House of Gathering. It is not called a Beit Hashem (House of G-d) or even a Beit Tefilla (House of Prayer.) This is because a Synagogue is not exclusively about being a place of worship or a place where they go to meet with G-d. Of course, it is the place where the members pray, but it is much more than that. It is also a place where we meet and learn and socialise. A place where we come together to celebrate our heritage and culture. It is a place where we become a community.

As we reflect on the illustrious history of the Central Synagogue, it is also an opportunity to look forward to the future and the next chapter in the life of this remarkable community. With the new building works complete we will have not just a beautiful Synagogue but a wonderful state of the art facility, and a community hub where we will plan educational events, social activities and much more, helping to ensure that Central is exactly that – the centre of Jewish life in London.

Naomi Lerer said:

> It is no coincidence that the day after the 150th anniversary celebrations of Central Synagogue, the Shul is going on a three-day trip to Poland accompanied by a survivor, for a moving, inspirational and powerful journey. And it is no coincidence that the day of the 150th anniversary marks the opening of the newly refurbished downstairs facility, which is set to be a vibrant community hub, not just for Central Synagogue, but for the wider London Jewish community.
>
> Because that is the very essence of Central. It remembers and respects its past, placing huge importance on honouring and learning from all those who have come before us. At the same time, it recognises and values the next generation, making them a priority and fully committing and investing in their future.
>
> It is only with this essential combination of remembering the past and building for the future that we are ensuring the long-term success of this Shul.
>
> It is such an honour to be the Rebbetzin during this remarkable time and I look forward to being part of this exciting new chapter for Central Synagogue.

Another new initiative has been the PJ Library. This was started by Harold Grinspoon in Massachusetts in 2005 and spread to Britain in 2016. It sends families Jewish books every month and Raquel Amit. at Central has masterminded their distribution to the children in the community as a whole. A half million children get the books nowadays. Titles include *Bagels from Benny* and *Dinosaur on Passover*, so the education comes with a satisfactory layer of entertaining sugar. As Raquel explained:

> PJ Library has enabled us to bring beautiful stories with positive morals to Central's children services and parties, giving our children further insights into Jewish holidays, concepts and traditions and laying a foundation for Jewish learning in a simple yet engaging way.

As one mother reported:

> PJ Library have totally captivated my three-and-a-half-year-old
> daughter. She recounts the stories to us about the Jewish holidays
> with such detail as if they were fairy stories.

Retaining one's Jewish identity is, perhaps, most difficult when going to
university. Divorced, perhaps for the first time, from the family home,
offered so many new attractions and without the local friendships, it is
very easy for students to drift away from their Jewish heritage. To
counteract this there are the Jewish societies at the Universities and twelve
teams of rabbis and rebbitzens around the country to look after their
involvement.

There is a problem with a very few academics whose lectures include
material which could well be considered antisemitic, and some Jewish
societies feel under pressure. While most universities only have very
occasional incidents to report, a few, like Bristol and London, have been
the centre for causes célèbre.

There are now 160 centres of higher education in Britain and in 2000
there were about 150 antisemitic incidents reported to the Community
Security Trust. The highest number was 11 which made the average for
universities as a whole well under one a year.

Many of the instances tend to receive a great deal of publicity and
further legislation is promised to make anything racist illegal. The necessity,
however, to protect freedom of speech makes the whole subject very
contentious in academic circles.

There is one new problem which makes demands on the members.
That is the extension of the congestion charge to £15 a day, covering almost
all of the hours of the day and evening and every day of the week. The result
is, of course, that it becomes expensive to attend services unless members
use public transport. Those with Blue Badges, which usually means the
elderly, can largely avoid the cost but for those without the benefit, it is a
burden.

The women members of the Synagogues are far more important than
they were. They may not be wardens but then there is insufficient
understanding of the role of women in Judaism. A child is only Orthodox
Jewish if its mother is Orthodox Jewish. This is the Biblical ruling and it
makes women far more important than men.

The faith places great emphasis on the importance of the family, an
institution which has suffered with increased secularism. It is believed that

women are fundamental in building the strength of the unit and, therefore, any other activities which demand their time should be kept to a minimum. One such responsibility is looking after the Synagogue and Orthodox women are relieved of the task. It is delegated to the men.

It is not that Orthodox women are deprived of the opportunity, but that it has always been considered that there are more important things with which they need to deal. Women can now be chairs of United Synagogues which is very different from the situation that existed during most of the years that Central has existed.

The image of Central has, of course, changed markedly over the years. Initially it was a Branch community, which worked for years to be independent of the older Great Synagogue. It also set out to be superior to many of the members' humble foundations in the East End. New generations, however, were often embarrassed at the culture of their parents and grandparents. There was a world of difference between the original Wolfson family in the Gorbals in Glasgow and a string of members of the House of Lords; Lord Leonard Wolfson, Lord David Wolfson, from the days of Margaret Thatcher and now Lord Simon Wolfson.

Most of the new generation admired the progress their parents and grandparents had made in their lives, but their Synagogue moved from the attractions of novelty to the benefits of tradition. If, of course, you could continue to improve the status and activities of the community, you might get both benefits and Central has achieved this. One can be proud of being a member of such an old established community and still participate in every new venture of the United Synagogue as a whole.

The level of observance of the members is the decision of every individual. It is a generalisation to say that the standards of observance expected of Honorary Officers have increased over the years. Where wardens, like Sir Robert Waley Cohen, might drive to Synagogue on Shabbat, other wardens at the time might go to work on the sabbath afternoon. Whether this is still the situation remains the decision of the individual. It is certainly the case that many congregants on a shabbat have ridden to shul, but it is not a subject for criticism from the pulpit as it was in Chief Rabbi Hart Lyon's 18th century days.

Some elements of the Din remain contentious. Cyril Shine publicly attacked the insistence of a rabbi on there being no mixed dancing at a wedding which is the din. The overall level of observance still depends very much on the views of the congregation, whose contrary opinions are always readily available if there is a cause célèbre.

Where the Sephardim decided initially not to join with the Ashkenazim to create a joint Synagogue, there is now a Sephardi minyan once a month at Central and Chazan Raphael Berdugo conducts the service with the traditional Sephardi melodies.

There have been thousands of members of the Central over the 150 years and it would be naive to suppose that they have all been pillars of rectitude. There have been wrongdoers as well. The other side of the coin is that there is a far greater family feeling in Central congregation than was present in the early years. Looking after the weaker members was always the contribution of many fine congregants, but it was normally their independent decisions to lend a helping hand. Today the help is organised and structured, with Susan Grant taking the responsibility of ensuring the support is in place.

The same is true of the programmes for keeping the children involved with the Synagogue. It is no longer a question of bringing them to shul and hoping that their parents enthuse them. For years there have been services aimed to involve them, and for them to enjoy.

Originally, the Branch Synagogue was simply a new venue in which to worship. Now the programme of events throughout the year covers a whole range of interests. The children have fun, the members can make new friendships, there is every opportunity to learn or simply to enjoy oneself. It doesn't make attending services any less important but it keeps an extended family together. Central has also linked with Spiro Ark, whose programme of lectures provides light in a lot of darkness.

In every life there are going to be periods of stress of one kind or another, and knowing that help is available if needed, is a great comfort. For individuals on their own this can be particularly important Central sets out to help.

Over the years, the education of the minister has improved and it is now sine qua non that he will have semicha. The days of the minister as a servant of the congregation are long gone, though the stress of comforting the bereaved and the sick are still a day-to-day part of the rabbi's life.

One unattractive development over the years had been the increasing need to protect the building and Central is looked after, like all Jewish buildings, by the Community Security Trust, who in 2018 had a grant from the Home Office of no less than £13.4 million to provide security guards for over 400 schools, Synagogues, and Jewish communal buildings throughout the country. The CST trains volunteers from Jewish communities and has 1,400 cameras to monitor the situation in the buildings. In this regard the Jewish community is better organised than the Moslems, but then they have been dealing with the problem for much longer.

So Central remains a pillar of Anglo-Jewry and as its traditions are now 150 years old; there is no reason to expect that there is any danger of that changing. The late Chief Rabbi, Lord Jonathan Sacks, wrote a book asking if we would have Jewish grandchildren. As long as there are strong institutions like Central, there is no reason to doubt it.

During 2021 The Wolfson Hall, which had been the Wix Hall, was totally modernised and turned into a function room which could take 200 guests. The King David Suite at the Marble Arch Synagogue had been a major venue for many years for every kind of function, but eventually it was not profitable and was sold to a nearby hotel. That left a vacancy for a hall for Jewish functions, if people did not want to pay the substantial hire costs of West End hotels with kosher licences. Only time will tell if Central can do better than the Marble Arch.

The Jewish recognition of the plight of refugees stretched across all the world. Afghanistan is a long way from London but when the Taliban took over the country in 2021, the Bushey United Synagogue collected a vast amount of food and clothing for those fleeing Kabul. There was a great deal of publicity for their support but as their Rabbi, the American Elchanon Feldman, said, we had been refugees before the war and the support we had received at that time from the non-Jewish world could now be reciprocated.

Looking back over the centuries, by all logical reasoning though, Judaism should not have survived. How could it not have been subsumed into the Greek empire or vanish like the Carthaginians in the days of the Roman empire. With the power of the church over the centuries, using every weapon to eliminate their Jewish citizens, how could the Jews not be completely destroyed?

It has to be the greatest example of the victory of pure faith in the world's history. All the great empires have vanished into historical footnotes, but the Jews still maintain the Talmud. Central is one of the indomitable homes of that philosophy.

It is a truism that you can only live life forwards and only understand it backwards. The importance of Central Synagogue after 150 years certainly bears this out. For the initial idea was to create a Branch Synagogue for people moving to the West End, not to change the structure of the community.

When the Central was built, the Great was still the most important synagogue in London, the oldest Ashkenazi Synagogue and the most influential. It was a Rothschild warden who ensured that Nathan Marcus Adler was elected Chief Rabbi. This, effectively, remained the position until the Synagogue was blitzed in 1941.

At the turn of the 20th century there were five major synagogues in the West End of London; the Central, Bayswater, New West End, St. Johns Wood and Western. The Bayswater was compulsorily purchased for a road development and the Western joined with the new Marble Arch Synagogue. This left the Central as the single survivor of the Synagogues who made up the original United Synagogue.

There was another major change though. The oldest families in the community had always provided the leaders but, for the first time, a descendent of a poor immigrant family was appointed president of the United Synagogue. This was Sir Isaac Wolfson and he was also one of the two wardens at the Central. The Synagogue now had history on its side, as well as the community leader. Attempts to have it join up with the Marble Arch Synagogue were firmly resisted and it remains today part of the West End heritage.

Today there is a woman's shiur and the ladies have an equal share in the running of the Synagogue. Recently the shul, for the first time, offered four services during weekdays; shacharit, a lunchtime service, the afternoon service and the evening. All are supported and this is particularly helpful for those in the West End of London who have yahrzeit.

The concept of a Ladies' Guild, divorcing the women from the important decisions the men had traditionally made, is out-of-date. It is more likely that a committee of both sexes will now continue to act together and equally.

What of the future? When older people downsize, they might well move to the West End but the membership is likely to drop over the years. What will increase is the number of tourists who want a Synagogue when they come to London on holiday. The Central is ideal. The descendants of the original Central families will also come to the Synagogue to remember their relatives, because nostalgia is a powerful attraction.

There is also a need for those working in the West End who want to find a minyan when they have yahrzeit. Central will continue to provide services on weekdays for them and for those who want to just attend services in the mornings, afternoons and evenings.

The students in the nearby colleges will always know that they will be welcome at the Synagogue. It is a counter to loneliness, and it provides companionship for those older people who would otherwise have little support. Those who visit patients in the hospitals nearby will also welcome a Synagogue where they can pray for the recovery of their relatives.

Where people are without relatives, they will continue to be able to find themselves welcomed into the Synagogue family. It will be a change in the original purpose of the Synagogue, but it will be no less important for that. The Synagogue has able ministers who should be at their post for many years yet and the younger generation of members will provide the Honorary Officers to take over from the incumbents.

That is likely to be the future and the Synagogue, like Bevis Marks, will continue to be part of a tradition of British Jews which. now stretches over many. centuries. When there are important events for the entire community they will probably be held at Bevis Marks, but when only the Ashkenazi are involved, Central is likely to be their chosen venue.

There are much older Synagogues around the world, in cities like Safed, Prague and Providence, Rhode Island, but Britain has its own heritage and will, please G-d, continue to grace London.

ב"ה

**CENTRAL SYNAGOGUE
LONDON**

*The Honorary Officers
have pleasure in inviting you to attend
the service celebrating the 150th Anniversary of
the Central Synagogue
and the Induction of Rabbi Barry Lerer
by the Chief Rabbi Ephraim Mirvis
on Shabbat, 25th April 2020 ~ 1 Iyar 5780*

R.S.V.P. by 8th April
020 7580 1355
36-40 Hallam Street, London w1w 6nw
bookings@centralsynagogue.org.uk

Service to commence at 9.00 am
Kiddush in the Wolfson Hall
Please be seated by 10.00 am

14. The 150th service invitation

בס"ד

Office of The
CHIEF RABBI

MESSAGE FROM THE CHIEF RABBI ON THE OCCASION OF
THE 150th ANNIVERSARY OF THE CENTRAL SYNAGOGUE

Valerie and I are delighted to extend our very best wishes to the entire congregation of the Central Synagogue, on the occasion of your 150th anniversary.

The number 150 is best known in Jewish thought as the number of Psalms composed by King David and other great Jewish scholars. The Psalms provide a remarkable resource of guidance and inspiration for us through all of life's varying experiences. Through the Psalms we express our joy, pain, despair, hope and triumph. Whenever our emotions peak, you can be sure that there is a Psalm to help us express them and they provide sanctuary for us when we need them most.

The Central Synagogue is not just a Beit Tefillah – a house of prayer. It is a veritable Beit Knesset – a house of assembly. Just as we draw strength from the 150 Psalms, so too have many drawn strength over the last 150 years from the Central Synagogue. Within the Shul, congregants have joined together to experience every possible human emotion, united in their belief in the Almighty and deep pride in their Jewish tradition. In addition, for 150 glorious years, the Synagogue has provided inspiration and guidance to all of British Jewry and well beyond, as an historic beacon of Jewish communal excellence.

Under the outstanding spiritual leadership of Rabbi and Rebbetzen Lerer and Chazan Steven Leas and lay leadership of Barry Townsley and his team, yours is a community which is truly blessed to have a rich history and a bright future.

With my warmest best wishes,

Chief Rabbi Ephraim Mirvis
April 2020 • Nisan 5780

15. Message from Chief Rabbi Ephraim Mirvis

The Ambassador's Office
Embassy of Israel
London

לשכת השגריר
שגרירות ישראל
לונדון

Message from HE Mark Regev, Ambassador of Israel to the Court of St James's

I wish Rabbi Lerer, Rebbetzen Naomi and the entire community of Central Synagogue a very heartfelt *Mazal Tov* as you celebrate 150 years to the consecration of your present site.

The laying of Central Synagogue's foundation stone on Great Portland Street in 1869, and its completion the following year, forms an important part of your congregation's story and the remarkable history of British Jewry.

For generations, your members have undoubtedly made a real contribution both in the Diaspora and to our homeland, and as you celebrate this century and a half, I hope you are proud of the strong bond you have built with the Jewish state these past 71 years.

Mark Regev
Ambassador of Israel to the Court of St James's

2 Palace Green, London, W8 4QB

16. Message from His Excellency, Mark Regev

Index

The lists off Honorary Officers, Officers and those who died in wars are to be found at the front of the book and not always in the Index.

Tilbury, 41.
Tisha b'Av, 11.
Tokyo, 93.
Top Hats, 24.
Tottenham Home for Jewish Incurables,
    150.
Tourists, 1.
Townsley, Barry, CBE, 229, 245.
Tractate Berakhot, 190.
Traders, 4.
Training Ministers Committee, 65.
Tredegar 108.
Trees, 207.
Trenner, Elizabeth, 53.
Trenner, Joseph, 89, 92, 106.
Tribe, 215.
Truck System, 108,.
Truman, Harry,192,.
Trzaskowsky, Rafał, 230.
Trustees, 176.
Tuck, Siri Adolph, 33, 89, 91, 117, 118,
    120, 146.
Tuck, Desmond, 125, 128, 136, 143, 146,
    148,194.
Tuck, Lady, 125.
Tuck, Raphael, 121,
Tucker, Sophie, 184.
Turgel, Jonny, 229.

Uganda, 94.
Ukraine, 212, 213.
Understanding Shabbot, 232.
Union of Jewish & Religious Classes,
    125, 135.
Unionist Conservative Alliance, 73.
United Africa Company, 156.
United Synagogue, 1, 15,18, 24, 25, 28,
    31-33, 37, 42, 47-49, 54, 58, 62, 65,
    67, 69, 72, 75, 80, 81, 84, 89, 92, 93,
    97, 102-108, 114, 115, 124, 128, 134,
    141, 143-146, 150-154, 156-159, 161-
    163, 166, 172-174, 181, 183, 187, 195,
    197, 203, 204, 206, 208, 213, 215, 219,
    221, 222, 224, 229, 237, 238, 240, 243,
    244, 251, 254.
    Act, 81,
    Burial Society, 43,

Chesed Bursary Fund, 215,
Community Service, 202,
Council, 203,
H..M. Forces Committee, 135,
Ministers, 186,
Visitation Committee, 56, 64. 90, 208,
Welfare Committee, 142,
Young, 228,
United Synagogue Act, 58.
Universities Test Act, 13, 14.
University College Hospital, 140.
University College, London, 90, 136, 152,
    197.
University of Pennsylvania, 132.
University Zionist Federation, 129.
Upper Berkeley Street Synagogue, 67, 82,
    83, 124, 125.

V1 & V2, 143.
Valentine Cards, 121.
Valentine, Isaac, 46, 101.
Valentine, Philip, 36, 46, 94,101.
Vallentine's Almanack, 101.
Variety Club, 243.
Victoria, Queen, 18, 23, 86, 121,
    .Gaon, 198, 232.
Visiting Committee of the Hebrew
    Congregations, 102.
Visitation Committees, 42.
Visitors among the Jewish Poor, 80.
Vzous Hatorah, 55.
Voysey, Rev. Charles, 54.

Waddesdon Manor, 59, 74 .
Wakefield, William, 219.
Waley, Elizaberth, 105.
Waley Cohen, Lady Alice, 134 .
Waley Cohen Bernard, 177.
Waley Cohen, Dorothea, 106.
Waley Cohen, Robert, 95, 104-106, 115,
    118, 120, 134, 141, 143-145, 150, 153,
    154-157, 251.
Waley, Jacob, 58, 95.
Walthamstow & Leyton Synagogue, 160.
War Damage Reparations, 141, 161.
War Damages Committee, 141.
War Memorial Candelabrum, 117.